WHAT DRIVES
CURRENCY MARKETS

FINANCIAL TIMES

Prentice Hall

In an increasingly competitive world, it is quality
of thinking that gives an edge – an idea that opens new
doors, a technique that solves a problem, or an insight
that simply helps make sense of it all.

We work with leading authors in the fields of
management and finance to bring cutting-edge thinking
and best learning practice to a global market.

Under a range of leading imprints, including
Financial Times Prentice Hall, we create world-class
print publications and electronic products giving readers
knowledge and understanding which can then be
applied, whether studying or at work.

To find out more about our business and professional
products, you can visit us at www.business-minds.com

For other Pearson Education publications, visit
www.pearsoned-ema.com

Pearson
Education

WHAT DRIVES CURRENCY MARKETS

After the euro

BRIAN KETTELL

FINANCIAL TIMES
Prentice Hall

An imprint of Pearson Education

London · New York · San Francisco · Toronto · Sydney · Tokyo · Singapore
Hong Kong · Cape Town · Madrid · Amsterdam · Munich · Paris · Milan

PEARSON EDUCATION LIMITED

Head Office:
Edinburgh Gate
Harlow CM20 2JE
Tel: +44 (0)1279 623623
Fax: +44 (0)1279 431059

London Office:
128 Long Acre
London WC2E 9AN
Tel: +44 (0)20 7447 2000
Fax: +44 (0)20 7240 5771
Website: www.business-minds.com

First published in Great Britain in 2000

The right of Brian Kettell to be identified as author
of this work has been asserted by him in accordance
with the Copyright, Designs and Patents Act 1988.

ISBN 0 273 63071 7

British Library Cataloguing in Publication Data
A CIP catalogue record for this book can be obtained from the British Library.

This publication is designed to provide accurate and authoritative information
in regard to the subject matter covered. It is sold with the understanding that
neither the author nor the publisher is engaged in rendering legal, investing,
or any other professional service. If legal advice or other expert assistance is
required, the service of a competent professional person should be sought.

The publisher and contributors make no representation, express or implied,
with regard to the accuracy of the information contained in this book and
cannot accept any responsibility or liability for any errors or omissions
that it may contain.

10 9 8 7 6 5 4 3 2 1

Typeset by Northern Phototypesetting Co. Ltd, Bolton
Printed and bound in Great Britain by Redwood Books, Trowbridge, Wiltshire

The Publishers' policy is to use paper manufactured from sustainable forests.

ABOUT THE AUTHOR

Brian Kettell (MSc, BSc Econ) has many years' experience working in financial markets and banking. A graduate of the London School of Economics, he has worked for Citibank, American Express, Arab Banking Corporation (Vice President) and Shearson Lehman (Vice President). This experience has since been applied in providing training courses on international financial markets. He has delivered training courses on the markets for a variety of organizations including Chase Manhattan Bank, Nomura, Morgan Stanley, Kleinwort Benson, Banque Indosuez and The Euromoney Institute of Finance. He is now Senior Lecturer at London University and a visiting Professor of Finance at several French business schools.

He has published widely (over 80 articles) in numerous journals including *Central Banking*, *The Banker*, and *The Securities Journal*. His previous books include *What Drives Financial Markets*, *Fed-Watching*, *The International Debt Game* (with George Magnus, Chief Economist, Warburg, Dillon, Read), *Businessman's Guide to the Foreign Exchange Market*, *Monetary Economics*, *The Finance of International Business*, *Gold*, and *The Foreign Exchange Handbook* (with Steve Bell, Chief Economist, Deutsche Morgan Grenfell). In addition he has published a large number of case studies on financial markets.

The author would like to dedicate this book to his wife Nadia, without whose support it would not have been written, and to his sister Pat without whom it would not have been typed.

CONTENTS

ACKNOWLEDGEMENTS

I wish to acknowledge: the Bank of England for permission to reprint Appendix 2.1; Central Banking, Professor Gregory D. Hess of Oberlin College and Dr Owen D. Humpage of the Federal Reserve Bank of Cleveland for permission to reprint Appendix 3.1; and the International Monetary fund for permission to reprint Appendix 9.1. In addition I wish to acknowledge drawing on an article on the October 1998 report of the Deutsche Bundesbank for many of the ideas on the discussion of ERM II in Chapter 2.

I would also like to acknowledge the extensive help provided to me by Gavin Wells, foreign exchange dealer, Citibank London, for his patience and help with the sections in the book referring to the dealing room implications of the introduction of the euro, and to many other related issues.

INTRODUCTION

Throughout the 1990s, currency crises of differing degrees of severity have erupted, from the UK, Italy, Spain and Sweden in 1992, to Mexico and Argentina in 1995; to Thailand, Malaysia, Indonesia and South Korea in 1997 to Russia in 1998 and to Brazil in 1998–9. The lessons of these currency upheavals (which in many cases resulted in severe economic upheavals) have not, so far, been reflected in existing texts on the foreign exchange market. In addition to these developments, Europe introduced a new currency – the euro – on 1 January 1999.

Many books have been written about the foreign exchange market and any new book has to justify its position. This book does so based on two considerations. First, it is the first book published on the subject, in which the introduction of Europe's new currency, the euro, is incorporated into every chapter. Books which devote chapters and examples using the 11 former European currencies, the Deutsche mark, French franc, Italian lira, etc are now history.

Second, the text treats many of the topical, sometimes controversial topics regarding the foreign exchange market, in a reader-friendly way. Before publication of this text, these issues were largely discussed in academic journals or obscure sources but were certainly not easily accessible even to the most serious reader. A list of the topics discussed in each chapter illustrates this point.

Chapter 1   Where does the foreign exchange market fit into the global financial system?

Chapter 2   What is the ideal exchange rate system for a country and to what extent do the existing arrangements meet these criteria?

Chapter 3   Where does volatility in the foreign exchange market come from?

Chapter 4   What are the long-term factors affecting exchange rates and to what extent are they influenced by short-term considerations?

Chapter 5   How does economic news affect the foreign exchange market?

Chapter 6   What makes a great currency?

Chapter 7   What do we know about currency arbitrage?

Chapter 8   What goes on inside a foreign exchange dealing room?

Chapter 9   What are the advantages and disadvantages for a country of introducing either a Currency Board or Dollarization?

Chapter 10   Will the euro succeed or will it collapse?

Chapter 11   How does the introduction of the euro affect the way spot and forward exchange rates are quoted?

Chapter 12   How has the introduction of the euro affected the money markets?

Chapter 13   Can currency collapses be predicted?

CHAPTER 1

The evolution of the foreign exchange market

Its role in the globalization of international finance

- Some early history
- The evolution and role of international capital markets
- Recent trends in global financial integration

SOME EARLY HISTORY

The first foreign exchange markets consisted of meeting places of money changers functioning in commercial centres. The money changers were familiar figures in marketplaces and harbours in the ancient Middle East and Greece, with their tables, scales and weights, displaying a variety of domestic and foreign coins. Money changers usually combined their functions with those of bullion dealers, serving the requirements of international trade and finance in a dual capacity.

According to Einzig,[1] the profession of money changer came into being in countries of the ancient Middle East at a relatively early stage of their monetary evolution. Even during the period when foreign coins were only accepted at their bullion value in centres of foreign trade, there was a need for the services of specialists able to weigh the coins with a high degree of precision. It was also necessary to ascertain their fineness by some primitive method of assaying, such as the use of the Lydian stone. It can be argued that these specialists, on the basis of their superior experience, were the earliest form of foreign exchange dealers.

Foreign coins circulated in ample supply within the Roman Empire. In particular the provinces adjoining foreign countries were in the habit of using coins from across the border as token moneys with or without official exchange rates against the denarius. The large number of hoards of Roman coins found in Germany, in the countries adjoining the Black Sea, in Scandinavia, Iran, India, Sri Lanka, Egypt and in many other countries outside the confines of the Roman Empire indicates the extent to which such coins must have been used in payments abroad.

The Roman gold coin, the aureus, was the first currency to attain worldwide fame. After the currency reforms of Augustus, the silver denarius also came to be regarded as highly acceptable abroad, even in distant China. Since its introduction late in the 3rd century BC, the denarius became universally accepted throughout the Roman Empire, even when faced with competition from local currencies. The denarius was the denomination used for serious business and, indeed, was the US dollar of the day. It was eventually superseded by the base silver radiate around AD 240.

According to Einzig,[2] Vienna was the first modern market where forward exchange business was transacted systematically, and on a large scale, during the various periods when the Austrian currency was subject to fluctuations, between

1850 and 1890. Rouble notes are also known to have been actively dealt for forward delivery on the Vienna bourse throughout the 1880s and 1890s, and there was also a market in forward sterling. A forward exchange market was functioning also in Berlin during the 1880s. There was keen interest arbitrage between Vienna and Berlin, with the exchange risk covered, in view of the instability of the Austrian Gulden.

The more recent globalization of financial markets is a development that has radically transformed the way the international financial markets and international business operate. This chapter examines how global finance has changed in recent years, highlighting the causes, consequences and recent trends.

As already suggested, international finance is not new. Its origins date back at least to the late Middle Ages when a burgeoning European wool trade and other transnational enterprises provided the economic underpinning for financial intermediation. Efficient resource mobilization, as well as existing threats to established trade routes, encouraged the Crusades. Later, the wealth of Florentine merchants and bankers assisted in financing the Renaissance.[3]

More recently, between the years 1984 and 2000 there has been a tenfold increase in cross-border debt and bond issues, a significant increase in the trade of international equities on most markets, a huge increase in currency trading and an explosion in the number, and trading volume, of derivatives with a cross-border component, including currency swaps, options and futures. The reasons for this acceleration are discussed in this chapter.

THE EVOLUTION AND ROLE OF INTERNATIONAL CAPITAL MARKETS

The trend towards closer cross-border integration has been clearly in evidence over the past half century, and can indeed be traced back directly to the years following the end of the Napoleonic Wars. Evidence for this can be seen in Table 1.1, which shows comparative annual average growth rates for world output and the volume of world exports in each of six periods spanning the years 1820–1997. In Table 1.1, there is only one time phase, from 1913–50, in which export growth fell short of output growth; and here exceptional factors were at work, in the form of two world wars and the Great Depression of the 1930s. In these six periods, the ratio of export growth to output growth, which is one indicator of the speed with which integration was going ahead, appears highest for the half century to 1870, while the growth rate of world exports was appreciably higher, both absolutely and relatively, for the period 1950–73 than in 1973–92. Since that time it has risen again.

Central to this economic integration has been the role played by international capital markets. International capital markets, like their domestic counterparts,

Table 1.1 ● Growth rates of world output and exports, 1820–1997 (average annual compound percentage rates of growth)

	1820–70	1870–1913	1913–50	1950–73	1973–92	1992–97
Output	1.0	2.1	1.9	4.9	3.0	3.7
Exports	4.2	3.4	1.3	7.0	4.0	8.1

Sources: For 1820–1992, Madison, *Monitoring the World Economy*; for 1992–7, IMF, *World Economic Outlook*. The final figure in the table relates to world merchandise trade rather than world exports

serve several key functions (see Goldstein and Mussa).[4] They channel resources from units (households, firms, governments) that are savers to units that are dissavers, thereby loosening the constraints imposed by self-finance and enabling increases both in the overall productivity of investment and in the smoothing of consumption. They provide liquidity. They allocate and diversify risk. They may even help to "discipline" errant borrowers, either by subjecting them initially to a rising default premium and ultimately, to the threat of credit rationing, or by forcing adjustments in exchange rates. By permitting trade in financial assets to take place without regard to either national boundaries or the nationalities of market participants, there is a strong presumption that the efficiency, liquidity, risk-pooling, and disciplinary attributes of capital markets will be enhanced.

Ultimately international capital markets are central to the smooth working of a liberal competitive financial system. The key elements of a liberal competitive financial system are summarized in Figure 1.1.

International commercial banking began when Italian banks established operations in the City of London in the late thirteenth century. The road at the heart of the city, Lombard Street, recalls the origins of banking in the city. Following the expulsion of the Jews under King Edward I, Italian funds and financial expertise were required to pay for his wars. Two groups, Bardi and Peruzzi, volunteered this support and looked to a tax on wool exports as a source of repayment. The intermediation of the Italians continued until the reign of Edward III when the King decided to rely on the domestic merchant class to provide needed finance. Exercising his right as sovereign he promptly repudiated the Italian debt, precipitating the collapse of both the Bardi and Peruzzi banks.[5]

International lending has always incurred risks. Historically few banks appear to have avoided this pitfall. A chronicler of the Medici Bank, for example, observes that "rather than refuse deposits, the Medicis succumbed to the temptation of seeking an outlet for surplus cash in making dangerous loans to princes."[6]

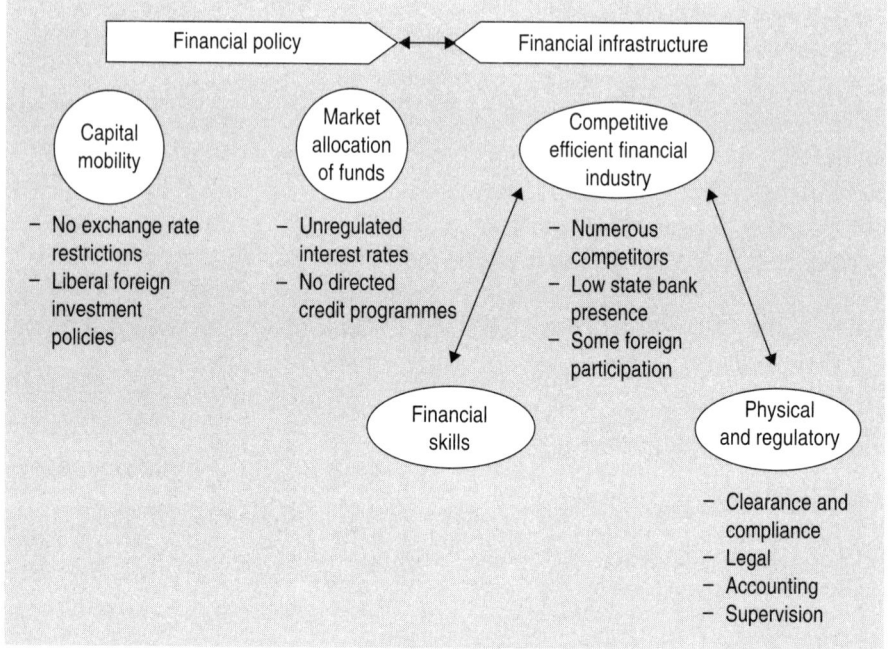

Fig 1.1 ● **Elements of a liberal, competitive financial system**

Source: McKinsey Analysis

During the period when European powers colonized the New World, international lending was directed towards development finance. Capital transfers were bilateral in nature, linking individual European countries to their respective colonies and trading outposts. Funds for these development loans were raised essentially from wealthy individuals. The unequal distribution of wealth at the time produced a high domestic savings rate.[7] A relatively stable economic and social environment in Europe also encouraged people to invest. Early intermediaries tapped these resources of surplus capital and organized direct loans for foreign borrowers, typically sovereign states or top-quality enterprises.

Chief financial centres during this period were London, Paris and Berlin. New York joined the market, too, but at a later stage. There were also smaller financial centres in Italy, the Netherlands, Switzerland, Belgium and Sweden.[8]

European merchant banks, which have since evolved into international bond houses and other financial intermediaries, benefited from their location in capital-rich countries that enjoyed virtually uninterrupted balance-of-trade surpluses. The early institutions thus performed a "recycling" function, by moving capital investments from the established economies of Europe in order to finance growth in what were then the developing countries of the world. Among other achievements, the railways of Russia, South America and China were built largely by virtue of bond financings subscribed for by European investors. The rapid industrial expansion of the US towards the end of the nineteenth century also owes much to this transnational financing.[9]

Following the Second World War, the international financial markets remained in disarray. Transnational capital investment chiefly took the form of official aid, such as the Marshall Plan, and a limited number of foreign bond offerings. Directly after the war the financing activities of major borrowers such as the World Bank, the European Coal and Steel Community, and some governments served to re-establish investor confidence in international securities offerings.[10]

Through the 1960s and 1970s the international bond market started to evolve and with the imposition of the Interest Equalization Tax on 18 July 1963 the Eurobond market was born.

BOX

1   What are all these international financial instruments?

International bonds are securities sold largely outside the country of residence of the borrower. Such offerings may be divided into two categories: "Eurobonds" and "foreign bonds".

Eurobonds are offered to the general public, where permitted by law, through an international syndicate of financial intermediaries, and sold principally, and at times exclusively, in countries other than the country of the currency in which the bonds are denominated.

Foreign bonds by contrast, are underwritten by a syndicate of financial intermediaries from one country only. They are distributed in much the same fashion as domestic issues in that country and are denominated in the national currency. Both Eurobonds and foreign bonds are usually available in bearer form, preserving anonymity of beneficial ownership, and interest is payable free and clear of withholding and other taxes at source.

The other major form of international financing is, the **syndicated loan** (or medium-term credit) which typically refers to a loan of two or more years' maturity provided by a group or syndicate of international commercial banks.

There are, additionally, a plethora of hybrid instruments such as floating-rate notes and Euronotes.

The first step towards the internationalization of financial markets was the introduction of Eurodollar markets in the 1960s and 1970s and the development and growth of the Eurobond market. Undoubtedly the major push to global financial markets came from deregulation, particularly in the form of the removal of exchange controls in many countries in the 1980s and in the removal of the barriers to entry to foreign firms. The globalization of financial markets has to a large extent been on the back of growth in multinational corporations. As companies grow and become international in scope, they tend to look for finance on an international scale.

The Eurocurrency market

A Eurocurrency is a dollar or other freely convertible currency deposited in a bank outside its country of origin. Thus, US dollars on deposit in London become Eurodollars. These deposits can be placed in a foreign bank or in the euro branch of a domestic US bank. The Eurocurrency market then consists of those banks – called Eurobanks – that accept deposits and make loans in euro currencies. Following the introduction of the euro on 1 January 1999, the interpretation of the term "euro" has been somewhat altered and we return to the implications of this in later chapters.

The Eurobond and Eurocurrency markets are often confused with each other, but there is a fundamental distinction between the two. In the Eurobond market, Eurobonds, which are bonds sold outside the countries in whose currencies they are denominated, are issued directly by the final borrowers. The Eurocurrency market enables investors to hold short-term claims on commercial banks, which then act as intermediaries to transform these deposits into long-term claims on final borrowers. However, banks do play an important role in placing Eurobonds with the final investors.

The origin of the post-Second World War Eurodollar market is often traced to the fear of Soviet Bloc countries that their dollar deposits in US banks might be frozen by US citizens with claims against Communist governments. To avoid this risk, it has been suggested, they left their dollar balances with banks in France and England.

Whatever its post-war beginnings, the Eurocurrency market has thrived for one reason: government regulation. By operating in Eurocurrencies, banks and suppliers of funds are able to avoid certain regulatory costs and restrictions that would otherwise be imposed. These costs and restrictions include the following.

1. Reserve requirements that lower a bank's earning asset base (that is, a smaller percentage of deposits can be lent out).
2. Special charges and taxes levied on domestic banking transactions, such as the requirement to pay US Federal Deposit Insurance Corporation fees.
3. Requirements to lend money to certain borrowers at concessionary rates, thereby lowering the return on the bank's assets.
4. Interest rate ceilings on deposits or loans that inhibit the ability to compete for funds and lower the return on loans.
5. Rules or regulations that restrict competition among banks.

The Eurobond market, a market which has been subject to radical innovation, survives largely because, unlike any other major capital market, it remains unregulated and untaxed. The Eurobond market, like the Eurocurrency market, as discussed earlier, exists because it enables borrowers and lenders alike to avoid a variety of monetary authorities regulations and controls, as well as providing them with an opportunity to escape the payment of some taxes. As long as governments attempt to regulate domestic financial markets but allow a (relatively) free flow of capital among countries, then external financial markets will survive. If tax and regulatory costs rise, these external markets will grow in importance.

Figure 1.2 provides a summary of how the factors affecting the globalization of financial markets are interconnected.

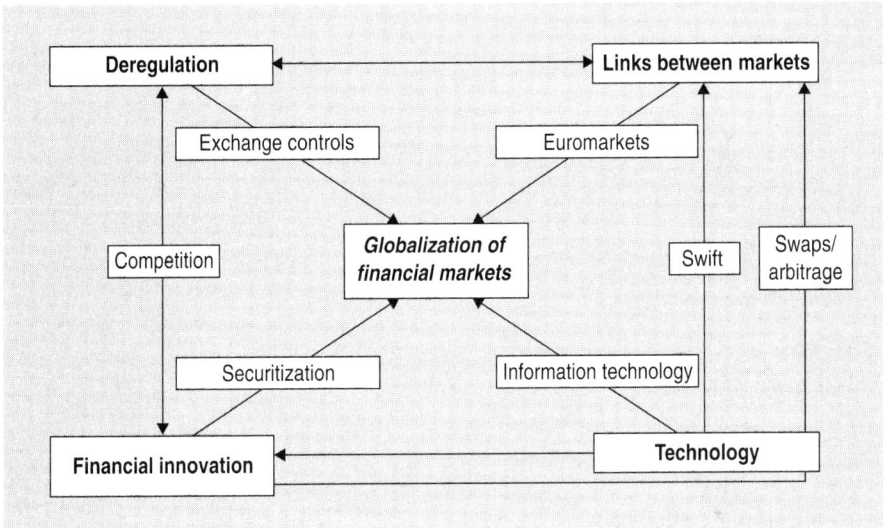

Fig 1.2 ● The role of deregulation, technology and financial innovation in the globalization of financial markets

RECENT TRENDS IN GLOBAL FINANCIAL INTEGRATION

The structural changes that have occurred in the national and international finance during the past two decades should be seen, as already indicated, as part of a complex process best described as the globalization of finance and financial risk. The IMF[11] stressed that the key elements of this ongoing transformation have been:

● an increase in the technical capabilities for engaging in precision finance, that is, for unbundling, repackaging, pricing and redistributing financial risks

● the integration of national financial markets, investor bases, and borrowers into a global financial marketplace

- the blurring of distinctions between financial institutions and the activities and markets they engage in
- the emergence of the global bank and the international financial conglomerate, each providing a mix of financial products and services in a broad range of markets and countries.

These changes have radically altered both investor and borrower perceptions of financial risks and rewards around the world, and their behaviour across national and international financial markets.

Closer integration of financial markets

Liberalization of domestic capital markets and of international capital flows since the early 1970s (coupled with rapid gains in information technology) has been the catalyst for financial innovation and the growth in cross-border capital movements. In part, the globalization of financial intermediation has occurred in response to the demand to intermediate these growing cross-border capital movements, as discussed above. Firms in most countries currently enjoy access to financial services from a more diverse and more competitive array of providers, and at lower cost, while investors have better information and access to an expanded menu of investment opportunities.

There are many ways of assessing the extent of globalization of financial markets, given that markets become integrated in a number of ways: through the increasing web of connections among financial institutions, through exchange linkages, and through less formal trading and information linkages. Some of these assessment methods are applied below.

Cross-border finance in a global securities market

The integration of national financial systems into a single global financial system is indicated by more diversified investment portfolios, the larger the number of firms tapping foreign sources of funds, and the growth of highly sophisticated asset managers, an important subset of which focus exclusively on identifying and exploiting arbitrage opportunities around the globe. Gross flows and net flows of capital increased markedly between 1970 and 1997 (see Table 1.2). The 32 times increase in gross direct investment in the industrial countries is impressive, from $14.45 billion in 1970 to $448.32 billion in 1997, but it pales in comparison to the growth in gross portfolio flows, which has increased by almost 200 times, from $5.26 billion in 1970 to $1,040.19 billion in 1997.

Table 1.2 ● Major industrial countries: gross and net flows of foreign direct and portfolio investment*

(in billions of US dollars)

	1970	1975	1980	1985	1990	1995	1996	1997
Gross flows								
Foreign direct investment	14.45	34.25	82.82	75.94	283.24	369.01	357.53	448.32
Portfolio investment	5.26	27.10	60.93	233.44	329.63	764.34	1162.64	1040.19
Net flows								
Foreign direct investment	–4.05	–9.93	–8.14	–12.66	–59.58	–83.41	–87.41	–92.60
Portfolio investment	1.42	8.53	16.02	25.03	41.36	186.53	267.37	272.51

Source: International Monetary Fund, *Balance of Payments Statistics Yearbook*
*Group of Seven countries

Another measure of capital market integration is cross-border securities transactions, defined as gross purchases and sales of securities between residents and non-residents. Cross-border transactions in bonds and equities in the major advanced economies amounted to less than 5 per cent of GDP in 1975, but in 1997 they amounted to between one and seven times GDP (see Table 1.3). Foreign participation in securities markets in Europe is even higher than in the US and Japan. This accords with the stylized fact that about half of all equity transactions for firms located in the European Union (EU) take place outside the home country. See Goldstein and Mussa.[12]

Table 1.3 ● Selected major industrial countries: cross-border transactions in bonds and equities*

(in per cent of GDP)

	1975	1980	1985	1989	1990	1991	1992	1993	1994	1995	1996	1997
US	4	9	35	101	89	96	107	129	131	135	160	213
Japan	2	8	62	156	119	92	72	78	60	65	79	96
Germany	5	7	33	66	57	55	85	170	158	172	199	253
France	–	5	21	52	54	79	122	187	197	187	258	313
Italy	1	1	4	18	27	60	92	192	207	253	470	672
Canada	3	9	27	55	65	83	114	153	208	189	251	358

Source: Bank of International Settlements (1998)
*Gross purchases and sales of securities between residents and non-residents

International securities markets

Mirroring the expansion in cross-border trading in financial assets, firms are increasingly turning to international securities markets to raise funds. Inter-

Table 1.4 ● International equity issues by selected industrial and developing countries and regions

(in billions of US dollars except as noted)

	1990	1991	1992	1993	1994	1995	1996	1997	1990–7 Change (per cent)
Industrial countries									
US	990	2,230	4,228	4,664	3,731	4,470	4,072	3,081	211.2
Japan	480	0	47	28	0	111	438	792	65.0
Germany	57	981	400	469	2,795	6,023	7,028	3,614	6,240.4
France	777	1,109	1,213	3,421	5,850	4,348	5,278	7,336	844.1
Italy	132	583	756	797	2,664	2,281	4,488	8,441	6,294.7
UK	3,103	4,028	3,003	1,775	870	3,966	6,281	8,656	179.0
Canada	111	450	205	471	780	1,477	1,345	2,365	2,030.6
Netherlands	432	536	65	1,267	3,330	4,071	5,817	3,693	754.9
Sweden	211	6	13	940	2,101	1,121	2,141	2,246	964.5
Switzerland	0	0	353	472	75	671	0	1,449	–
Belgium	0	0	0	265	0	210	845	845	–
Luxembourg	0	0	0	109	363	115	797	341	–
Total	6,293	9,923	10,283	14,678	22,559	28,864	38,530	42,859	581.1
Developing countries and regions									
Africa									
South Africa	0	143	154	0	176	331	609	698	
Asia									
Hong Kong SAR	0	271	230	837	320	1,206	3,278	3,568	
Indonesia	586	117	119	299	1,359	1,112	1,215	462	
Korea	40	200	150	328	1,168	1,310	1,051	630	
Malaysia	0	0	385	0	0	1,294	155	314	
Philippines	40	77	333	126	947	886	489	265	
Singapore	152	184	283	564	301	475	344	702	
Thailand	83	91	4	725	759	531	151	28	
Europe									
Czech Republic	0	0	0	0	10	32	104	0	
Hungary	52	81	21	8	200	274	227	1,589	
Poland	0	0	0	0	0	70	17	695	
Turkey	46	0	0	178	375	52	12	368	
Latin America									
Argentina	0	360	392	2,655	735	0	217	1,627	
Brazil	0	0	133	0	1,028	296	387	2,251	
Chile	98	0	129	288	799	224	297	563	
Mexico	0	3,531	3,077	2,913	1,679	0	668	550	
Venezuela	0	0	146	42	0	0	904	95	
Middle East									
Israel	0	506	281	336	89	222	544	538	

Sources: Capital Data Bondware; author's own calculations

national issues of equity have risen almost sixfold during the 1990s for firms located in the industrial countries (see Table 1.4). Total international equity issues by firms located in industrial countries rose from $6,293 million in 1990 to $42,859 million in 1997, a growth rate of 581 per cent. Within individual countries, the growth rates for some were much larger, with Italy (6,294 per cent) and Germany (6,240 per cent) being the countries with the highest growth.

The nominal increase in outstanding issues of international debt securities has been even more impressive than that of international equity issues (see Table 1.5). In early 1998, the outstanding amount of international bonds was $3.7 trillion, or more than six times larger than in 1985. In this case the fastest growth between 1993 and March 1998 was on the part of the US, almost double that of the nearest contenders, the UK and Japan.

Non-resident holdings of public debt have also increased substantially. Such holdings in Belgium, Canada, Germany and the US have more than doubled since 1983, and in Italy there has been a threefold increase since 1990 (see Table 1.6).

Derivatives markets

Derivatives instruments are contracts in which the legal right to payment or delivery is dependent on the value of an underlying asset. The basic instruments which form the derivatives markets are forwards, futures, swaps and options. If we add the non-derivative instruments (equities and bonds) to this list, then applying modern corporate finance theory we can combine the individual risk profiles of these elementary instruments to create any type of risk exposure we wish.

In simple terms, once an investor has a view on the market direction, he or she can match this view by buying or selling a derivatives instrument. This is possible because derivatives have made many financial instruments and commodities fungible (ie interchangeable with each other).

Derivative securities, unlike securitized assets, are not obligations backed by the original issuer of the underlying security. Instead, derivative securities are contracts between parties other than the original issuer of the underlying security. The most common contracts are:

● futures
● options
● forward-rate agreements
● swaps

Table 1.5 ● Outstanding international debt securities by nationality of issuer

(in billions of US dollars except as noted)

	1993	1994	1995	1996	1997	March 1998
All countries	2,027.7	2,401.2	2,722.5	3,154.1	3,542.2	3,691.4
Industrial countries						
US	175.7	203.9	264.2	389.6	555.4	602.9
Japan	336.8	351.6	351.4	342.0	319.7	309.4
Germany	119.4	184.8	261.3	337.6	392.2	419.2
France	153.0	184.8	205.0	214.7	220.0	229.6
Italy	69.9	84.6	92.0	94.7	97.4	99.2
UK	186.5	211.4	224.6	272.0	307.0	327.2
Canada	146.7	163.9	174.8	180.4	184.8	190.1
Netherlands	52.6	79.1	101.2	119.0	140.4	149.9
Sweden	74.2	97.2	104.1	107.4	101.7	96.4
Switzerland	18.1	23.9	33.3	42.5	65.4	67.3
Belgium	28.0	34.1	44.7	51.8	52.5	51.4
Luxembourg	2.0	3.3	6.6	11.5	13.8	14.0
Developing countries and regions						
Africa						
South Africa	1.1	2.5	3.7	4.3	4.5	4.8
Asia						
Hong Kong SAR	7.5	13.7	15.4	26.1	33.2	34.2
Indonesia	2.3	4.2	4.3	10.2	16.0	15.7
Korea	15.2	19.6	27.5	43.9	51.5	50.2
Malaysia	4.7	4.2	5.7	10.1	13.2	12.7
Philippines	1.3	2.3	3.1	7.1	10.3	10.3
Singapore	0.8	0.9	1.0	3.0	4.5	4.4
Thailand	3.3	6.0	7.4	12.5	14.4	14.0
Europe						
Czech Republic	0.0	0.0	0.0	0.0	–	–
Hungary	10.3	13.8	19.4	29.8	41.6	44.6
Poland	0.0	0.0	0.3	0.6	2.3	2.2
Latin America						
Argentina	8.5	13.8	19.4	29.8	41.6	44.6
Brazil	10.0	12.9	17.1	28.9	38.6	41.9
Chile	0.8	0.8	0.8	3.1	4.8	4.8
Mexico	22.9	29.9	29.7	42.0	50.3	51.3
Venezuela	4.3	4.1	3.6	3.4	8.5	8.5
Middle East						
Israel	1.5	1.2	1.3	2.1	3.4	3.4

Source: Bank for International Settlements

Table 1.6 ● Non-residents' holdings of public debt*

(in per cent of total public debt)

	US	Japan	Germany	Italy	UK	Canada	Belgium
1983	14.9	–	14.1	–	–	10.7	13.2
1984	15.4	–	14.6	–	7.2	11.3	14.6
1985	15.2	3.7	16.3	–	7.0	12.4	13.9
1986	16.1	3.3	20.1	–	8.0	16.1	14.7
1987	16.6	3.3	21.2	–	10.7	15.5	15.5
1988	18.4	2.0	20.7	–	12.2	15.7	17.5
1989	20.8	3.0	22.1	–	13.7	16.3	19.2
1990	20.1	4.4	20.9	4.4	14.7	17.4	19.3
1991	20.1	5.8	23.1	5.2	15.2	19.0	22.7
1992	20.4	5.5	25.6	6.2	17.6	20.2	21.5
1993	22.2	5.4	32.8	10.1	19.6	21.8	23.3
1994	22.8	5.9	25.9	12.2	20.7	22.6	21.4
1995	28.3	4.3	28.2	13.2	18.8	23.3	21.5
1996	35.0	4.3	29.3	15.9	–	23.8	20.8
1997	40.1	–	–	–	–	23.1	21.9

Source: Bank for International Settlements

*End-of-year data; definitions vary across countries

● caps
● collars
● floors
● swaptions.

Figure 1.3 provides a summary of the key derivatives and an illustration of their functions.

While futures and some options are traded on exchanges, the majority of derivatives contracts are traded over-the-counter (OTC) directly between the participants. The differences between the two ways derivatives can be traded are summarized in Table 1.7.

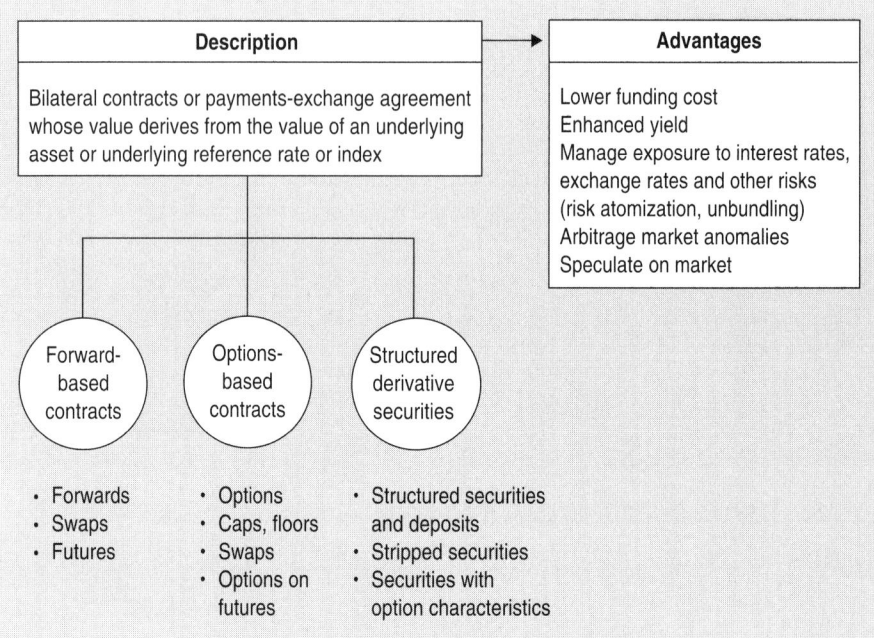

Description	Advantages
Bilateral contracts or payments-exchange agreement whose value derives from the value of an underlying asset or underlying reference rate or index	Lower funding cost Enhanced yield Manage exposure to interest rates, exchange rates and other risks (risk atomization, unbundling) Arbitrage market anomalies Speculate on market

Forward-based contracts	Options-based contracts	Structured derivative securities
• Forwards • Swaps • Futures	• Options • Caps, floors • Swaps • Options on futures	• Structured securities and deposits • Stripped securities • Securities with option characteristics

Fig 1.3 ● Derivatives: description and advantages

Table 1.7 ● Exchange-traded and over-the-counter options

Exchange traded	Over-the-counter
Standardized	Tailor-made
Margined	Not margined
Low credit risk	Credit risk
No penalty offset	Mutual agreement required for offset
Price transparency	Diffuse prices

Although the exchange traded options market and OTC options differ in respect of the features described in Table 1.7, they are still part of the same marketplace and are usually priced off the same underlying instrument. The transparency of pricing of the exchange traded option enables it to act as a benchmark for the OTC pricing. The closer the similarity between the exchange traded and OTC product the greater the OTC trader's confidence will be as to the accuracy of his price.

The exchange traded option can be employed by OTC traders as a hedging tool and so enable them to lay off their risk. Most OTC traders are adept at managing the mismatch which arises between the standard exchange traded and the non-standard OTC product.

Stages in the evolution of derivatives markets

As Table 1.8 illustrates, the growth of the derivatives markets has been phenomenal, averaging 26 per cent per annum growth for the period 1990–1998.

Table 1.8 ● Global exchange-traded contract volumes

Year	Number of contracts traded	Index (1990 = 100)
1990	777,195,380	100.0
1991	815,488,373	104.9
1992	967,380,722	124.5
1993	1,198,210,064	154.2
1994	1,592,779,422	204.9
1995	1,669,013,772	214.7
1996	1,673,632,379	215.3
1997	1,856,379,771	238.9
1998 (Jan–Nov)	2,104,313,325	270.8

Source: Futures and Options World

The evolution of the derivatives markets, while complex in detail, may be summarized according to a few basic themes.

1. There is usually a genuine business need or business risk that needs to be solved between a corporate party and counterparty. This business need could be characterized as a form of business risk, which a creative derivatives team then turns into an arbitrage opportunity. The problem is solved by a new product, which in its initial form is supported by lengthy and complicated documentation and intense involvement by senior management. In this process the transaction costs are very high. However, as soon as the transaction is completed, and other companies in similar circumstances discover its benefits, it is soon replicated and amplified throughout the markets.

2. Financial intermediaries will take advantage of this arbitrage opportunity until it is completely exhausted, resulting in a "boom and bust" cycle for particular derivatives strategies.

3. As a particular type of derivatives transactions or strategy becomes standardized, ie where the documentation and senior management involvement is greatly reduced, it becomes possible for the financial institutions to create portfolios of these instruments.

4. Sophisticated banks realize that they do not have to match any of the individual derivatives transactions, and, through the use of computer modelling, are able to determine their risk exposure and simultaneously hedge their overall position against any residual floating- or fixed-rate risk.

A central driving force of the globalization of the financial service industry has been a revolutionary change in the ability to manage financial risk – with the help of derivatives. The demise of the Bretton Woods exchange-rate arrangements, the liberalization of the financial sectors worldwide and the rapid internationalization of economic life during the last 20 years have created new uncertainties.

The risk management industry has allowed participants in the global financial markets, from multinationals with sophisticated treasury operations to households with floating-rate mortgages, to cope better with expanded financial risk, ie the risk of a change in commodity or stock prices, exchange rates, interest rates, or market liquidity.

The advances since the mid-1970s in the ability to identify and isolate the key financial risks commonly found in modern economies, together with the development of financial institutions and markets that can efficiently commoditize, trade and price such risk, can be said to be an important stage in the evolution of modern market economies. At a fundamental level, it allows those who would like to reduce the economic uncertainty surrounding them to do so at a market-determined price, while those who are better-equipped and willing to bear certain types of risk have vastly expanded opportunities.

The growing reach of the financial service industry is readily apparent. It has enabled the restructuring of industries through mergers, acquisitions and divestitures, and it has provided innovative solutions to massive privatization programmes. It has internationalized the raising and investing of funds and expanded the sources and types of financing to support the emergence of new industries. It has allowed the funding of economic development in emerging and transition economies around the world.

Foreign exchange market turnover

Financial globalization has been a counterpart to international trade in goods and services reflecting the growing financing needs of countries and the globalization of national economies. This is evidenced by the observation that trading in the global foreign exchange market has far outpaced growth in international trade in goods and services.

The average daily turnover in "traditional" global foreign exchange instruments (spot transactions, outright forwards and foreign exchange swaps) has been officially estimated at $1,490 billion in April 1998, compared with $590 billion in April 1989 (see Table 1.9).

Although the rate of growth in other OTC foreign exchange derivative instruments (currency swaps and options) was considerably higher than in traditional ones, they remained, as of April 1998, at $97 billion, a small fraction of overall trading. Meanwhile, the notional value of transactions in interest rate deriva-

Table 1.9 ● The global foreign exchange and over-the-counter derivatives markets

(average daily turnover in billions of US dollars; notional amounts for derivatives)

Category	April 1989	April 1992	April 1995	April 1998
A. Traditional foreign exchange Instruments	**590**	**820**	**1,190**	**1,490**
Spot transactions*	350	400	520	590
Outright forwards and forex swaps†	240	420	670	900
B. Other foreign exchange derivative Instruments	–	–	**45**	**97**
Currency swaps	–	–	4	10
Options	–	–	41	87
Other	–	–	1	0
C. Interest rate derivative instruments	–	–	**151**	**265**
FRAs	–	–	66	74
Swaps	–	–	63	155
Options	–	–	21	3
Other	–	–	2	0
D. Total B + C	–	–	**196**	**362**
Memorandum items: exchange-traded Derivatives				
Currency instruments	*13*	*14*	*17*	*12*
Interest rate instruments	*374*	*640*	*1,205*	*1,360*

* Adjusted for local cross-border double counting
† Includes estimates for gaps in reporting

Sources: BIS; Futures Industry Association; various futures and options exchanges

tives, ie forward rate agreements (FRAs), swaps and options, amounted to $265 billion, compared with $151 billion in 1995.

The growth in size of this daily turnover dwarfs volume sizes in all other financial markets (see Table 1.10).

Table 1.10 ● Growth of foreign exchange market turnover

Currency	1992	1995	1998
	(%)	(%)	(%)
US dollar	34	47	33
Deutsche mark	91	12	37
Japanese yen	24	–4	72
Global	**41**	**29**	**46**

Source: BIS (1998)

The growth between 1986 and 1995 in daily nominal foreign exchange turnover has been of the order of sixfold (see Table 1.11). World annual exports of goods and services in 1995 totalled about $6.1 trillion, compared with almost $1.2 trillion in daily foreign exchange market turnover. Put on the same basis, daily turnover in foreign exchange markets was of the order of 50 times that of the value of exports of goods and services, almost three times what it was a decade earlier. Foreign exchange trading growth rates of these magnitudes, net of the growth rate in trade in goods and services, provide a clear indicator of the globalization of financial markets.

Table 1.11 ● Foreign exchange trading volumes and world trade

	1986	1989	1992	1995
Global estimated turnover (in billions of US dollars)	188	590	820	1,190
As a per cent of				
World exports of goods and services	7.4	15.8	17.4	19.1
Total reserves minus gold (all countries)	36.7	75.9	86.0	84.3

Sources: Bank for International Settlements; International Monetary Fund (1997)

Finally, the integration and globalization of capital markets has been reinforced by the yield-seeking behaviour of investors across national borders, most apparent by the cross-border arbitraging of differences in yields on investments with similar risks. Onshore/offshore interest differentials have declined markedly since the 1970s, and are now negligible for most advanced economies. Similarly, covered interest parity holds more tightly across most advanced economies than in the early 1980s.[13] Indeed, a sophisticated and significant segment of the financial industry in the major international financial centres is singly concerned with arbitraging often minute mispricing of financial assets around the globe.

References

1. Einzig, P. (1970) *The History of Foreign Exchange*. Macmillan.
2. Ibid.
3. Sampson, A. (1982) *The Money Lenders*. Coronet, 29.
4. Goldstein, M. and Mussa, M. (1993) "The Integration of World Capital Markets," IMF Working Paper No. 93/95.

5. Prestwich, M. (1979) "Italian Merchants in England," in *The Dawn of Modern Banking*. New Haven, CT: Yale University Press.

6. de Roover, R. (1948) *The Medici Bank*. New York: New York University Press.

7. Park, Y. S. (1974) *The Eurobond Market: Functions and Structure*. New York: Praeger, Chapter 1.

8. Einzig, P. (1969) "Pre-war Markets in Foreign Issues," in *The Eurobond Market*. London: St Martin's Press, Chapter 3.

9. US Joint Economic Committee (1964) "Economic Policies and Practices," Paper No. 3: "A Description and Analysis of Certain European Capital Markets." Washington DC: US Government Printing Office, 6.

10. Park, Y. S. (1974) *The Eurobond Market: Functions and Structure*. New York: Praeger, Chapter 3.

11. International Monetary Fund (1997) "A Survey by the Staff of the International Monetary Fund," *World Economic Outlook*, May 1997.

12. Goldstein, M. and Mussa, M. (1993) "The Integration of World Capital Markets," IMF Working Paper No. 93/95.

13. International Monetary Fund (1997) "A Survey by the Staff of the International Monetary Fund," *World Economic Outlook*, May 1997.

CHAPTER 2

The global exchange rate system

The principles, the existing system and the "Euroization" of the currency markets

WHAT IS THE IDEAL EXCHANGE RATE SYSTEM THAT A COUNTRY SHOULD ADOPT?

The economics literature has identified a number of factors that influence the relative desirability of alternative exchange rate regimes. These relate to an economy's structural characteristics, its susceptibility to external shocks, and its macroeconomic and institutional conditions.

The early literature on the choice of exchange rate regime, which was based on the theory of optimum currency areas, focused on the characteristics that determine whether a country would be better off, in terms of its ability to maintain internal and external balance, with a fixed or with a flexible exchange rate arrangement. That literature generally indicated that small open economies, ie economies where trade represents a large proportion of GNP, are better served by a fixed exchange rate, and that the less diversified is a country's production and export structure and the more geographically concentrated its trade, the stronger also is the case for a fixed exchange rate. The attractiveness of a fixed exchange rate is also greater the higher is the degree of factor mobility, the less a country's inflation rate diverges from that of its main trading partners, and the lower is the level of economic and financial development (see Table 2.1 on page 29).

Another approach to the choice of exchange rate regime has focused on the effects of various random disturbances on the domestic economy. The optimal regime in this framework is the one that stabilizes macroeconomic performance, ie one that minimizes fluctuations in output, real consumption, the domestic price level, or some other macroeconomic variable. The ranking of fixed and flexible exchange rate regimes depends on the nature and source of the shocks to the economy, policy makers' preferences (ie, the type of costs they wish to minimize), and the structural characteristics of the economy. An extension of this approach assumes that the choice of exchange rate regime is not simply one between a perfectly fixed or a freely floating exchange rate. Rather, it is suggested that there is a range of regimes of varying degrees of exchange rate flexibility reflecting different intensities of official intervention in the foreign exchange market. The typical finding is that a fixed exchange rate (or a greater degree of fixity) is generally superior if the disturbances impinging on the economy are predominantly domestic nominal shocks, such as sudden changes in the demand for money, whereas a flexible rate (or a greater degree of flexibility) is preferable if disturbances are predominantly foreign shocks or domestic real shocks, such as shifts in the demand for domestic goods.

Credibility versus flexibility

A more recent strand of analysis has emphasized the role of credibility and political factors in the choice of exchange rate regime. A key point that emerges from this analysis is that when the domestic rate of inflation is extremely high a pegged exchange rate, by providing a clear and transparent nominal anchor, can help establish the credibility of a stabilization programme. An exchange rate anchor may also be preferable because of instability in the demand for money as inflation is reduced sharply. This contrasts with the more traditional view that the less a country's inflation rate diverges from that of its main trading partners the more desirable is a fixed exchange rate.

In some circumstances, a fixed exchange rate can help to discipline a country's economic policies, especially its fiscal policy. This is particularly relevant for developing countries that do not have the same capacity as advanced economies to separate fiscal and monetary policy. A fixed exchange rate constrains the author-ities' use of what is known as the "inflation tax" as a source of revenue, the more so if the exchange rate is rigidly fixed as in a monetary union or a currency board. The idea that inflation is a form of tax is based on the principle that individuals need to hold more cash when inflation rises. For example when inflation is 10 per cent per year, a person who holds currency for a year loses 10 per cent of the purchasing power of that money and thus effectively pays a 10 per cent tax on the real money holdings. The beneficiary here being the government as they have purchased goods and services which was presumably the cause of the inflation in the first place. The advantage of the fixed exchange rate here is that if the commitment not to use the inflation tax implied by the adoption of a rigidly fixed exchange rate is credible, it allows the authorities to tie down private sector expec-tations of inflation. In contrast, a flexible exchange rate provides the authorities with greater scope for revenue from seigniorage, the revenue that the government raises by printing money, but at the expense of a lack of precommitment as regards future inflation. An adjustable peg provides the authorities with the option to devalue and tax the private sector by generating unanticipated inflation. The risk here, however, is that the peg may become unsustainable if confidence in the authorities' willingness, or ability to maintain it, is lost.

In this framework, the choice of exchange rate regime involves a trade-off between "credibility" and "flexibility", and may depend not only on the nature of the economy and the disturbances to which it is subject but also on political considerations. For instance, it may be more costly politically to adjust a pegged exchange rate than to allow the nominal exchange rate to move by a corre-sponding amount in a more flexible exchange rate arrangement – because the former is clearly visible and involves an explicit government decision, while the latter is less of an event and can be attributed to market forces. When the political costs of exchange rate adjustments are high, it is therefore more likely that a more flexible exchange rate arrangement will be adopted, the more so the larger and more frequent the expected adjustment under a pegged regime.

Choice of peg: single currency or basket?

When the choice of regime has been made in favour of a pegged exchange rate, a further choice arises between pegging to a single currency and pegging to a basket of currencies. When the peg is to a single currency, fluctuations in the anchor currency imply fluctuations in the effective (trade-weighted) exchange rate of the economy in question. By pegging to a currency basket instead, a country can reduce the vulnerability of its economy to fluctuations in the values of the individual currencies in the basket. Thus, in a world of floating exchange rates among the major currencies, the case for a single currency peg is stronger if the peg is to be the currency of the dominant trading partner. However, in some cases, a significant portion of the country's debt service may be denominated in other currencies. This may complicate the choice of currency to which to peg. For instance, for a number of East Asian countries, the US is the major export market, but debt is often serviced largely in Japanese yen. With their currencies typically pegged to dollar-denominated baskets, movements in the yen–dollar rate in recent years have thus posed difficulties for some of these countries.

MACROECONOMIC CHARACTERISTICS OF EXCHANGE RATE REGIMES

Traditionally a distinction in discussing exchange rate arrangements is to differentiate between "pegged" and "flexible" exchange rate systems. The former comprises arrangements in which the domestic currency is pegged to a single foreign currency or to a basket of currencies, including the Special Drawing Right, discussed below. The latter exchange rate arrangement consists of arrangements in which the exchange rate is officially classified as "managed" or "independently floating".

The major difference in economic performance between these two groupings of exchange rate arrangements is with respect to inflation. Inflation in countries with pegged exchange rates has historically been consistently lower and less volatile than in countries with more flexible exchange rate arrangements, but the difference narrowed substantially in the 1990s. In contrast to the marked difference in inflation performance across exchange rate regimes, there is no clear relationship between the exchange rate regime and output growth over the past two decades as a whole. During the 1990s, however, the median growth rate in countries with flexible exchange rate arrangements appears to have been higher than in countries with pegged exchange rates.

Countries that have officially declared flexible exchange rate regimes are, on average, larger economies. They are also less open, where openness is measured by the ratio of trade to output, which partly reflects the fact that larger economies tend to be more self-sufficient. These findings accord with the theory of optimal currency areas, which predicts that, all else being equal, the smaller and more open is an economy, the stronger is the case for a fixed exchange rate.

WHAT ARE THE LESSONS WITH RESPECT TO THE CHOICE OF AN EXCHANGE RATE REGIME?

In an era when countries are becoming increasingly linked to one another through trade and capital flows, the functioning of a country's exchange rate regime is a critical factor in economic policy making. At issue is the extent to which a country's economic performance and the mechanism whereby monetary and fiscal policies affect inflation and growth are dependent on the exchange rate regime.

There is no perfect exchange rate system. What is best depends on a particular economy's characteristics. A useful analysis in the IMF's May 1997 *World Economic Outlook* considers some of the factors which affect the choice. These would include the following.

- **Size and openness of the economy**. If trade is a large share of GDP, then the costs of currency instability can be high. This suggests that small, open economies, may be best served by fixed exchange rates.

- **Inflation rate**. If a country has much higher inflation than its trading partners its exchange rate needs to be flexible to prevent its goods from becoming uncompetitive in world markets. If inflation differentials are more modest a fixed rate is less troublesome.

- **Labour market flexibility**. The more rigid wages are the greater the need for a flexible exchange rate to help the economy to respond to an external shock.

- **Degree of financial development**. In developing countries with immature financial markets a freely floating exchange rate may not be sensible because a small number of foreign exchange trades can cause big swings in currencies.

- **The credibility of policymakers**. The weaker the reputation of the central bank, the stronger the case for pegging the exchange rate to build confidence that inflation will be controlled. Fixed exchange rates have certainly helped economies in Latin America to reduce inflation.

- **Capital mobility**. The more open an economy to international capital, the harder it is to sustain a fixed rate.

Table 2.1 summarizes many of these ideas.

Table 2.1 ● Considerations in the choice of exchange rate regime

Characteristics of economy	Implication for the desired degree of exchange rate flexibility
Size of the economy	The larger the economy, the stronger the case for a flexible rate
Openness	The more open the economy, the less attractive is a flexible exchange rate
Diversified production/export structure	The more diversified the economy, the more feasible is a flexible exchange rate
Geographic concentration of trade	The larger the proportion of an economy's trade with one large country, the greater is the incentive to peg to the currency of that country
Divergence of domestic inflation from world inflation	The more divergent a country's inflation rate from that of its main trading partners, the greater is the need for frequent exchange rate adjustments. (But for a country with extremely high inflation, a fixed exchange rate may provide greater policy discipline and credibility to a stabilization programme)
Degree of economic/financial development	The greater the degree of economic and financial development, the more feasible is a flexible exchange rate regime
Labour mobility	The greater the degree of labour mobility, when wages and prices are downwardly sticky, the less difficult (and costly) is the adjustment to external shocks with a fixed exchange rate
Capital mobility	The higher the degree of capital mobility, the more difficult it is to sustain a pegged-but-adjustable exchange rate regime
Foreign nominal shocks	The more prevalent are foreign nominal shocks, the more desirable is a flexible exchange rate
Domestic nominal shocks	The more prevalent are domestic nominal shocks, the more attractive is a fixed exchange rate
Real shocks	The greater an economy's susceptibility to real shocks, whether foreign or domestic, the more advantageous is a flexible exchange rate
Credibility of policymakers	The lower the anti-inflation credibility of policymakers, the greater is the attractiveness of a fixed exchange rate as a nominal anchor

Source: IMF

Dollarization and the choice of an exchange rate regime

Dollarization, the holding by residents of a significant share of their assets in foreign currency denominated form, in this case the US dollar, is a common feature of developing and transition economies. It is a response to economic instability and high inflation, and to the desire of domestic residents to diversify their asset portfolios. In countries experiencing high inflation, dollarization is typically quite widespread as the public seeks protection from the cost of holding assets denominated in domestic currency. Dollarization is discussed further in

Chapter 9, but it is useful to introduce some of the ideas that are relevant to the choice of exchange rate regime in this chapter.

In order to understand the role of dollarization in influencing the choice of exchange rate regime, it is useful to distinguish between two motives for holding foreign currency assets: currency substitution and asset substitution. Currency substitution occurs when assets denominated in foreign currency are used as a means of payment, while asset substitution occurs when assets denominated in foreign currency serve as stores of value. Currency substitution typically arises during high inflation, when the cost of holding domestic currency for transactions purposes is high. Asset substitution results from portfolio allocation decisions and reflects the relative risk and return characteristics of domestic and foreign assets. In many developing countries, assets denominated in foreign currency have often provided residents with the opportunity to insure against major domestic macroeconomic risks.

Dollarization introduces additional complications into the choice of an exchange rate regime. A key implication of currency substitution is that exchange rates will tend to be more volatile. One reason for this is that there may be frequent and unexpected shifts in the use of domestic and foreign money for transactions, given the ease of switching between domestic money and the dollar. Another is that demand for the domestic-currency-denominated component of the money stock will be more sensitive to changes in its expected opportunity cost. Using the jargon of economics, the interest elasticity of domestic money demand will be higher when there is significant currency substitution, meaning that as domestic and foreign interest rates change, investors will switch quickly between assets, depending on expected returns.

In a floating exchange rate regime, this higher elasticity and instability of money demand would be likely to result in greater exchange rate volatility. This strengthens the argument for the adoption of a pegged exchange rate when currency substitution is extensive. Nevertheless, the broader considerations, discussed earlier in this chapter, that should guide the choice of exchange rate system, still apply. In particular, if shocks originate mostly in financial markets, then fixed exchange rates provide more stability but, if shocks are mostly real in nature, floating rates are superior in stabilizing output.

There is a clear case for fixing the exchange rate when a highly dollarized economy is stabilizing from very high inflation or hyperinflation. Currency substitution is likely to be important, and monetary shocks are likely to predominate, especially as successful stabilization may result in a large but unpredictable increase in the demand for domestic currency. Moreover, during hyperinflation, foreign currency may assume the role of a unit of account, and the exchange rate may also serve as an approximate measure of the price level, making it a powerful guide for influencing expectations in the transition to a low inflation equilibrium. Argentina in 1991 (discussed further in Chapter 9) is an example of a country where an exchange rate anchor helped to stop hyperinflation in the context of extensive currency substitution.

Dollarization in the sense of asset substitution also has implications for the choice of an exchange rate regime. The most important of these may be that the availability of foreign currency deposits, in domestic banks, increases capital mobility, as the public can potentially shift between foreign currency deposits held with domestic banks to those abroad, as well as between foreign-currency- and domestic-currency-denominated deposits held in domestic banks. These various assets are likely to be close substitutes for savers, thereby strengthening the link between interest rates on dollar deposits at home, international dollar interest rates, and domestic currency interest rates. This would limit the control that the central bank can exert on monetary conditions, in particular on the level of interest rates on domestic currency. In contrast to the implications of currency substitution dollarization, in the sense of asset substitution, may thus increase the usefulness of a flexible exchange rate arrangement in enhancing monetary autonomy.

WHY DO CURRENCIES FACE SPECULATIVE ATTACKS?

Krugman's dilemma

Why are currencies repeatedly subject to speculative attacks? In searching for answers to this question Krugman[1] draws on what he calls his "matrix of opinion", which is defined by the different answers to two questions.

1. Whether flexibility of the exchange rate is useful. A country that fixes its exchange rate, in a world in which investors are free to move their money wherever they like, essentially sacrifices the opportunity to have its own monetary policy. Interest rates must be set at whatever level makes foreign exchange traders willing to keep the currency close to the fixed target rate. A country that allows its exchange rate to float, on the other hand, can reduce interest rates to fight recessions and raise them to fight inflation. So the first question Krugman asks, is whether this extra freedom of policy is useful or is it merely illusory.

2. Whether, having decided to float the currency, one can trust the foreign exchange market not to do anything crazy. Will the foreign exchange market set the currency at a value more or less consistent with the economy's fundamental strength and the soundness of the government's policies? Or will the market be subject to alternating bouts of "irrational exuberance and unjustified pessimism", to borrow the famous phrase of Chairman of the Fed, Alan Greenspan.

The answers one might give to these questions define four boxes, all of which have their adherents. Krugman's matrix is shown below.

		Krugman's Matrix	
		Is exchange rate flexibility useful?	
		No	Yes
Can the forex	Yes	Relaxed guy	Serene floater
market be trusted?	No	Determined fixer	Nervous wreck

Suppose that you believe that the policy freedom a country gains from a floating exchange rate is actually worth very little, but you also trust the foreign exchange market not to do anything silly. Then you will be a very "relaxed guy". You will not much care what regime is chosen for the exchange rate. You may have a small preference for a fixed rate or better yet a common currency, on the grounds that stable exchange rates reduce the costs of doing business, Krugman suggests, but you will not lose sleep over the choice.

Suppose on the other hand, that you believe that freedom gained by floating is very valuable, and that financial markets can be trusted. Then you will be, what Krugman calls, a "serene floater". You will believe in freeing your currency from the constraints of a specific exchange rate target, in order that you can get on with the business of pursuing full employment. This was the view held by many economists in the late 1960s and early 1970s.

You will be equally sure of yourself if you believe the opposite, that foreign exchange markets are deeply unreliable, dominated by those irrational bouts of optimism and pessimism, while the monetary freedom that comes with floating is of little value. You will then be a "determined fixer".

But what if you believe both that the freedom that comes from floating is valuable and that the markets that will determine your currency's value under floating rates are unreliable? Then you will be a "nervous wreck", subject to stress-related disorders. You will regard any choice of currency regime as a choice between evils, and will always worry that you have chosen wrongly.

So, given this matrix, in which quadrant is the international financial system? Krugman believes that the nervous wrecks have it. Yes, the monetary freedom of a floating rate is valuable. No, the foreign exchange market cannot be trusted. This reasoning starts with the case for floating currencies. The classic case against floating rates is that any attempt to make use of monetary autonomy will quickly backfire. Assume that a country drops its commitment to a fixed exchange rate and uses that freedom to cut interest rates, which in turn would lead to a decline in the value of the currency. Fixed exchange rate defenders would argue that instead of an increase in employment the result would be a surge in inflation, wiping out both any gain in competitiveness vis-à-vis foreign producers and any stimulus to real domestic demand. The evidence from the UK which exited the Exchange Rate Mechanism in 1992 and painlessly stimulated the economy afterwards provides a counter argument to this view. So floating exchange rates, it can be argued, do work.

Krugman then turns to whether or not the foreign exchange market can be trusted. The evidence, he suggests, is that the currency markets are not "efficient" and they are subject to all sorts of anomalies, speculative bubbles, etc. Foreign exchange markets do not exist in a vacuum. What creates an environment in which speculators can make money is the prevalence of finance ministers who decide to fix their currencies but are suspected of being less than total in their commitment to that policy. The original model of such attacks, Krugman stresses, imagined a country that was known to be following policies ultimately inconsistent with keeping its exchange rate fixed – for example, printing money to cover a budget deficit.

More recent research work, Krugman emphasizes, has drawn attention to three further concerns regarding the extent to which foreign exchange markets can be trusted.

1. Some economists have argued for the importance of self-fulfilling currency crises. They imagine a country whose government is prepared to pay the cost of sticking to an exchange rate indefinitely under normal circumstances, but which is not willing and/or able to put up with the pain of keeping interest rates high enough to support the currency in the face of speculators guessing that it might be devalued. In that case the fixed rate will survive if investors think it will, but it will also collapse if they think it will!

2. If markets are subject to irrational shifts in opinion, for example forgetting the "fundamentals" and simply running with the herd, this applies as much to speculative attacks on fixed exchange rates as to gyrations in the value of flexible exchange rates. One remarkable fact is that there was no sign in the markets that the great currency crises of the 1990s were anticipated. Until only a few weeks before Black Wednesday in the UK, or the Mexican crisis of 1994, investors were cheerfully putting their money into sterling or pesos without demanding any exceptional risk premium. Then quite suddenly everyone wanted out. Was this because of some real news, or was it simply the observation that everyone else suddenly wanted out?

3. The return of the "gnomes of Zurich". Finance ministers whose currencies are under attack invariably blame their problems on the nefarious schemes of foreign exchange market manipulators. Economists usually treat such claims with derision. But casual perusal of business magazines in the last few years would suggest that there appear to be investors who not only move money in anticipation of a currency crisis but also actually do their best to trigger that crisis for fun and profit.

There are, of course, two ways to defeat all of these speculative pressures. One is to be basically indifferent to the exchange rate pressure. The other is to lock in the exchange rate beyond all question – something best done by simply creating a common currency, leaving nothing to speculate in.

Which of these is the better solution? This Krugman suggests, is a peculiarly difficult question to answer. The theory of optimum currency areas, discussed further in Chapter 10, gives us a checklist of the things that ought to matter. However, it is notoriously difficult to turn that checklist into an operational set of criteria. What recent theorizing, backed by recent experience, Krugman goes on to argue, does seem to indicate, is that a country should make a choice one way or the other. That is, in a world in which hot money can move as easily as it now does, an imperfectly credible fixed exchange rate combines the worst of both worlds. You forsake the policy freedom that comes with a flexible rate, yet you remain open to devastating speculative attacks.

THE IMF EXCHANGE RATE ARRANGEMENTS

Every member of the International Monetary Fund (IMF) is obliged to notify the IMF of its exchange rate arrangements within 30 days of becoming a member and promptly thereafter of any subsequent changes.

Since 1973, exchange rate regimes adopted by members have covered a broad spectrum, ranging by degree of flexibility from single currency pegs to free floats. Most countries have adopted regimes that fall fairly readily into one or another of the major categories of the classification system adopted by the IMF in 1982. Countries with dual or multiple exchange markets normally have one market that is clearly the most important, and the IMFs classification refers to that market.

Within the group of fixed-rate arrangements, several deserve separate discussion. In the most pure form of a single currency peg, the currency of another country circulates as legal tender, for example, the Australian dollar in Kiribati, and the US dollar in Liberia, the Marshall Islands, the Federated States of Micronesia, and in Panama. In these countries, the financial stability provided by unifying the currency with the currency of the larger country, and thereby reducing administrative costs, was judged to be more important than the loss of seigniorage and the inability to pursue an independent monetary policy.

A closely related type of peg is a currency board arrangement, whereby the country in question pegs its currency to the currency of a larger country, and simultaneously its issue of domestic currency is fully backed by the foreign currency. Argentina, Estonia, Hong Kong, Lithuania, Bulgaria and Singapore, among others, use modified versions of currency boards. Currency boards are discussed in more detail in Chapter 9.

A currency union is an arrangement under which a common currency circulates at par among the members. The seven currencies that make up the West African Economic and Monetary Union (WAEMU) maintain a common currency, the CFA franc, which has a fixed exchange rate against the French franc/euro. The countries in the WAEMU are Benin, Burkina Faso, Côte d'Ivoire, Guinea-Bissau, Mali, Niger, Senegal and Togo. The CFA franc was, prior to the introduction of the euro, also issued at the same fixed exchange rate to the six member countries of the Central African Monetary Area in which the CFA franc was also the common currency. These countries are Cameroon, Central African Republic, Chad, Republic of Congo, Equatorial Guinea and Gabon. Similarly, six Caribbean countries also maintain fixed exchange arrangements and use a common currency, the Eastern Caribbean dollar, which is issued by the Eastern Caribbean Central Bank and is pegged to the US dollar. These countries are Antigua and Barbuda, Dominica, Grenada, St Lucia, and St Vincent and the Grenadines.

At the other end of the spectrum, the distribution between managed and independently floating arrangements reflects the policy stance for full, or limited, market determination of the exchange rate. In countries with managed regimes, as with pegged and other less flexible regimes, the foreign exchange market does not necessarily clear, even in the limited sense of equalizing supply and demand in the presence of restrictions on foreign exchange flows, and the result has often been the emergence of a parallel, or black market, exchange rate. In contrast, under independently floating regimes, supply and demand is in continuous equality, albeit in the very short run. Currency market intervention is limited in the independently floating group because, by definition, the authorities may intervene only to smooth the exchange rate and not to establish a particular level for it.

The number of member countries that peg their currencies to a single currency or a basket of currencies has decreased in recent years. This decrease is even more marked if one excludes individual country peggers that adhere to some form of regional arrangement and thus have less true discretion regarding their choice of regime. At the other extreme, the number of countries with more flexible exchange rates (particularly independently floating) regimes has increased. In some cases, a currency can be classified into more than one category.

Exchange rate classifications

The IMF sets out its exchange rate classifications using the following taxonomy (*International Financial Statistics*, January 2000).

Exchange arrangements with no separate legal tender (37 countries)

Under this system, the currency of another country circulates as the sole legal tender or alternatively, the member belongs to a monetary or currency union in which the same legal tender is shared by the members of the union.

It is useful to break down this group into countries that use another currency as legal tender. This includes the following groupings:

Group One: Kiribati   Palau

Marshall Islands   Panama

Micronesia   San Marino

Group Two

The East Caribbean Common Market (ECCM).[1] This includes the following countries:

Antigua & Barbuda   St Kitts & Nevis

Dominica   St Lucia

Grenada   St Vincent & the Grenadines

Group Three

The West African Economic and Monetary Union (WAEMU). This includes the following countries:

Benin   Mali

Burkina Faso   Niger

Côte d'Ivoire   Senegal

Guinea-Bissau   Togo

Group Four

The Central African Economic Monetary Community (CAEMC). This includes the following countries:

Cameroon   Congo, Republic of

Central African Republic   Equatorial Guinea

Chad   Gabon

Group Five

Euro Area.

The classification of the Euro area in this category is based on the fact that, until they are withdrawn in the first half of 2002, national currencies will retain their status as legal tender within their home territories.[2] This classification includes the following countries:

Austria   Italy

Belgium   Luxembourg

Finland   Netherlands

France   Portugal

Germany   Spain

Ireland

Currency board arrangements (8 countries)

A currency board arrangement is defined by the IMF as a monetary regime based on an implicit legislative commitment to exchange domestic currency for a specified foreign currency at a fixed exchange rate, combined with restrictions on the issuing authority to ensure the fulfilment of its legal obligation.

Countries applying a currency board arrangement are:

Argentina	China, Peoples' Republic and Hong Kong
Bosnia and Herzegovina	Djibouti
Brunei Darussalam	Estonia
Bulgaria	Lithuania

Other conventional fixed peg arrangements (44 countries)

Under this system the country pegs its currency (formally or *de facto*) at a fixed rate to a major currency or a basket of currencies where the exchange rate fluctuates within a narrow margin of at most ±1 per cent around a central rate.

Countries adopting this system can be broken down into countries that adopt a single peg against a single currency and those that adopt a single peg against a currency composite, such as the SDR – see below. Countries applying a fixed peg against a single currency are:

Aruba	Lesotho
Bahamas[3]	Macedonia, FYR[4]
Barbados	Malaysia
Bahrain[4,5]	Maldives[4]
Belize	Namibia
Bhutan	Nepal
Cape Verde	Netherlands Antilles
China, P.R. Mainland[4]	Oman
Comoros[6]	Qatar[4,5]
Egypt[3,4]	Saudi Arabia[4,5]
El Salvador[4]	Syrian Arab Republic[3]
Iran[3,4]	Swaziland
Iraq	Trinidad & Tobago
Jordan[4]	Turkmenistan[4]
Lebanon[4]	United Arab Emirates[4,5]

Countries applying a fixed peg arrangement against a composite currency, defined below, are:

• Botswana[3]	Myanmar[3]
Burundi	Samoa
Fiji	Seychelles
Kuwait	Solomon Islands
Latvia	Tonga
Malta	Vanuatu
Morocco	

The **Special Drawing Right** (SDR), also known as a currency composite, is an international reserve asset created by the IMF in 1969 and allocated to its members to supplement existing reserve assets.

The value of the SDR, determined daily on the basis of a basket of currencies, tends to be more stable than that of any single currency in the basket. Movements in the exchange rate of any one component currency will tend to be partly or fully offset by movements in the exchange rates of the other currencies.

The composition of the basket is reviewed every five years to ensure that the currencies included in it are representative of those used in international transactions and that the weights assigned to the currencies reflect their relative importance in the world's trading and financial systems. Since 1981, the currencies of five countries, France, Germany, Japan, the UK and the US, have been included in the basket because successive reviews have determined that these are the five countries with the largest exports of goods and services. The reviews also specify the initial weights of the currencies in the basket, reflecting their relative importance in international trade and reserves, as measured by the value of exports of goods and services of the countries issuing them and the balances of the currencies held as reserves by members of the IMF.

With the introduction of the euro on 1 January 1999, the currency amounts of the Deutsche mark and the French franc in the SDR basket were replaced with equivalent amounts of euros, based on the fixed conversion rates between the euro and the Deutsche mark and the French franc announced by the European Council on 31 December 1998. The SDR valuation as at 31 August 1999 is given in Table 2.2.

Table 2.2 ● SDR valuation on 31 August 1999

Currency	Currency amount*	Exchange rate On 31 August[†]	US dollar equivalent[††]
Euro (Germany)	0.2280	1.05450	0.240426
Euro (France)	0.1239	1.05450	0.130653
Japanese yen	27.2000	109.55000	0.248288
Pound sterling	0.1050	1.60370	0.168389
US dollar	0.5821	1.00000	0.582100
		Total	1.369856

SDR 1 = US$1.36986
US$1 = SDR 0.730004[†††]

[*] The currency components of the SDR basket.
[†] Exchange rates in terms of currency units per US dollar, except for the euro and the pound sterling, which are expressed in US dollars per currency unit.
[††] The US dollar equivalents of the currency amounts.
[†††] The official SDR value of the US dollar, which is the reciprocal of the total of the US dollar equivalents – that is, US$1÷1.3986, rounded to six significant digits.

Source: IMF Treasurer's Department

Pegged exchange rates within horizontal bands[7] (8 countries)

Under this arrangement the value of the currency is maintained within margins of fluctuation around a formal or *de facto* fixed peg that are wider than ±1 per cent around a central rate. Countries applying this system can be broken down into two groups: those within a co-operative arrangement, usually referred to as ERM II, discussed in detail below; and those falling under what the IMF calls "Other Band Arrangements".

Countries falling into ERM II are Denmark and Greece.

Countries falling into Other Band Arrangements are Cyprus, Iceland, Libyan AJ, Ukraine and Vietnam.

Crawling pegs (5 countries)

Under this arrangement, the currency is adjusted periodically in small amounts at a fixed, preannounced rate or in response to changes in selective quantitative indicators. Countries applying this system are:

Costa Rica	Tunisia
Nicaragua	Turkey
Bolivia	

Exchange rates within crawling bands[8] (7 countries)

Under this arrangement, the currency is maintained within certain fluctuation margins around a central rate that is adjusted periodically at a fixed preannounced rate or in response to changes in selective quantitative indicators. Countries applying this system are:

Honduras	Sri Lanka
Hungary	Uruguay
Israel	Venezuela
Poland	

Managed floating with no preannounced path for the exchange rate (26 countries)

Under this arrangement, the monetary authority influences the movements of the exchange rate through active intervention in the foreign exchange market without specifying, or precommitting to, a preannounced path for the exchange rate. Countries applying this system are:

Algeria	Uzbekistan[3]
Belarus[3]	Azerbaijan
Cambodia[3]	Ethiopia
Dominican Republic[3]	Kenya
Mauritania	Kyrgyz Republic
Nigeria	Malawi
Norway	Pakistan[3]
Paraguay	Tajikistan
Romania	Czech Republic
Singapore[4]	Lao PDR[3]
Slovak Republic	Jamaica
Suriname	Slovenia
Guatemala	Croatia

Independent floating (51 countries)

Under this arrangement, the exchange rate is market determined, with any foreign exchange intervention aimed at moderating the rate of change and preventing undue fluctuations in the exchange rate, rather than at establishing a level for it. Countries applying this system are:

Gambia	New Zealand	Tanzania
Ghana	Sweden	Thailand
Guinea	UK	Uganda
Guyana	Albania	Yemen, Republic of
India	Armenia	Zambia[3]
Korea	Brazil	Afghanistan[3]
Mauritius[4]	Georgia	Congo, Democratic
Mongolia	Colombia	Republic of
Peru	Haiti	Eritrea
Philippines	Indonesia	Japan
São Tomé and Principe[3]	Kazakhstan	Liberia
Sierra Leone	Madagascar	Papua New Guinea
South Africa	Mexico	Somalia[3]
Switzerland	Moldova	US
Zimbabwe	Mozambique	Russian Federation
Australia	Rwanda	Chile
Canada	Sudan	Angola
		Ecuador

Notes

1 These countries also have a currency board arrangement within the common market.
2 Until they are withdrawn in the first half of 2002, national currencies will retain their status as legal tender within their home territories.
3 Member maintained exchanged rate arrangement involving more than one market. The arrangement shown is that maintained in the major market.
4 The indicated country has a *de facto* arrangement under a formally announced policy of managed or independent floating. In the case of Jordan, it indicates that the country has a *de jure* peg to the SDR but a *de facto* peg to the US dollar. In the case of Mauritius, the authorities have a *de facto* policy of independent floating, with only infrequent intervention by the central bank.
5 Exchange rates are determined on the basis of a fixed relationship with the SDR, within margins of up to ±7.25%. However, because of the maintenance of a relatively stable relationship with the US dollar these margins are not always observed.
6 Comoros has the same arrangement with the French Treasury as do the CFA Franc Zone countries.
7 The band width for these countries is Cyprus (±2.25%), Denmark (±2.25%), Greece (±15%), Iceland (±6%), Libya (±77.5%), Ukraine (Hrv 3.4-4.6 per US dollar), and Vietnam (7%, one sided).
8 The band for these countries is Hungary (±2.25%), Honduras (±7%), Israel (symmetric band of 30%), Poland (±15%), Sri Lanka (±1%), Uruguay (±3%), and Venezuela (±7.5%).

CHANGING PATTERN OF EXCHANGE RATE ARRANGEMENTS IN DEVELOPING COUNTRIES

Over the past two decades, the mix of exchange rate arrangements in developing countries has changed significantly. Following the breakdown of the Bretton Woods par value system and the widespread adoption of floating exchange rates by the major advanced economies in the early 1970s, most developing countries initially continued to peg their currencies either to a key currency – predominantly the US dollar or the French franc – or to a basket of currencies. Starting in the late 1970s, however, a number of developing countries moved away from these arrangements.

At first, the shift was mainly away from single currency pegs to pegs defined in terms of baskets of currencies, for example, the SDR, or to limited flexibility with respect to a single currency (see Table 2.3). But since the early 1980s, there has been a marked shift toward more flexible exchange rate arrangements. Thus, whereas in 1976, 87 per cent of developing countries had some type of pegged exchange rate, while only 10 per cent had flexible exchange rates, by 1986 the proportions were 71 per cent and 25 per cent, respectively, and by the mid 1990s most countries had reportedly adopted a flexible exchange rate regime. When the relative economic size of countries is taken into account, the shift in exchange rate regimes appears to have been even more pronounced. Thus, in

1976 developing countries with pegged exchange rates accounted for 70 per cent of developing countries' total trade, while countries with flexible exchange rates accounted for only 8 per cent. By 1996, this pattern had been virtually reversed.

Table 2.3 ● Developing countries: officially reported exchange rate arrangements

	1976	1981	1986	1991	1996
Pegged	**86**	**75**	**67**	**57**	**45**
US dollar	42	32	25	19	15
French franc	13	12	11	11	11
Other	7	4	4	3	4
SDR	12	13	8	5	2
Composite	12	14	18	20	14
Limited flexibility	**3**	**10**	**5**	**4**	**3**
Single	3	10	5	4	3
Co-operative	–	–	–	–	–
More flexible	**11**	**15**	**28**	**39**	**52**
Set to indicators	6	3	4	4	2
Managed floating	4	9	13	16	21
Independently floating	1	4	11	19	29
Number of countries	**100**	**113**	**119**	**123**	**123**

Based on end-of-year classification

Source: IMF

These figures are based on officially declared exchange rate arrangements. In some countries, however, an arrangement may be officially classified as "managed floating" or even "independently floating", even though the exchange rate continues to be used actively as a policy instrument and is effectively set by the authorities. Indeed, some of these countries continue to informally peg their exchange rate to one of the major reserve currencies, particularly the US dollar. The shift toward more flexible exchange rate regimes since the 1970s may therefore be less pronounced than indicated by official statements and classifications, but it is still significant.

Notwithstanding the increasing adoption of more flexible exchange rate arrangements, some countries have continued to maintain pegged exchange rate regimes, the prime example being the 14 sub-Saharan countries of the CFA zone, which have pegged their currencies to the French franc since 1948, and are now pegging to the euro. Also, a few countries have reverted to a fixed exchange rate regime. The most notable examples are Argentina, which adopted a currency-board-type arrangement in 1991 and has maintained it since, and Hong Kong, China, which has had a currency board type arrangement since 1983. All developing countries that switched from flexible to a pegged exchange rate subsequently reverted to flexible arrangements.

Table 2.4 ● Geographical distribution of officially reported exchange rate arrangements

	Africa	Asia	Middle East and Europe	Western Hemisphere	Total
			1976		
Pegged	39	15	13	19	86
To a basket of currencies	12	7	5	–	24
Limited flexibility	–	1	2	–	3
More flexible	1	1	2	7	11
Independently floating	–	–	1	–	1
Total	**40**	**17**	**17**	**26**	**100**
			1986		
Pegged	34	14	11	21	80
To a basket of currencies	15	9	6	2	32
Limited flexibility	–	2	4	–	6
More flexible	13	7	2	11	33
Independently floating	8	1	1	3	13
Total	**47**	**23**	**17**	**32**	**119**
			1996		
Pegged	25	11	8	11	55
To a basket of currencies	5	9	5	–	19
Limited flexibility	–	–	4	–	4
More flexible	25	13	5	21	64
Independently floating	20	5	2	9	36
Total	**50**	**24**	**17**	**32**	**123**

Source: IMF

The shift towards more flexible exchange rate arrangements has been broadly based across geographic regions (see Table 2.4). In 1976, pegged rate regimes were dominant in all four of the IMF's *World Economic Outlook's* regional groupings of developing countries: Africa, Asia, the Middle East and Europe, and the Western Hemisphere. This was still true in 1986, especially in Africa and the Middle East and Europe region. But by 1996, flexible exchange rate regimes had become dominant in all regions. Pegged rate regimes are now most common among countries in Africa and the Middle East and least prevalent among countries in the Western Hemisphere. In Africa, countries with currencies pegged to the French franc or the South African rand now account for the bulk of pegged regimes. The exchange rate arrangements of a few Middle eastern countries (Bahrain, Qatar, Saudi Arabia and the United Arab Emirates) are formally classified as ones of "limited flexibility", but in fact the currencies of these countries are tightly linked to the US dollar.

Of the countries in the Western Hemisphere with pegged exchange rates, all peg their currencies to the US dollar. In Asia, although no country formally pegs to the dollar, in many cases the dollar appears to have a very large weight in currency baskets, at least until recently. Among the Asian economies with flexible exchange rate arrangements, the majority have always favoured managed floating, but in the 1990s a number of countries adopted "independently floating" rates. Arrangements in which the exchange rate is adjusted according to a set of indicators were prevalent in Western Hemisphere countries in the 1970s and early 1980s, but they have since become less common. Instead, Western Hemisphere countries with flexible arrangements are evenly divided between those with managed and those with independently floating rates. In Africa, the great majority of countries with flexible exchange rate arrangements have chosen to float independently.

THE "EUROIZATION" OF THE FOREIGN EXCHANGE MARKET

The introduction of the euro on 1 January 1999 has meant that relationships between members of the euro bloc, mostly the former EMS currencies, have now altered. In this section we describe the impact of the euro on the exchange rate regimes applied in both non-participating European countries and on other countries affected by the change. We then provide a summary of Central and Eastern Europe exchange rate regimes. Finally we describe the operational features of the new European Exchange Rate Mechanism (ERM II).

The introduction of the euro has meant that changes to the pegging arrangements, formerly in place, have had to be made. These changes range from the introduction of the euro as their own currency to the adoption of exchange rate regimes involving the use of the euro. These arrangements are mainly a legacy of past links to the former euro area national currencies. The new arrangements are summarized in Tables 2.5, 2.6 and 2.7.

Various *ad hoc* arrangements have been introduced largely relating to French territorial communities to the Vatican City, the Republic of San Marino and to the Principality of Monaco. Besides these *ad hoc* monetary agreements, some 30 countries around the euro area currently have exchange rate regimes involving the euro. These can be broken down into four groups.

1. The first group includes countries the currency of which is pegged to the euro. This group comprises four countries. Since January 1999 two EU Member States, Denmark and Greece, have been participating in the new exchange rate mechanism (ERM II) that links the currencies of the EU

Member States to the euro on a bilateral and voluntary basis. Two other countries (Cyprus and Macedonia) unilaterally peg their currencies to the euro.

2. The second group (Bosnia-Herzogovinia, Bulgaria and Estonia) have adopted euro/Deutsche mark-based currency boards. The formal substitution of the euro for the Deutsche mark in these exchange rate regimes is planned to take place, at the latest, upon the introduction of the euro banknotes in 2002.

3. A third group (including Hungary, Iceland and Poland) consists of 17 countries that peg their currency to a basket of currencies including the euro or one of its national denominations. This group also includes those countries with currencies pegged to the Special Drawing Right (SDR). When it was introduced, the euro, as discussed below, automatically replaced the fixed currency amounts of the Deutsche mark and the French franc in the SDR basket, which in turn also includes the US dollar, the Japanese yen and sterling. The components of the SDR are illustrated in Table 2.2.

4. The fourth group (including the Czech Republic, the Slovak Republic and Slovenia) has adopted a system of managed floating with the euro used informally as the reference currency.

Table 2.5 ● Central and Eastern Europe: exchange rate regimes

Country	Exchange rate regime	Basket/target	Fluctuation band (%)
Albania	Independent floating		
Bulgaria	Currency board	DM	0
Croatia	Managed floating	*De facto* narrow target band vis-à-vis DM	
Czech Republic	Managed floating		
Estonia	Currency board	DM	0
Hungary	Crawling peg*	Euro	±2.25
Latvia	Fixed peg	SDR	0
Lithuania	Currency board	US$	0
FYR Macedonia	Managed floating	*De facto* peg to DM	±7.00
Poland	Independent floating		
Romania	Independent floating		
Slovak Republic	Independent floating		
Slovenia	Managed floating	*De facto* shadowing of DM, combined with real exchange rate rule	

* Midpoint of band is devalued monthly by 0.8 per cent

Source: IMF, Monetary and exchange rate policy of transition economies of Central and Eastern Europe after the launch of EMU, May 2000

Table 2.6 ● European countries "euro" exchange rate arrangements

Country	Exchange rate regime	Peg against	Features of the arrangement	Remarks
Bosnia-Herzegovina	Currency board	EUR/DEM		Formally introduced on 20 June 1997. National legislation provides that the euro will replace the Deutsche mark upon the introduction of the euro banknotes in 2002 at the latest.
Bulgaria	Currency board	EUR/DEM		Formally introduced on 1 July 1997. National legislation provides that the euro will replace the Deutsche mark upon the introduction of the euro banknotes in 2002 at the latest.
Croatia	Managed floating (EUR/DEM used informally as reference currency)			The managed float has been in place since the stabilization plan was introduced in October 1993.
Czech Republic	Managed floating (EUR/DEM used informally as reference currency)			In May 1997 the peg with a ±7.5% fluctuation band to a currency basket (DEM (65%) and USD (35%)) that had been introduced in February 1996 was abandoned. The peg to a currency basket had been introduced in 1991.
Cyprus	Peg	EUR	±2.25% fluctuation band	The Cypriot pound (CYP) was pegged to the ECU between June 1992 and December 1998. The CYP has been pegged to the euro since 1 January 1999 with the same central parity previously adopted for the ECU.
Denmark	Peg within co-operative arrangement	EUR	±2.25% fluctuation band	Participation in ERM II since 1 January 1999.
Estonia	Currency board	EUR/DEM		Introduced in June 1992. National legislation provides that the euro will replace the Deutsche mark upon the introduction of the euro banknotes in 2002 at the latest.
Greece	Peg within co-operative arrangement	EUR	±15% fluctuation band	Participation in ERM II since 1 January 1999.
Hungary	Crawling fluctuation band	EUR	±2.25% pre-announced crawling fluctuation band with a 0.5% monthly depreciation rate	Introduced in December 1994, the monthly rate of depreciation of the central rate and accordingly of the crawling fluctuation band has been frequently reduced over time. As of 1 January 2000 the euro replaced the currency basket.

Iceland	Peg	Trade-weighted currency basket including the euro	±6% band (widened from ± 2.25% in 1995)	Currency basket peg in effect since early 1992. Until September 1995 the currency basket was: ECU (76%); USD (18%); JPY (6%).
Latvia	Peg	SDR		De facto peg to the SDR since February 1994, formalized in 1997.
Macedonia	De facto peg	EUR/DEM		Monetary policy based on an exchange rate objective, with a de facto peg to the Deutsche mark in force since early 1994.
Malta	Peg	Currency basket: EUR (56.8%) USD (21.6%) GBP (21.6%)	±0.25% fluctuation band	Currency basket peg in effect since 1971. The euro was substituted for the ECU, with effect from 1 January 1999.
Slovak Republic	Managed floating (euro used informally as reference currency)			Between 14 July 1994 and 1 October 1998 the Slovak crown (SKK) was pegged to a basket of two currencies (60% DEM and 40% US dollar). In 1996 the fluctuation band was widened from ±1.5% to ±7%. On 2 October 1998 the system of pegging was abolished and replaced by managed floating; on 1 January 1999 the Deutsche mark was replaced by the euro as reference currency.
Slovenia	Managed floating (euro used informally as reference currency)			Since 1992 the exchange rate has remained within an unannounced narrow band against the Deutsche mark (the euro since 1 January 1999).
Turkey	Managed floating with a de facto crawling peg	Currency basket including US$ and EUR/DEM		In effect since approximately 1993 although interrupted by floating during 1994. The present band was defined in the Stand-by Arrangement with the International Monetary Fund in 1995. Exchange rate policy aims at minimizing fluctuations of the real effective exchange rate.

Source: ECB Monthly Report, September 1999

Table 2.7 ● Non-European countries "euro"rate arrangements

Country	Exchange rate regime	Peg against	Features of the arrangement	Remarks
14 African countries of which the CFA franc is the legal tender	Peg	EUR	Fixed	The CFA franc is issued by the Central Bank of West African States and the Bank of Central African States. The first institution issues the currency for Benin, Burkina Faso, Côte d'Ivoire, Guinea-Bissau, Mali, Niger, Senegal and Togo, and the second for Cameroon Central African Republic, Chad, Republic of Congo, Equatorial Guinea, and Gabon. The CFA franc was pegged to the French franc until 31 December 1998.
Bahrain	Peg	SDR	±7.25% fluctuation band	The dinar is *de jure* pegged to the SDR, although, *de facto*, it closely follows the US dollar.
Bangladesh	Peg	Basket of trading partners' currencies including the euro		
Botswana	Peg	SDR and basket of trading partner currencies, including the euro		
Burundi	Peg	Basket of currencies of its major trading partners, including the euro		
Cape Verde	Peg	EUR	Fixed	The escudo was pegged to the Portuguese escudo until 31 December 1998.
Chile	Crawling fluctuation	Basket USD EUR/DEM/JPY	±16% band	
Comoros	Peg	EUR	Fixed	The Comorian franc was pegged to the French franc until 31 December 1998.

Country	Regime	Reference	Fluctuation band	Notes
Israel	Crawling fluctuation band	Basket (in terms of units of each currency in the basket): USD (0.6741) EUR (0.2282) GBP (0.0589) JPY (6.5437)	±15% crawling fluctuation band. Under this system, there is a gradual, constant and predetermined adjustment to both the midpoint and the band.	The number of units of each currency in the basket is determined according to its share in external trade during the previous calendar year and to international cross rates at the time the basket's composition is fixed. The euro replaced the Deutsche mark with effect from 1 January 1999.
Jordan	Peg	*De jure* peg to the SDR	Fixed	The dinar has been *de jure* pegged to the SDR since 1995, although *de facto* it closely follows the US dollar.
Libyan Arab Jamahiriya	Peg	SDR	Broad fluctuation band	
Morocco	Peg	Undisclosed basket	The rate can fluctuate daily by 0.3% either way.	The euro is likely to be included in the currency basket.
Myanmar	Peg	SDR	±2% fluctuation band	
Qatar	Peg	SDR	±7.25% fluctuation band	
Saudi Arabia	Peg	SDR	Fixed	The riyal is officially pegged to the SDR, although *de facto* it follows the US dollar.
Seychelles	Peg	Weighted basket including the euro		
United Arab Emirates	Peg	SDR	±7.25% fluctuation band	
Vanuatu	Peg	Undisclosed transactions-weighted currency basket		The euro is likely to be included in the currency basket.

Source: ECB Monthly Report, September 1999

THE NEW EUROPEAN EXCHANGE RATE MECHANISM – ERM II

As discussed in more detail in Chapter 10, on 1 January 1999, at the start of Stage Three of European Economic and Monetary Union (EMU), the currencies of 11 EU Member States merged into the euro, forming a common and independent currency. Previously those 11 currencies had been linked by the Exchange Rate Mechanism (ERM) of the European Monetary System (EMS). On that date, the euro superseded the European Currency Unit (ECU), which was defined in principle as a basket currency, in the ratio of 1:1, as provided in the EC Treaty. In practice some adjustments had to be made as the components of the ECU were not identical to those of the euro. At the same time, the EMS ceased to exist. However in order to foster the convergence process in the Member States that are not yet participating in the single monetary policy, and to strengthen and underpin the single market, some Member States which are not introducing the euro from the outset (Denmark and Greece) are being given an opportunity to prepare themselves for full integration into the euro area by linking their currencies to the euro in the context of a new, modified exchange rate mechanism. This section provides an overview of the structural and operational features of the new exchange rate mechanism, known as "ERM II".

Legal basis

In legal terms the new exchange rate mechanism rests on two pillars. The first is the "Resolution of the European council on the establishment of an exchange rate mechanism in the third stage of economic and monetary union" of June 1997, which defines the principles and objectives of the system and its main structural features. Second, the decision-making bodies of the European Central Bank (ECB) – the Governing Council and the General Council – agreed on 1 September 1998 on the text of an agreement between the ECB and the central banks of the EU Member States outside the euro area. This specifies the operating procedures of ERM II. Subsequently, that agreement was signed by the relevant parties, ie by the ECB President and the Governors of the central banks of the four non euro-area Member States – Denmark, Greece, Sweden and the UK.

Objectives

The introduction of the euro, in 11 of the 15 EU Member States, has given rise to a fundamentally new situation for European monetary policy. The vast majority of the Member States have transferred their monetary policy sovereignty to the European central bank, while Denmark, Greece, Sweden and the UK continue to pursue autonomous monetary and foreign exchange policies for the time being. Even so, Article 109 of the EC Treaty requires those Member States to treat their exchange rate policy as a matter of common interest.

Linking the currencies of the Member States which are not participating in the euro area from the outset (the "pre-ins") to the euro will, it is hoped, give those countries a strong incentive to pursue stability-oriented economic and monetary policies. That principle is particularly important for those EU Member States which are seeking to join the euro area in the foreseeable future but which have not yet reached the degree of economic convergence required by the EC Treaty. Equally, the new reference system, it is hoped, will counteract possible speculative exchange rate fluctuations that are unwarranted, given the economic fundamentals. Thus, foreign exchange market turmoil within the EU such as has often occurred in the past, can, again it is hoped, be largely avoided.

Principles

In much the same way as in the previous EMS, "pre-ins" are, in principle, free to actively participate in the new exchange rate mechanism. Countries which do not participate from the outset can do so at a later stage. However, the European Council has drawn attention to the fact that Member States with a derogation, that is those states not participating in the full euro arrangement, will be expected to join ERM II. Participation is compulsory for those EU Member States which are seeking to introduce the euro in the foreseeable future, since the convergence criterion spelled out in Article 109 of the EC Treaty requires their participation in the Exchange Rate Mechanism for at least two years without devaluation and also to keeping their exchange rates within the "normal" fluctuation margins.

At their request, Denmark and Greece are participating in the new exchange rate mechanism from 1 January 1999. This was the outcome of an informal agreement between the ministers of the euro-area Member States, the ECB and the ministers and central bank governors of Denmark and Greece, involving the European Commission and after consulting the Monetary Committee, in September 1998. The Greek drachma is participating in ERM II with a fluctuation band of ±15 per cent around its central rate against the euro, while a fluctuation band of ± 2.25 per cent has been agreed for the Danish krone.

Against the background of the experience gained with the former EMS, the new exchange rate mechanism has been designed to be more flexible in a number of areas. The underlying motive here was that the objective of maintaining price stability, which has been given priority by the ECB and the national central banks, must in no circumstances be jeopardized. Thus, the generally automatic and quantitatively unlimited obligation to intervene in support of exchange rates, once the limits of the fluctuation bands have been reached, may be suspended, if there is a risk of conflict with the ESCB's primary objective, namely price stability.

In addition, all the parties involved in central rate decisions, including the ECB, have the right to initiate a confidential procedure aimed at reconsidering central rates, in order that necessary adjustments can be carried out in good time. Furthermore, it is now possible for different degrees of progress in convergence on the part of the "pre-ins" to be taken into consideration. There is a fixed procedure enabling Member States whose economic performance has converged very closely with that of the euro-area Member States to agree with the ECB on fluctuation bands for their currencies that are narrower than the standard bands envisaged in ERM II.

Structural features: central rates and fluctuation bands

Unlike the situation in the former EMS, which provided for reciprocal central and intervention rates in the form of a parity grid for all the participating currencies, in the new exchange rate mechanism, the euro has expressly been given the role of the anchor currency. Central and intervention rates are all defined in terms of the euro. Hence, the new system is sometimes likened to a "hub and spokes approach". Around the central rate of the currency of every "pre-in" country vis-à-vis the euro a ±15 per cent standard band for exchange rate fluctuations is fixed. In the case of the standard fluctuation band, the intervention rates are determined by simply adding the 15 per cent margin to or subtracting it from the bilateral central rates, and subsequently rounding the result to six significant digits. The central and marginal rates are quoted as the countervalue of one euro and are announced in the markets.

For future participants, a further implication of the new system is that the assessment of their currency's exchange rate stability within ERM II depends only on the relation to the euro. Under the old system, a currency's exchange rate stability was assessed by reference to what was termed a "divergence indicator", which was based on the deviation of the ECU market rates from the ECU central rates, and therefore incorporated weighted deviations from all other participants in the system.

According to the Resolution of the European Council, decisions on central rates and the standard fluctuation band are taken by mutual agreement between the ministers of the euro-area Member States, the ECB and the ministers and central bank governors of the "pre-in" Member States participating in the new exchange rate system.

Interventions and central rate adjustments

As a matter of principle, the central banks concerned will automatically intervene when the upper or lower intervention points are reached. In the euro area, such operations are normally carried out by the central banks of the "ins", acting on behalf of the ECB. In each individual case, the initiative for such support measures, which are generally unlimited in amount, proceeds from the market participants, who offer their central bank, at which they are required to maintain an account, the weak currency at the marginal rate, or seek to buy the strong currency at the intervention rate. However the notion underlying the Resolution of the European Council and the Central Bank Agreement makes it clear that foreign exchange market intervention to defend central rates are only designed to bolster other policy measures. A stability orientated monetary and fiscal policy, it is stressed, must be at the heart of any central rate stabilization. In particular, the interest rate instrument has to be employed flexibly in this context in order to stabilize exchange rates. As described above, the central banks involved may suspend intervention if the overriding objective of maintaining price stability appears to be at risk. Any decision to suspend compulsory intervention would have to take due account of the particular circumstances and of the credible functioning of ERM II.

In the event of shifts in the economic fundamentals between participants in the system (such as changes in the purchasing-power parities), thereby applying pressure to the currencies participating in ERM II, central rates are, it is stressed, to be adjusted to the new economic situation faster than had been the case in the EMS. Thus, all the parties involved in decision making have the right to initiate a confidential procedure aimed at reconsidering central rates. This new element of granting initiator rights to the ECB and national central banks is designed to help de-politicize central rate adjustments and to accelerate adjustment procedures, which are thought to have been sluggish in the former EMS.

Very short-term financing

To enhance the credibility of the intervention commitments assumed automatically accessible "very short-term financing facilities" have been established between the ECB and the central banks of the "pre-ins" participating in ERM II. They serve to ensure that all participants in the system have access to a sufficiently large amount of partner currencies so as to be able to intervene in the foreign exchange market in favour of their currencies, if necessary. However, central banks which seek recourse to short-term financing are required to make appropriate use of their own foreign reserve holdings for their support operations before taking up such loans. In the event of compulsory intervention, the financing is in principle unlimited in amount, has an initial maturity of three months and is denominated in the currency of the creditor central bank. In much the same way as the interventions, it may be suspended if the target of price stability would otherwise be at risk.

This very short-term financing facility may also be used in the event of intra-marginal interventions, but only up to specified ceilings fixed for the central banks of the "pre-in" Member States. These ceilings for cumulative borrowing are defined as twice the amount formerly made available to the respective national banks in the context of the short-term monetary support mechanism. Under this arrangement, the ceilings for the central banks amount to euro 520 million for Denmark, euro 300 million for Greece, euro 990 million for Sweden and euro 3,480 million for the UK. These amounts are notional for the central banks of the Member States which are not participating in ERM II, the UK and Sweden. The ceilings for the ECB and the central banks of the "ins" have been set at zero, which also indicates that the ECB, as the anchor central bank, and the other central banks of the "ins" will not engage in intramarginal intervention as a matter of principle.

Monitoring

The General Council of the European Central Bank (which comprises the central bank governors of the "ins", the ECB's president and vice president, and the central bank governors of the "pre-ins") monitors the functioning of the new exchange rate mechanism. Equally, the General Council serves as a forum for monetary and exchange rate policy co-ordination between all EU central banks, and for assessing the administration of the intervention and financing mecha-nisms specified in the Agreement. In addition, it has to monitor, on a permanent basis, the sustainability of exchange rate relations between every currency par-ticipating in ERM II and the euro.

The future

ERM II is also likely to be of significance in the light of the expected enlargement of the EU to include a number of countries in Central and Eastern Europe. Once these countries have joined the EU, they will be able, in principle, to adjust their currencies to the euro by participating in ERM II. It remains to be seen how fast the individual countries will be able to adapt their economic and monetary policies to conditions in the euro area, thus meeting the requirements for adopting the euro at a later stage.

The exchange rate regimes for Central and Eastern Europe are illustrated in Tables 2.5, 2.6 and 2.7.

Reference

1. Krugman, P. (1998) *The Accidental Theorist*. W.W.W. Norton.

The foreign exchange and over-the-counter derivatives markets in the UK*

In April this year, the Bank of England conducted its regular survey of turnover in the United Kingdom foreign exchange and over-the-counter (OTC) derivatives markets,[1] as part of the latest worldwide survey organized by the Bank for International Settlements (BIS). The foreign exchange market survey has been conducted triennially since 1986, and a parallel survey of the OTC derivatives markets was first conducted in 1995. This article sets out the results (in US$ billion), and compares them with the 1995 survey and results for other major centres.[2]

The survey shows that:

- Average daily spot and forward foreign exchange turnover for April 1998 was $637 billion, 37 per cent higher than the $464 billion per day recorded three years earlier (an annualized growth rate of 11 per cent).

- Average daily turnover in the UK for OTC currency and interest rate derivatives was $171 billion, 131 per cent higher than the $74 billion per day recorded three years earlier (an annualized growth rate of 32 per cent).

- The UK has consolidated its position as the world's largest centre for foreign exchange and OTC derivatives business, accounting for 32 per cent and 36 per cent of the global foreign exchange and OTC derivatives markets respectively.

- The forward foreign exchange market continued to grow more rapidly than the spot market, which now represents only 35 per cent of total foreign exchange turnover.

- US dollar/Deutsche mark retained its position as the most widely traded currency pair (22 per cent of all spot and forward foreign exchange transactions). The share of sterling trading rose, and sterling/US dollar regained its position as the second most actively traded currency pair (14 per cent turnover). Cross-trading of ERM currencies generally declined.

- The proportion of interest rate OTC derivatives turnover accounted for by swaps increased from 32 per cent to 56 per cent; the proportion accounted for by forward rate agreements (FRAs) fell from 59 per cent to 35 per cent.

- ERM currencies dominated the UK interest rate derivatives market, making up 56 per cent of all trades. The Deutsche mark almost doubled its share of the market, growing from 18 per cent to 32 per cent; all other major currencies lost market share.

*This appendix was reprinted, with permission, from the *Bank of England Quarterly Bulletin*, November 1998. By Jamie Thom of the Bank's Foreign Exchange Division and Jill Paterson and Louise Boustani of the Bank's Markets and Trading Systems Division.

The London survey

Participants
293 banks and securities houses participated in the UK foreign exchange survey (40 with nil returns, ie reporting "no activity" in April), and 10 foreign exchange brokers. 317 principals took part in the OTC derivatives markets survey (120 with nil returns). As in previous years, the Bank of England asked all banks active in the UK, and some non-bank financial firms believed to be active in the wholesale markets, to participate in the survey. Other institutions did not take part directly, but their transactions with principals taking part, or through brokers, will have been reported by those institutions. It is reasonable to assume that little trading took place between non-participating entities.

The questionnaire
Survey participants were requested to complete a questionnaire prepared by the Bank of England, based on a standard format agreed with other central banks and produced by the Bank for International Settlements (BIS). Participants were asked to provide details of their gross turnover for the 20 business days in April 1998. Gross turnover is the absolute total value (measured in nominal terms) of all deals contracted; there was no netting of purchases against sales. Data were requested in terms of US dollar equivalents. The basis of reporting was the location of the trade, regardless of where it was booked. The questionnaire asked for data broken down by currency, instrument and type of counterparty.

The survey distinguished the following types of transaction:

Foreign exchange
- *Spot transaction:* single outright transaction involving the exchange of two currencies at a rate agreed on the date of the contract, for value or delivery (cash settlement) within two business days – including same-day and next-day value transactions.

Forwards
- *Outright forward:* similar to a spot deal except that it is for value more than two business days after the deal was struck.
- *Foreign exchange swap:* transaction that involves the actual exchange of two currencies (principal amount only) on a specific date at a rate agreed at the time of the conclusion of the contract (the short leg), and a reverse exchange of the same two currencies at a date further in the future at a rate agreed at the time of the contract (the forward leg). Only the unsettled forward part of the deal was reported, and the spot leg was *not* included as a spot transaction.

OTC derivatives
- *Currency swap:* contract that commits two counterparts to exchange streams of interest payments in different currencies for an agreed period of time and to exchange principal amounts in different currencies at a pre-agreed exchange rate at maturity.
- *Currency option:* option contract that gives the right to buy or sell a currency with another currency at a specified exchange rate, during a specified period or on a specified date. This category also includes exotic foreign exchange options, such as average rate options and barrier options.
- *Forward rate agreement (FRA);* interest rate forward contract in which the rate to be paid or received on a specific obligation for a set period of time, beginning at some time in the future, is determined at contract initiation.

- *Interest rate swap:* agreement to exchange periodic payments related to interest rates on a single currency; can be fixed for floating, or floating for floating, based on different indices. This group includes swaps where the notional principal is amortized according to a fixed schedule, independent of interest rates.

- *Interest rate option:* option contract that gives the right to pay or receive a specific interest rate on a predetermined principal for a set period of time. This group includes options written on interest rate securities, interest rate warrants or swaptions and caps, floors, collars, corridors or other synthetic products created by the grouping of different options.

Reporting institutions were asked to distinguish between transactions with *banks and securities firms, other financial institutions* (all categories of financial institution other than banks or securities firms) and *non-financial customers*, in each case separating local and cross-border transactions (determined according to the location, rather than nationality, of the counterparty) to permit adjustment for double-counting. Additionally, participants in the foreign exchange survey were asked how much business was done through brokers – including that through automated dealing systems – and to indicate whether they operated netting arrangements (and if so, to provide details). Brokers were also asked how much of their business was done through their own branches and subsidiaries abroad.

The *gross* aggregate responses to the main sections of the questionnaire are reproduced in Tables M, N and O (at the end of this article). These data can also be obtained in electronic form from the Bank's web site at www.bankofengland.co.uk/pr98100.htm. The BIS intends to publish an analysis of the global survey results next spring. A survey of global outstanding positions in the derivative markets (measured at the end of June 1998) has also been undertaken, and results for this will be released by the BIS at the same time.

Introduction

The Bank's foreign exchange and derivatives market surveys in April were the latest in a triennial series co-ordinated globally by the BIS. On this occasion, 43 countries undertook market surveys, and have each reported their results to the BIS, which has produced estimates of the size of the global markets.[3] These global results are adjusted for the fact that trades between participants in the surveys reporting to two different central banks will appear in both national surveys (local double-counting is deducted "at source").

Foreign exchange
Daily turnover in the UK

Average daily turnover during April 1998 was $637 billion per day ($217 billion in the spot market and $420 billion in the forward market). This was 37 per cent higher than in the previous survey in 1995, a slower rate of growth in dollar terms than the 60 per cent increase reported between 1992 and 1995. However, there have been large exchange rate movements since 1995: in sterling terms, the overall growth was 32 per cent, whereas in Deutsche mark terms it was 80 per cent.[4]

About 47 per cent of firms taking part in the survey thought that the overall level of turnover during the survey period was normal; 5 per cent considered it to be above normal; and 15 per cent below normal. The remaining 33 per cent did not comment.

Global turnover

Table A shows that average daily turnover in the UK market is almost as great as that of the US, Japan and Singapore combined. The growth of turnover in the US was marginally faster than in the UK, partly because of the slower growth of ERM cross-currency and Ecu-denominated trading (which represented 10 per cent of UK turnover in 1995, double that in the US). The slower growth reported by the Banque de France and the Bundesbank was largely because of a fall in both centres in Deutsche mark/French franc turnover. Several centres, including Japan, Hong Kong and Switzerland, reported a fall in foreign exchange turnover in dollar terms. In domestic currency terms, however, turnover in Japan and Switzerland rose by 45 per cent and 25 per cent respectively between 1995 and 1998.

Table A ● Average daily foreign exchange turnover

US$ billions

	1992	1995	1998	Percentage change 1995–98
UK	291	464	637	37
US	167	244	351	43
Japan	120	161	149	−8
Singapore	74	105	139	32
Germany	55	76	94	24
Switzerland	66	87	82	−5
Hong Kong	60	90	79	−13
France	33	58	72	24

It would be misleading simply to aggregate the individual results from countries to produce a figure for global turnover; this would double-count deals between centres. The BIS estimate of global turnover eliminates such double-counting and shows that global turnover was $1,490 billion per day in April 1998, an increase of 26 per cent from $1,190 billion in April 1995. The UK's share of the global foreign exchange market continued to rise: it reached 32 per cent in April 1998, compared with 30 per cent in 1995, 27 per cent in 1992, and 26 per cent in 1989.

Types of transactions

Table B shows a further fall in the proportion of foreign exchange business transacted for spot value. Forward transactions made up 65 per cent of total gross turnover, continuing the substantial rise since the first survey in 1986, when the share of forwards stood at 27 per cent. Most of these transactions are swaps, in which neither counterparty assumes currency risk. They are closely linked to money-market deals (most are short-dated), and

Table B ● Proportion of gross foreign exchange turnover by transaction type

Per cent

	1992	1995	1998
Spot	52	41	35
Forward: outright	6	7	7
Forward: swaps	42	52	58
Maturity of forwards:			
Up to and for 7 days	33	42	51
7 days and up to and for 1 month	4	5	5
1 month and up to 6 months	} 10		
3 months up to and for 1 year		6	4
Over 1 year	1	1	1

Note: Percentage shares have been rounded to the nearest whole number.

are often used to hedge currency risk and manage liquidity. A similar trend was evident in the US, where the proportion of turnover accounted for by forwards rose from 45 per cent to 58 per cent between 1995 and 1998.

Currency composition

Table C shows that US dollar/Deutsche mark retained its position as the most widely traded currency pair. Its share of currency trading has remained stable at around one-fifth since 1986. The importance of US dollar/yen trading diminished, reversing a rise between 1992 and 1995. But the derivatives survey indicates that this currency pair now has the largest share of the currency options market; this may partly reflect higher expected volatility of the US dollar/yen exchange rate. Most activity in Japan was also in the options markets. For example, average daily US dollar/yen turnover fell in Japan, from $122 billion to $113 billion, but US dollar/yen volumes in the foreign exchange options market grew by more than 90 per cent over the same period.

The proportion of UK turnover involving sterling increased slightly, from 16 per cent to 18 per cent, largely because of a rise in the share of sterling/US dollar transactions. But the importance of sterling trading to the UK market has declined significantly in the longer term (from 24 per cent of turnover in 1992, and 27 per cent in 1989). Overall, the UK market's reliance on domestic currency business is modest, compared with other major centres. In continental Europe, domestic currency trading represents a much higher proportion of total turnover: the figures for Germany, France and Switzerland are 66 per cent, 41 per cent and 39 per cent respectively.

Cross-trading between ERM currencies generally declined, ahead of EMU. Table C illustrates that the proportion of total turnover attributable to trading the Deutsche mark

Table C ● Relative shares of total net turnover by currencies traded

Per cent

	1989 Total	1992 Total	1995 Total	1998 Spot	Forward	Total
£/US$	27	17	11	4	10	14
US$/DM	22	24	22	10	12	22
US$/¥	15	12	17	5	7	13
US$/SwFr	10	6	5	1	4	6
US$/FFr	2	3	5	1	4	5
US$/Can$	2	2	2	1	2	2
US$/Aus$	2	1	2	1	1	2
US$/Lit	2	n.a.	3	1	5	6
US$/Pta	n.a.	n.a.	2	0	2	2
US$/other ERM	n.a.	9	6	1	8	8
US$/other	7	3	4	1	5	7
£/DM	3	5	3	3	1	3
£/other	1	1	1	0	0	1
DM/¥	2	2	2	1	0	2
DM/other ERM	n.a.	4	6	2	1	3
Ecu-denominated	2	5	4	0	2	2
Other cross-currencies	3	4	3	2	2	4
Total	**100**	**100**	**100**	**34**	**66**	**100**

n.a. = not available.

Note: Percentage shares have been rounded to the nearest whole number.

against other ERM currencies fell to 3 per cent, from 6 per cent in 1995. This was almost entirely attributable to a fall in Deutsche mark/French franc business, from 3 per cent of turnover to around 0.5 per cent. Currency options business also declined: Deutsche mark/French franc turnover as a proportion of total currency derivatives business fell from 5 per cent to less than 1 per cent. But Charts 1 and 2 show that the proportion of principals' turnover attributable to US dollar/ERM-currency trading increased (it is standard practice to swap non-dollar currencies using the US dollar as a conduit) and this may partly reflect the integration of national money markets within the prospective euro area.

Trading of the US dollar against "other currencies" as a proportion of overall turnover increased to 7 per cent, from 4 per cent in 1995. The Federal Reserve Bank of New York reported an identical increase. This is consistent with more rapid growth of emerging market currency trading, relative to overall turnover. By way of background, Table D, reproduced from the BIS's 68th Annual Report, shows that local daily turnover in emerging market currencies rose from around $25 billion to $60 billion between April 1995 and October 1997. (Within this total, the dollar value of Asian currency trading generally declined between April 1997 and October 1997; the Thai baht was devalued on 1 July 1997 and other currencies came under pressure soon thereafter.)

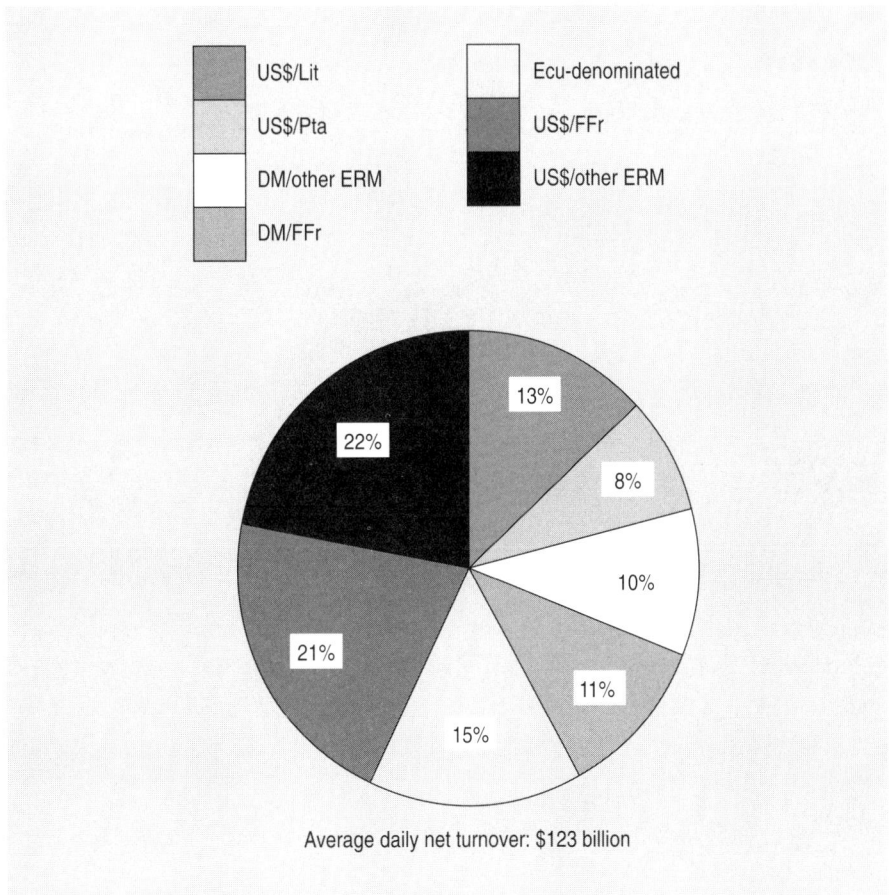

Chart 1 ● ERM currencies in 1995

For the first time, the UK survey included a memorandum item on emerging market currencies. Estimated gross turnover in these currencies was $12.5 billion per day,[5] compared with aggregate gross turnover of $798 billion per day. Chart 3 illustrates that UK trading of the US dollar against Asian and eastern European currencies represented four fifths of emerging market turnover. Principals were also asked to identify currencies with turnover exceeding $100 million during April, equivalent to $5 million per day. Using this as a guide, the most actively traded currencies at that time were the Czech koruna (20 dealers reported monthly turnover in excess of $100 million), Malaysian ringgit (19), Thai baht (16), Indonesian rupiah (13), and Polish zloty (12). The ranking for Asian currencies in the New York survey is similar, but eastern European currencies appear to be more actively traded in London, and Latin American currencies in New York.

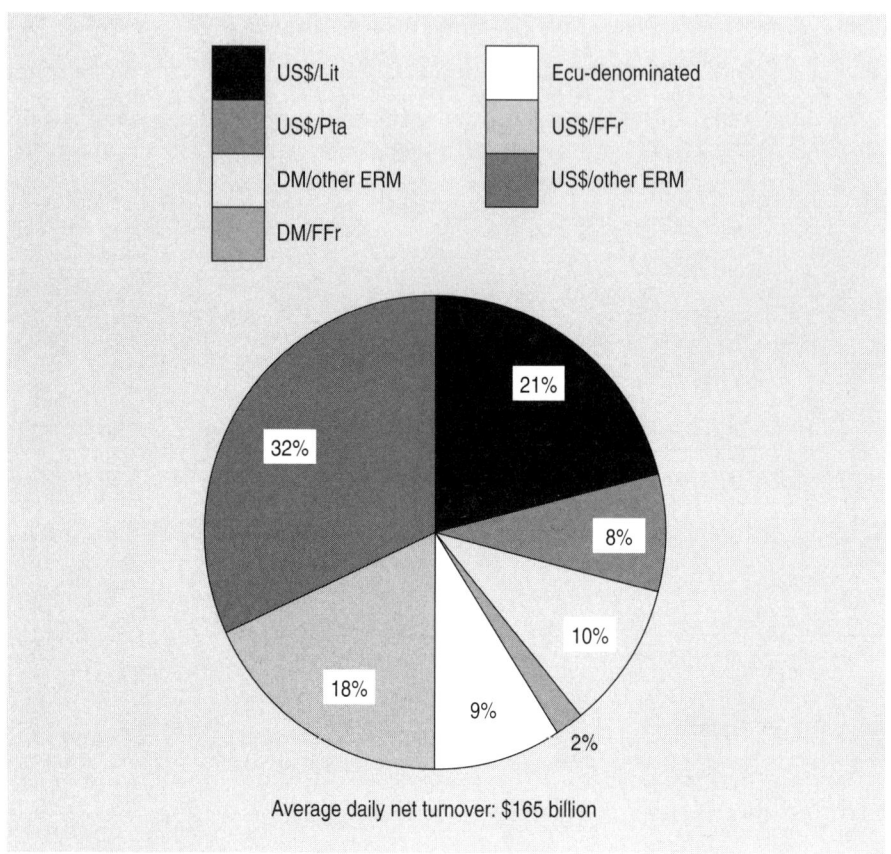

US$/Lit	Ecu-denominated
US$/Pta	US$/FFr
DM/other ERM	US$/other ERM
DM/FFr	

Average daily net turnover: $165 billion

Chart 2 ● ERM currencies in 1998

Table E ● Average daily turnover by counterparty

US$ billions; percentage of total net turnover in italics

	1989		**1992**		**1995**		**1998**	
Gross turnover	241		357		571		798.2	
of which:								
Domestic interbank[a]	108		134		215		322.7	
Net domestic turnover[b]	187		290		464		637.3	
of which:								
Other financial institutions	16	*9*	42	*14*	85	*18*	60.5	*9.5*
Non-financial institutions	10	*5*	24	*8*	30	*7*	46.6	*7.3*
Cross-border interbank	107	*57*	158	*55*	241	*52*	369.3	*57.9*
Net domestic interbank	54	*29*	67	*23*	108	*23*	160.9	*25.2*

[a] Domestic interbank deals are those between two banks located in the UK.
[b] Net domestic turnover is after adjustment for double-counting of such deals.

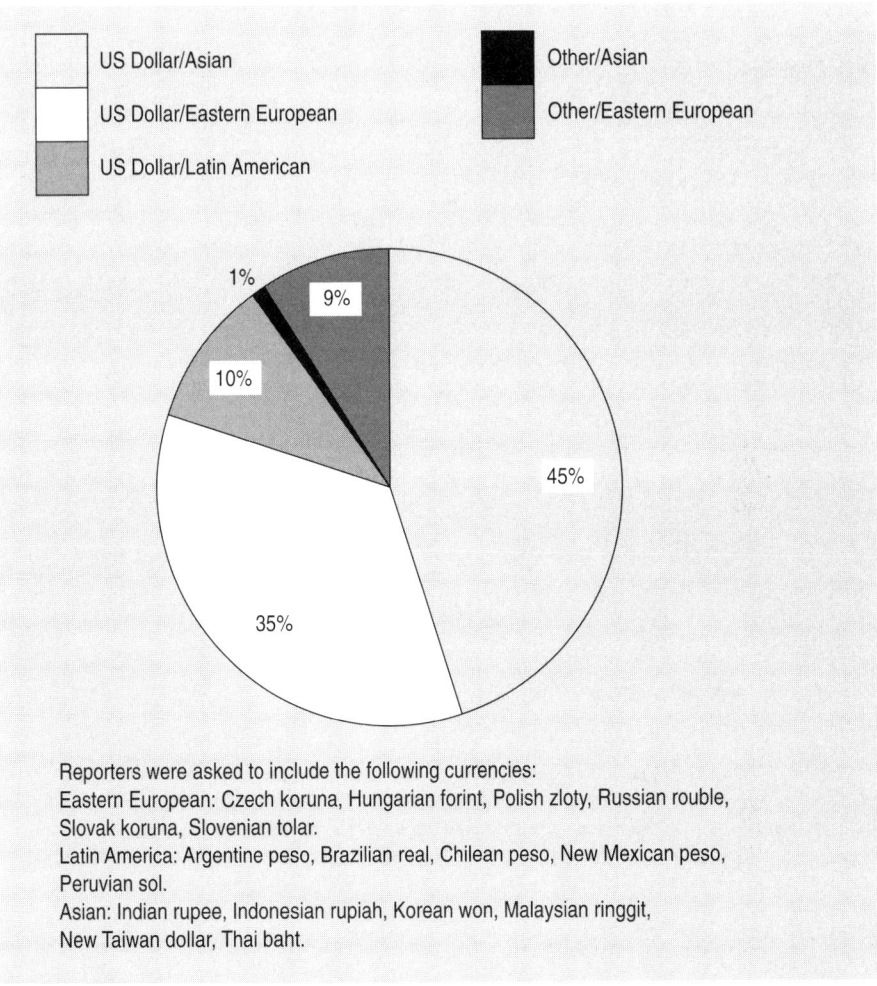

Reporters were asked to include the following currencies:
Eastern European: Czech koruna, Hungarian forint, Polish zloty, Russian rouble, Slovak koruna, Slovenian tolar.
Latin America: Argentine peso, Brazilian real, Chilean peso, New Mexican peso, Peruvian sol.
Asian: Indian rupee, Indonesian rupiah, Korean won, Malaysian ringgit, New Taiwan dollar, Thai baht.

Chart 3 ● Turnover in currencies of the emerging market economies

Counterparties

As Table E shows, the proportion of principals' turnover accounted for by domestic and international interbank business rose from 75 per cent to 83 per cent. The rise was attributable to the faster growth of cross-border business. Overall, cross-border transactions accounted for 66 per cent of net turnover. The global results show that cross-border deals account for a relatively high proportion of UK turnover. The comparable figure reported by the BIS was 54 per cent of global turnover.

The share of business with other financial institutions, such as pension funds, fell to 9.5 per cent. This reverses the trend between 1989 and 1995. The share of business with non-financial institutions was steady at 7 per cent. The results of the derivatives survey were similar: other financial institutions and non-financial institutions accounted for 13 per cent and 8 per cent respectively of turnover in currency derivatives.

Market concentration

The combined market share of the top 10 principals, which was stable in the previous survey, rose from 44 per cent to 50 per cent. The top 20's share – 15 of which were in the top 20 in 1995 – reached 69 per cent (68 per cent in 1995, and 63 per cent in 1992). But the number of firms individually accounting for more than 1 per cent of total turnover has remained stable at around 25 since 1992. So business remains well dispersed among the largest institutions. The results of the US survey were similar. For example, the top 10 principals' market share in the US rose from 48 per cent to 51 per cent. In contrast, other markets are more concentrated than those in either the UK or the US: in France, for example, the top 10 institutions accounted for four-fifths of turnover.

Previous surveys found that business was more widely dispersed in the most actively traded currencies than in others. But Table F shows that the top 10 principals' market share in a range of different currencies converged: the range is now between 52 per cent and 57 per cent.

Table F ● Percentage share of the 10 principals most active in individual currency pairs

	1986	1989	1992	1995	1998
£/US$	40	34	48	50	57
US$/DM	38	37	43	40	54
US$/¥	46	39	48	47	52
US$/SwFr	57	60	66	66	55
US$/FFr	70	61	54	51	55

Foreign-owned institutions operating in the UK market account for 85 per cent principals' aggregate turnover in the UK in 1998, compared with 79 per cent in 1995. North American principals remain the most active, with a 49 per cent market share, and their share rose in all US dollar pairs (see Table G). In contrast, UK principals' share of sterling trading declined, partly reflecting mergers between UK principals and institutions from the rest of the European Union (reducing the number of UK principals). The proportion of turnover transacted by Japanese principals fell from 10 per cent to 7 per cent and their share of the US dollar/yen market fell from around one third to less than one quarter. A similar trend was evident in Japan: foreign firms' share of customer transactions more than doubled, to 65 per cent of customer business transacted by principals.

Brokers

The proportion of principals' total foreign exchange business handled by brokers fell to 27 per cent. In 1995, the proportion of principals' total foreign exchange business transacted by brokers was 35 per cent, little changed from 34 per cent in 1992. The electronic brokers' share of principals' total foreign exchange business rose from 5 per cent to 11 per cent (they were not active at the time of the 1992 survey), and the proportion of business conducted by traditional voice brokers declined from 30 per cent to 16 per cent.[6] The

Table G ● Principals' share of the London market in different currencies by country grouping

Per cent	US dollar against:											
	£		DM		¥		SwFr		Can$		Aus$	
Nationality of principal												
UK	28	38	15	18	11	14	8	13	5	7	15	27
Other European Union	20	13	21	17	11	8	11	7	6	15	8	2
North American	39	33	46	44	46	40	64	54	77	69	41	34
Japan	5	6	8	10	23	30	5	2	1	1	1	1
Other	8	9	10	11	9	8	12	25	11	8	36	36

	Sterling against:		DM against:				Total	
	DM		¥		SwFr			
Nationality of principal								
UK	26	31	21	23	29	16	15	21
Other European Union	24	14	26	6	16	4	18	15
North American	38	36	26	28	33	42	49	42
Japan	5	7	20	31	3	2	7	10
Other	7	12	8	11	20	37	11	12

Note: Figures for 1995 are in italics.

number of voice brokers in the foreign exchange market was little changed from 1995, although several withdrew from the spot market. Overall, the structure of brokers' business, in terms of the relative proportion of spot and forward business transacted by brokers, changed little between 1995–98 (see Table H). The proportion of short-dated swaps business increased, in line with the rise in short-dated swaps' share of total turnover. Table I shows that the proportion of brokered transactions involving a UK principal has declined slightly between 1995–98, from 90 per cent to 86 per cent.[7]

Electronic brokers now handle 70 per cent of principals' spot deals transacted via brokers. And almost one quarter of spot transactions in the UK market are conducted by the electronic brokers (the proportion is almost one-third in the US). The scope of electronic brokers' business has become more diverse: a wider range of currency pairs and products (eg forwards) is available. However, spot trading of the US dollar against the Deutsche mark and yen still account for most of the two electronic brokers' volumes. In contrast, more than 95 per cent of volumes transacted via electronic brokers in certain currency pairs (such as sterling/US dollar and US dollar/Swiss franc) are handled by a single system.

Table H ● Types of transaction – all brokers' turnover

Percentage of total turnover

	1992	1995	1998
Spot	52	46	46
Forwards: outright	2	1	4
Forwards: swaps	46	53	50
of which:			
Up to and for 7 days	31	35	43
7 days and up to and for 1 month	4	5	4
1 month and up to 6 months	9	8	4
6 months up to and for 1 year	3	5	3
Over 1 year	1	1	0

Table I ● Counterparties to all brokers' turnover

Percentage of total turnover

	1989	1992	1995	1998
Between two principals in the UK	36	33	38	34
Between a principal in the UK and a principal abroad	50	49	52	52
Between two principals abroad	13	10	7	12
Other customers	1	8	3	2

OTC derivatives

Daily turnover in the UK

Average daily turnover in the UK for OTC currency and interest rate derivatives was $171 billion, 131 per cent higher than the $74 billion recorded by the previous survey. Overall, currency derivatives grew by 218 per cent over the three-year period, compared with 110 per cent for interest rate derivatives. The interest rate derivatives market is still larger, however, now accounting for $123 billion per day (up from $59 billion) – some 2.5 times the size of the currency derivatives market, at $48 billion per day (up from $15 billion).

Just over half the firms taking part in the survey thought that the overall level of turnover during the survey period was normal; 22 per cent considered it to be above normal; and 5 below normal. The remaining 21 per cent did not comment. Some participants reported that they undertook some unusually large interest rate trades in ERM currencies in April, ahead of the decisions at the start of May on the initial members of EMU and the bilateral rates at which they would join. This will have inflated both these firms' turnover values and share of the interest rate markets, and overall UK turnover in ERM interest rate products.

Global turnover

The results from the eight largest centres in 1995 show that the UK has consolidated its position as the world's largest centre for OTC derivatives business (see Chart 4).

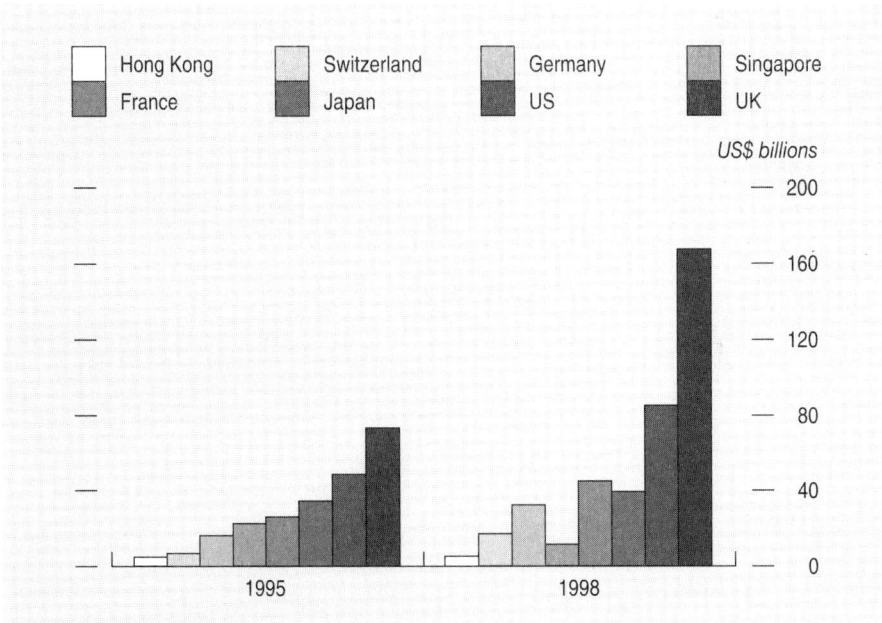

Chart 4 ● OTC derivatives turnover – UK and other centres

Table J shows that growth between the two surveys was slower outside Europe than within it: the US and Japan both recorded slower growth than the major European centres, and turnover in both Singapore and Hong Kong fell. Of the eight largest centres, the Swiss market grew most rapidly, although it remains small relative to the UK market. The BIS's estimate of global turnover (which eliminates double-counting between countries) was $362 billion per day in April 1998, an increase of 85 per cent from $196 billion in April 1995.

Table J ● Average daily OTC derivatives turnover in major financial centres

US$ billions

	1995	1998	Percentage change
UK	74	171	131
US	52	91	75
France	22	46	107
Japan	33	42	28
Germany	13	34	162
Switzerland	4	16	257
Singapore	18	11	–38
Hong Kong	4	4	–10

The UK's share of the global OTC currency and interest rate derivatives market rose to 36 per cent in April 1998, compared with 27 per cent in 1995.

By way of comparison, BIS figures[8] show that the value of global turnover in interest rate and currency products on organized derivatives exchanges grew by less than 1 per cent between 1994 and 1997. Average daily turnover of these – typically shorter-maturity – products in the first quarter of 1998 was $1,399 billion.

Type of transaction

There has been a significant shift in the balance of business between interest rate swaps and FRAs: in 1998, interest rate swaps dominated the market (see Chart 5), with 40 per cent turnover (up from 25 per cent in 1995), in contrast with 1995, when FRA business accounted for the largest share, with 47 per cent (this share has now dropped to 25 per cent). The dominance of interest rate swaps in 1998 is not unique to the UK – there has been a similar change in a number of the other major financial centres (eg Germany, France, Japan and Hong Kong).

The overall market shares reflect changes within the interest rate derivatives sector, which accounted for 72 per cent of total turnover in April 1998, compared with 80 per cent in 1995: swaps increased their share of interest rate trading from 32 per cent to 56 per cent, with growth of 271 per cent over the three-year period. Conversely, FRA's market share dropped from 59 per cent to 35 per cent, though turnover in FRAs grew by 22 per cent between the surveys. The share of interest rate options rose from 9 per cent to 10 per cent.

In the currency derivatives sector, there has been little change in the breakdown between instruments: currency options accounted for 89 per cent (down from 91 per cent in 1995) and currency swaps 11 per cent (up from 9 per cent in 1995). Though turnover in currency swaps has grown by 263 per cent, the growth of 213 per cent in currency options

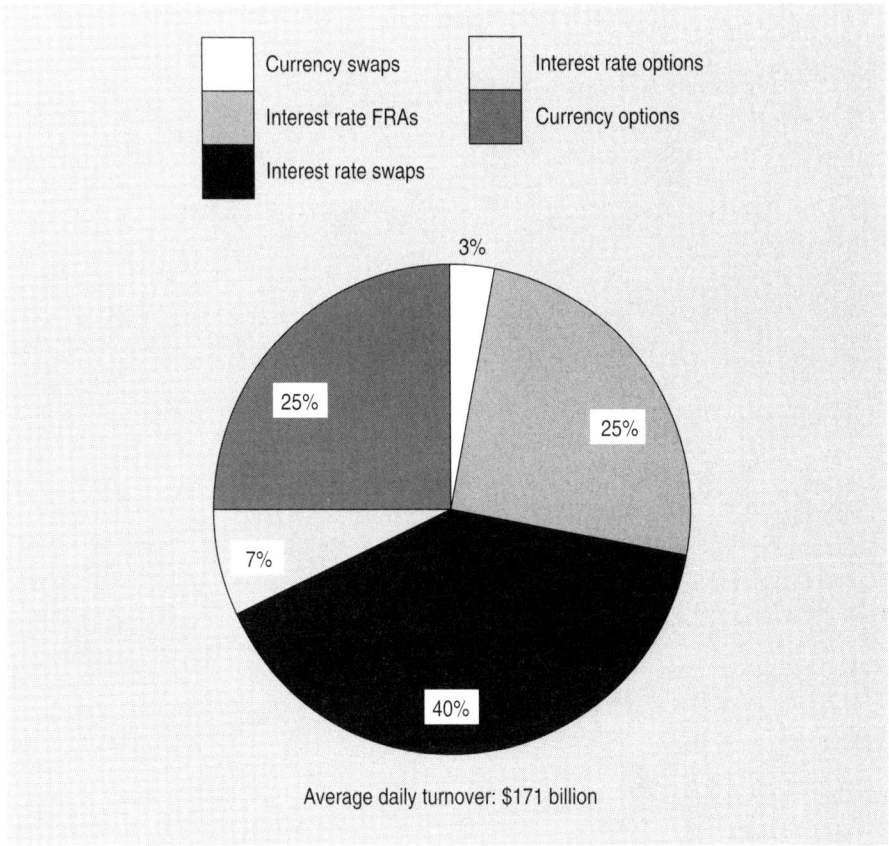

Chart 5 ● OTC derivatives turnover – product breakdown

– typically with shorter maturities – has contributed most to the absolute increase in turnover in the currency derivatives market.

Currency composition

ERM currencies dominated trading in the UK interest rate derivatives market, accounting for 56 per cent of all business[9] (see Chart 6). Within ERM currencies, the Deutsche mark alone accounted for 32 per cent, almost doubling its share of the interest rate derivatives market since the previous survey. Deutsche mark business also grew in other centres: in Germany, the market share of Deutsche mark interest rate business grew by 10 percentage points, to almost three quarters; in France, Deutsche mark business grew from 4 per cent to 19 per cent of the market. In the UK, only the FRA market was not dominated by ERM currencies – in FRAs, the US dollar and sterling accounted for 39 per cent between them, compared with only 24 per cent for interest rate swaps and 27 per cent for interest rate options.

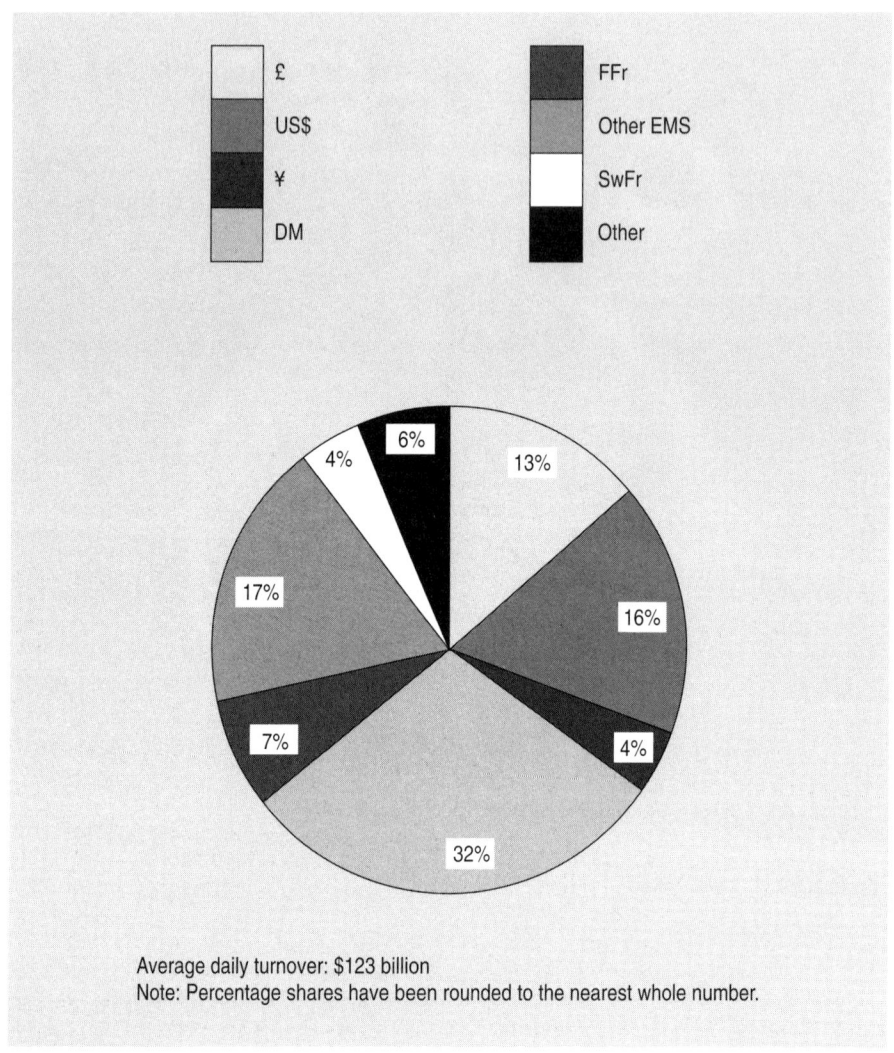

Average daily turnover: $123 billion
Note: Percentage shares have been rounded to the nearest whole number.

Chart 6 ● OTC interest rate derivatives turnover – currency breakdown

The only currency where the value of interest rate derivatives trading in the UK fell between 1995 and 1998 was the yen, where total turnover (in US dollar terms) fell by 4 per cent. But this owes much to the decline in the US dollar/yen exchange rate between the two survey periods – in yen terms, turnover rose by 53 per cent.

The picture was different in the currency derivatives market (see Table K), where the US dollar maintained its dominant position and the Deutsche mark lost market share. In the 1995 survey, the most active currency pairing was the US dollar/Deutsche mark. This was overtaken between the two surveys by the US dollar/yen pair, which grew particularly strongly in currency options, perhaps reflecting the market's expectation in April that this bilateral rate would become increasingly volatile.

Table K ● OTC currency derivatives – currency breakdown

Percentage of the market where the currency constitutes one leg of the trade		
	1995	**1998**
US$	77	76
DM	51	42
£	12	17

Note: As there are two currency legs to each trade, percentages will add up to more than 100.

As in the foreign exchange market, derivatives trades between the Deutsche mark and another ERM currency lost market share (falling from 9 per cent to 3 per cent). But in the derivatives market, this was not offset by an increase in US dollar/ERM trading. The US dollar/Deutsche mark pair fell from 31 per cent to 22 per cent of the currency derivatives market, while US dollar/other ERM maintained a steady 10 per cent of the market. This supports the foreign exchange findings that cross-trading between ERM currencies has declined – doubtless in anticipation of EMU – but suggests that the US dollar/ERM options market (as currency options dominate this sector) has not developed as rapidly as the corresponding spot, forward and swap markets.

Counterparties

Table L shows that the most active counterparties in the interest rate and currency derivatives markets were banks and securities firms, which accounted for 73 per cent (down from 84 per cent in 1995) of the total transactions in April 1998. Correspondingly, the share of business of other financial institutions increased to 21 per cent (up from 10 per cent in 1995). The share of business of non-financial institutions remained relatively steady at 6 per cent (down from 7 per cent in 1995).

The results in the overall market reflect the changes within the interest rate derivatives market. Banks and securities firms transacted most business, although their share fell from 86 per cent to 71 per cent over the three-year period. The share of interest rate business undertaken by other financial institutions grew to 24 per cent (from 9 per cent in 1995). It seems likely that this figure is distorted by a number of unusually large interest rate trades with other financial institutions in the ERM currencies in April, ahead of the May EMU announcements. Non-financial institutions' business was little changed at 5 per cent (down from 6 per cent in 1995).

In the currency derivatives market, there has been little change in the overall breakdown between counterparties. Interbank activity continues to dominate, with 79 per cent (up from 78 per cent in 1995) of the market. The levels of interbank activity undertaken locally and cross-border have, however, changed substantially: interbank cross-border trading still makes up the largest proportion of activity, but fell from 66 per cent of the market in 1995 to 53 per cent in 1998. The decline is mainly accounted for by the drop from 62 per cent to 48 per cent in the interbank cross-border activity in currency options (which comprise 89 per cent of the currency derivatives market).

Table L ● Average daily turnover by counterparty – currency and interest rate derivatives

US$ billions; percentage of net turnover in italics	Interest rate derivatives				Currency derivatives			
	1995		1998		1995		1998	
Gross turnover	77		152		17		60	
of which:								
Domestic interbank[a]	36		59		4		25	
Net domestic turnover[b]	59		123		15		48	
of which:								
Other financial institutions	5	9	30	24	2	12	6	13
Non-financial institutions	3	6	6	5	1	10	4	8
Cross-border interbank	32	55	58	47	10	66	26	53
Net domestic interbank	18	31	29	24	2	12	12	26

[a] Domestic interbank deals are those between two banks located in the UK.
[b] Net domestic turnover is after adjustment for double-counting of such deals.

Market concentration

Overall, concentration in the UK market has increased since 1995. The top 10 principals' combined market share rose from 52 per cent to 67 per cent, and the top 20's rose from 74 per cent to 82 per cent.

The currency derivatives market appears to be more concentrated than the interest rate market, with a smaller number of participants undertaking currency derivatives business than interest rate derivatives business during April 1998. Although the top five companies in the currency derivatives market hold 51 per cent of the market, compared with 54 per cent in the interest rate market, 20 companies hold 91 per cent of the currency derivatives market, compared with 82 per cent in the interest rate market.

Activity in currency derivatives during April 1998 was reported by 130 firms. Fourteen firms had 1 per cent or more of the currency market; 7 had between 1 per cent and 5 per cent; and 6 had between 5 per cent and 10 per cent. Activity in interest rate derivatives during April 1998 was reported by 178 firms. Twenty-four firms had 1 per cent or more of the interest rate market; 19 had between 1 per cent and 5 per cent; and 3 had between 5 per cent and 10 per cent.

Market share of foreign banks

Chart 7 shows that, as in the foreign exchange survey, foreign-owned institutions dominated the UK OTC derivatives market, with UK firms accounting for only 23 per cent of turnover[10] (down from 28 per cent in 1995). US principals continued to dominate, increasing their market share from 37 per cent to 47 per cent. Continental European firms also gained market share, led mainly by German and Swiss firms. Japanese banks, however, lost market share, falling from 9 per cent to 5 per cent – reflecting both the turbulence experienced by these firms around the time of the survey, and the fact that some Japanese firms consolidated in their home country and pulled out of the UK market in the three years between the two surveys.

There were some interesting developments within the different product types. US firms lost market share in currency derivatives, but compensated for this by increasing their share of the interest rate derivatives market from 37 per cent to 53 per cent. The main beneficiaries of US firms' relative decline in the currency derivatives market were Swiss firms (of which nine are active in the UK market), which increased their market share from 15 per cent to 32 per cent and now account for as much currency derivatives turnover in the UK as US firms do. UK principals lost market share (from 30 per cent to 22 per cent) in interest rate derivatives, and were the only major national group (compared with US, German, Japanese and Swiss firms) to have higher turnover in FRAs than in interest rate swaps – possibly suggesting that they have been concentrating their business at the shorter end of the market, which has suffered a relative decline in the period between the two surveys.

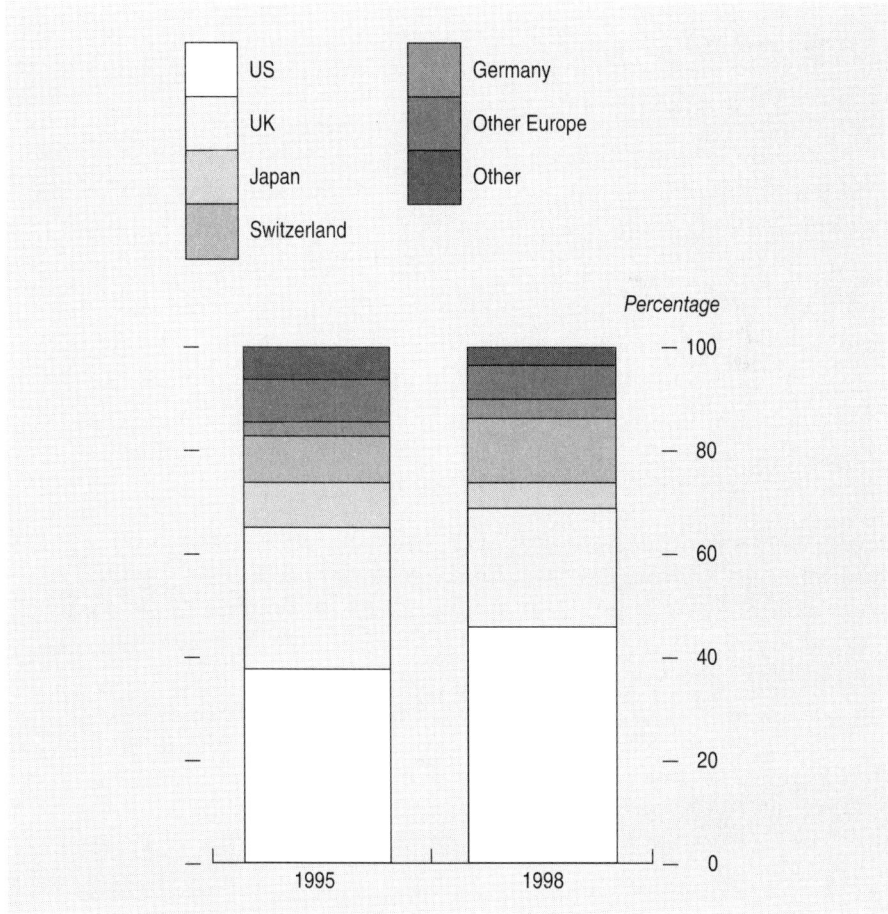

Chart 7 ● Derivatives market by nationality of bank

Notes

1. Only interest rate and currency OTC derivatives were covered by the 1998 turnover survey.
2. Unless specified otherwise, turnover figures published here are adjusted to remove double-countig of trades between UK principals that will have been reported by both parties.
3. Preliminary figures were released on 19 October 1998 and can be obtained from www.bis.org/press/p981019.htm
4. In April 1995, the average rates of sterling and the Deutsche mark against the US dollar were $1.61 and DM 1.38 respectively. In April 1998, the comparable figures were $1.67 and DM 1.81.
5. It was not possible to eliminate local double-counting for these currencies. The figure may underestimate turnover in emerging market currencies, because not all reporters completed the memorandum item.
6. Voice brokers quote prices over lines to principals' dealing rooms. The EBS Partnership and Reuters Transaction Services Ltd provide automated electronic order-matching systems.
7. The analysis of brokers' business excludes deals between principals abroad transacted by electronic brokers.
8. Data obtained from *International Banking and Financial Market Developments*, Bank for International Settlments, Table 20A.
9. This figure includes ECU and Swedish krona business.
10. All turnover figures in this section are gross.

CHAPTER 3

Volatility in the foreign exchange market

This chapter discusses the central role that volatility plays in understanding the behaviour of the foreign exchange market. After having discussed some of the more commonly used measures of volatility, Appendix 3.1 surveys the sources of exchange rate volatility and examines the empirical evidence. The terminology used to measure volatility can be confusing and/or mathematically demanding, and it is to this issue that we now turn.

VOLATILITY

Volatility is a measure of uncertainty about the future changes in the prices of assets and other economic variables. It is a fundamental parameter used to quantify risk in modern finance theory, and it is a critical input for virtually all decisions relating to risk management and to an understanding of the behaviour of financial markets.

Until 1973, volatility was generally estimated by using historical data. The appearance of exchange-traded options in 1973 and the concurrent development of the theory of contingent-claims pricing has made it possible to infer beliefs about the future volatility of an asset directly from the prices of options and other securities whose payoff structures depend on the asset's price. The estimate, extracted in this way, is called implied volatility, and is discussed below.

Standard deviation

Volatility is a measure of how the price of the underlying instrument varies. It can be defined as the standard deviation in price returns of the instrument.

What is the standard deviation? To find the standard deviation of a series of numbers we proceed as follows. Suppose we measure an overnight interest rate over two weeks, giving us ten observations. We want to measure how variable, or volatile, the interest rate is. Suppose we observe the following interest rates, in per cent: 6, 12, 11, 14, 7, 9, 11, 3, 12, 8. The first step is to work out the average or mean interest rate over the period: this is 9.30 per cent. Then we measure how much each rate varies from the mean. We need to average that variation, allowing for the negative as well as positive variations.

The easiest way to do this is to calculate the differences: 14 − 9.30 and square them. This ensures that we have positive numbers. Thus in this case we have 4.72 = 22.09. We add up the squared totals and average them (strictly speaking we divide by $n - 1$, where n is the number of observations). The result is called the variance. In this case, it is 11.12 (working to two decimal places). But because the variance is the result of squaring the percentage rates it is more meaningful to take the square root, which in this case is 3.33. The square root of the variance is called the standard deviation. We thus have a series of interest rates with an average, or mean, of 9.30 per cent and a standard deviation of 3.33 per cent. The standard deviation gives us a measure of how likely the interest rate is to stray away from its mean. Of course, this is a historical number. The following month's standard deviation could be quite different. Volatility itself can be volatile.

Measuring the volatility of an instrument in terms of its standard deviation gives us an idea of its likely trading range, all other things being equal. For example, if a currency priced at $1.00 has an annualized volatility of 20 per cent, then the most likely range of prices (ie within one standard deviation) by the end of the year is $0.85 and $1.20 ($1.00 divided by 1.2 and multiplied by 1.2, respectively). The application of normal distribution principles is where the idea of "most likely" originates.

HISTORIC VOLATILITY

Historic volatility measures volatility over the most recent past. It is formally defined as the annualized standard deviation of the logarithm of relative price movements. Table 3.1 provides an example of the calculation.

Table 3.1 ● Calculation of historic volatility

Given five daily price data for an exchange rate, the volatility is calculated as follows:

Day	Exchange rate	LN $\left(\frac{1.8345}{1.8220}\right)$ etc.	Difference from mean	(Difference)^2
1	1.8220			
2	1.8345	0.00684	0.00622	0.000039
3	1.8315	−0.00164	−0.00226	0.000006
4	1.8350	0.00191	0.00129	0.000002
5	1.8265	−0.00464	−0.00526	0.000028
	Mean =	0.00062	Total =	0.000074

$$\text{Variance} = \frac{\text{Sum of (differences)}^2}{(\text{number of data} - 1)} = \frac{0.000074}{3} = 0.000025$$

$$\text{Standard deviation} = \sqrt{\text{variance}} = 0.00497$$

$$\text{Volatility} = \text{standard deviation} \times \sqrt{\text{frequency of data per year}}$$

$$= 0.00497 \times \sqrt{252} = 7.9\%$$

The problem with historic volatility is that it reflects what has happened in the past, and thus may not be very relevant to current or future market conditions.

INTRA-DAY VOLATILITY

Intraday volatility can be measured either as the standard deviation of price quotations within the day (perhaps taken at half-hourly intervals), or as the scaled range of daily prices, ie the ratio between the day's high and low. These measures have the advantage of topicality but may be distorted by a small number of outlying trades within the day.

IMPLIED VOLATILITY

Implied volatility is normally measured as the volatility which would make the Black–Scholes options pricing formula hold exactly (see below). This is a forward-looking measure and may be interpreted as the market expectation of volatility over the option contract period.

THE BLACK–SCHOLES MODEL

Fischer Black and Myron Scholes developed a model for the valuation of call options that is widely accepted and used in the financial community. The formula itself is mathematical and appears to be very complex; however it is widely available on calculators and computers.

The Black–Scholes model uses five variables to value a call option on a non-dividend-paying stock. These five variables, all but the last of which are directly observable in the market, are as follows:

1. The price of the underlying stock, the spot price.
2. The exercise price of the option.
3. The time remaining to the expiration of the option.
4. The interest rate.
5. The volatility of the underlying stock – the implied volatility.

An option premium is made up of two components, the intrinsic value and the time value. The intrinsic value is simply the value of the option if it is exercised immediately. For a call option this is simply the strike price less the spot price. The intrinsic value for a call option = spot price minus strike price.

If intrinsic value for an option exists, then the option is said to be "in-the-money". A call option will be in-the-money if the strike price is below the spot price. If its strike price is above the spot price the call option will have zero intrinsic value and that is said to be "out of the money". If the strike price is equal to the spot price it is "at-the-money", with zero intrinsic value.

The *time value* of an option is the option premium less the intrinsic value. The time value reflects the fact that an option may have more ultimate value than its intrinsic value.

The time value for a call option = option premium minus intrinsic value.

An option buyer, even if the option is out of the money, will still have some hope that at some time prior to expiration changes in the spot price will move the option into the money, or further increase its value if it is already in the money. This prospect gives an option a value greater than its intrinsic value. Two examples to illustrate this are given below.

Example 1

Consider a call option valued at 18 pence in the stock of company ABC, with a strike price of 90 pence and a spot price for the underlying share of 100 pence. The option is in-the-money to the tune of 10 pence so that its intrinsic value is 10 pence and the other 8 pence represents its time value.

Example 2

Consider a call option valued at 11 pence in the stock of company XYZ, with a strike price of 85 pence and a spot price for the underlying share of 80 pence. The option is out-of-the-money and so has no intrinsic value. The whole value of the option, that is 11 pence, is time value.

Given data on the first four variables in the option-pricing model it is a simple exercise to calculate the fifth variable, the implied volatility.

WHAT DETERMINES VOLATILITY?

Four theories

It is useful to distinguish four classes of theory in relation to the determination of volatility as follows.

1. Information considerations – the arrival of information in the market results in price adjustment as market agents evaluate the implications of the information.

2. Hedging or speculative pressure – an increase in activity by one class of agents, say speculators, forces the price to adjust in such a way that the other group, in this case hedgers, can accommodate the increased speculative position.

3. Market liquidity – in liquid markets, large buy or sell orders can be absorbed with little or no price impact; in less liquid markets, large orders cause the price to move against the buyer.

4. The physical availability of the commodity. When a commodity is in short supply, a change in demand will have a larger price impact than when supplies are plentiful.

The first three explanations are common across financial markets, while the fourth, physical availability, relates more specifically to commodity markets where stocks can become very low.

These four explanations are not mutually exclusive, and indeed each is likely to be true to a greater or lesser extent. The importance of information arrival has been recognized across the entire range of financial markets. When markets receive news, they need to evaluate the information content of the news and translate this into price terms. This process is not instantaneous. Markets become like computers, processing the information by means of trading until, after perhaps half an hour but sometimes longer, a consensus has been reached such that no one wishes further to alter his position in relation to the news. Chapter 5 discusses the role of news on financial markets in much more detail.

The final, commodity-specific, factor determining volatility is the tightness of the market. The greater the availability of a commodity the lower the price and hence the greater the prospect of eventual capital gains from adding to inventory. The consequence is that when availability is high, small changes in availability are added to or taken from stocks and their price impact is small. By contrast, when availability is low the price will be high and the returns to holding inventory will be low or negative. In this circumstance, increments or decrements to availability are translated directly into the price. We should therefore expect an inverse relationship between availability and commodity volatility, with high volatility associated with low availability and vice versa.

Appendix 3.1 applies these ideas directly to the foreign exchange market.

Why are exchange rate markets volatile?*

Exchange rates, by their very nature, are volatile. While daily movements in exchange rates often seem unwarranted and excessive, a robust and healthy level of real foreign activity continues between countries. To what extent then should exchange rate volatility influence central bankers' decisions? The answer lies in the role that the transmission of information plays in exchange rate markets.

Foreign exchange traders face strong incentives to base their exchange rate quotations on all relevant information about current fundamentals and expectations about their future values. To the extent that dealers do so successfully, only new information that causes revisions in traders' expectations will influence exchange rates. One would expect that exchange traders would formulate their expectations without making systematic errors. To the extent that they can do so, revisions to their quotes will appear random, imparting a zigzag pattern to exchange rate movements. Over time, a net change in one direction or the other may emerge as exchange rates adjust to persistent shifts in underlying fundamentals. On a day-to-day basis, the exchange rate will bounce – in a seemingly random manner – around any such path (see Figures 3.1 to 3.4, described below).

The foregoing discussion is based on the implicit assumption that expectations are fairly uniform and firmly anchored to a set of generally recognized fundamentals. The widely recognized failure of exchange rate models to outperform a random walk in levels (white noise in growth rates), however, undermines the validity of this assumption (see Meese and Rogoff, 1983). Particularly damaging is the fact that since the inception of floating exchange rates, both nominal and real exchange rate volatilities have increased substantially (relative the Bretton Wood era), but the volatilities of their underlying fundamentals have changed little (see Frankel and Rose, 1995).

Although exchange traders are highly effective users of information, they probably do not conform to simple textbook models of "market efficiency". Indeed, why would trades occur, especially in such large volumes, if all traders had identical information at all times? Information about economic fundamentals (both its acquisition and interpretation) is costly, which may explain why many foreign exchange traders generate profits from technical trading rules – essentially rules of thumb – instead of from models based solely on economic fundamentals. Many of these rules project past trends into the future. Some, for example, require that traders buy when the exchange rate rises by some fixed percentage above its past trough, and sell when it falls some fixed amount below its past peak. Such

---

* This appendix was written by Professor Gregory D. Hess of Oberlin College and Dr Owen F. Humpage of the Federal Reserve Bank of Cleveland. It was originally published in *Central Banking,* Volume IX Number 4, May 1998, and has been reprinted with the permission of the authors.

trading rules could increase short-term volatility. As time passes and as information becomes freely accessible, traders may increasingly respond to fundamentals; initially, however, traders may not be linked to fundamentals in a fixed or even consistent way (see Hooper, 1997).

While it is generally accepted that exchange rate markets are volatile or uncertain, the measurement of volatility is problematic. The statistical modelling approach captures how *ex post* variability has evolved over time (eg GARCH models). Alternatively, *ex ante* uncertainty can be calculated from options price data, although the resulting measure of uncertainty is only as good as the options pricing formula. To keep our analysis as general as possible, the analysis below is based on simple calculations of the variance and covariance of exchange rate changes, and we allow for simple time variation in the Figures 3.1 to 3.4.

Tables 3.1 and 3.2 provide summary information on the volatility of the daily exchange rate growth for the pound/dollar, mark/dollar, yen/dollar and dollar index over the time period 1 June 1973 to 6 January 1999. The bilateral exchange rates are the spot ask, London close, and are quoted as the number of foreign currency units per US dollar. The Dollar index, constructed by the Board of Governors of the Federal Reserve System and published in the H.10 Tables, is a "weighted average of the foreign exchange values of the US dollar against a subset of currencies in the broad index that circulate widely outside the country of issue. The weights are derived from those in the broad index." The growth rates are calculated as 100 times the change in the log-level of the exchange rate.

Table 3.1 presents information about the variability and co-variation of daily exchange rate growth between these exchange rates. The variance of daily exchange rate growth is presented along the diagonal of the table while the elements below the diagonal are the co-variances between the exchange rates denoted in the relevant row and column. Above the diagonal we present the correlation coefficient between the exchange rates denoted in the row and column. Table 3.2 presents the standard deviations of exchange rate growth calculated for alternative non-overlapping horizons: daily, monthly, quarterly and annual.

To help with comparability, the change over the monthly, quarterly and annual horizons are converted into average business day changes. For example, the annual percentage change is divided by 260, as there are approximately 260 business days (52 weeks multiplied by 5) in a year. The monthly, quarterly and annual data are based on end of the period daily data. The data is expressed at a daily rate by dividing the changes in the data by the average number of business days. This ignores compounding, which would only strengthen our argument.

Quarterly and monthly changes are divided by 65 and 22, respectively.

Table 3.1 reveals three broad features about the volatility of exchange rates. First, at the daily level, the estimated daily variance of the growth of exchange rates is approximately 0.4 percentage points for each bilateral exchange rate, though is much lower for the dollar index (approximately 0.15 percentage points). This appears to be a rather high number. For example, assume for simplicity that exchange rate changes are normally distributed with mean zero. On the last day of 1998, the yen/dollar rate was 112.82. Then the associated 95 per cent confidence interval of plus or minus two standard deviations percentage points suggests that the yen/dollar rate would likely fluctuate between 114.2 and 111.5 on the first trading day of 1999 – an interval of over 2.5 yen.

Second, while the daily volatility of exchange rates may be large, the results in Table 3.2 reveal that many of these changes in exchange rates may be reversed over longer periods such as a month, quarter or year. This would suggest that the apparent daily (ie high frequency) volatility of exchange rates vastly overstates the longer term (ie low frequency) movements in exchange rates that occurs in any given day. In particular, the average daily standard deviation over a month is only approximately one-fifth as large as that for a given day. This fraction falls so that the average daily standard deviation over a quarter [year] is only about one-seventh [one-twelfth] as that for a given day. Returning to our earlier example, the 95 per cent confidence interval of plus or minus two standard deviations suggests that, based on the dollar's *average* daily movement over a year, the yen/dollar rate would likely remain within the interval 112.71 and 111.93 on the first trading day of 1999. Hence, when viewed from a long-term fundamental perspective, the interval over which the yen/dollar rate would likely fluctuate on a given day, approximately 0.2 yen, is much smaller.

Finally, the covariance (below the diagonal) and correlation (above the diagonal) terms suggest that these bilateral and dollar index exchange rates move together quite closely, even at the daily level. Among bilateral exchange rates, the UK/US and GR/US exchange rates co-vary the most with a correlation coefficient of over 0.66. Revealing their relative status as major currencies, all bilateral rates are closely correlated with the dollar index, with the Deutsche mark the most correlated, followed by the yen and finally the pound.

To demonstrate the stability of these findings, we present in Figures 3.1 to 3.4 plots of the moving standard deviation of exchange rates discussed above. Each plot is for a different exchange rate, and within each plot we present the moving daily standard deviation using horizons of one quarter and one year. Each figure reveals distinct changes in volatility. One interpretation is that the volatility changes indicate alterations in the flow of information to the market, with high volatility a mark of uncertainty. Volatility, for example, is high in the early 1980s and again around 1985 period. Uncertainty about the direction of US monetary policy, the Federal Reserve's operating procedure and the relative weight given to dollar exchange rates in the implementation of US policy characterized both of these episodes. Spikes also appear in the UK pound and German mark data near 1992, a period of uncertainty about German monetary policy and the viability of the European Monetary System.

For the bilateral dollar exchange rates presented in the figures, volatility seems low in recent years – UK pound and German mark – or at least no higher – with the Japanese yen – than that experience in the 1980s. Volatility of the dollar index, however, seems distinctly higher, owing to recent world financial crises and the safe-haven role of the dollar.

Does central bank intervention help?

Since the inception of generalized floating, central banks have often bought and sold foreign exchange in an attempt to "calm market disorder", an object that seems consistent with dampening short-term market volatility. Economists have remained fairly sceptical about the efficacy of official intervention because intervention does not appear to influence market fundamentals. While central banks can manipulate nominal exchange rates through unanticipated changes in relative money growth rates, most offset (or sterilize) the impact of official foreign exchange transactions on their monetary base, to avoid possible conflicts with their inflation objectives. The process of sterilizing intervention, however, alters the currency composition of publicly held debt. According to the portfolio balance approach to exchange rate determination, changes in the currency composition of outstanding government debt can affect exchange rates, independent of monetary policies. However, in general, empirical studies offer faint evidence that intervention alters exchange rates through a portfolio-balance channel. Relevant elasticities are either statistically insignificant or too small to be economically significant. Edison (1993) has surveyed this literature.

Even in the absence of the monetary and portfolio-balance channels, a central bank might still influence exchange rates by affecting the market's perception and interpretation of economic fundamentals. To do so, the central bank must possess better information than the market and must be able to convey that information to the market through its intervention.

Intervention might, for example, signal impending changes in monetary policies (see Mussa, 1981). Clearly, central banks may sometimes have better information than the market, but empirical tests suggest that central banks do not routinely enjoy such an advantage, even about monetary policy. Studies of intervention generally find neither strong nor consistent correlations between official intervention and either changes in exchange rates, exchange-rate risk premia, or measures of exchange-rate volatility. However, results are generally not robust across time periods, currencies, or differences in model specifications.

Recently, some empirical studies using GARCH models or option-pricing models have found some evidence that interventions increase exchange-rate volatility. These include Dominguez (1998) and Baillie and Osterberg (1997). Although these findings are not inconsistent with the idea that intervention transmits information to the market, they do not seem consistent with central bank attempts to "calm market disorder". Humpage (1999) finds some evidence that US interventions are successful in slowing the growth or reversing the direction of exchange rates, especially when co-ordinated with other central banks and large in size. Humpage (1998), however, found that most of these were concentrated in the immediate post-Plaza period and around the 1987 stock market crash. During both periods, the market seemed uncertain about the direction of US monetary policy. In contrast, he finds, however, that most other interventions have generally been unsuccessful.

Is volatility harmful?

To summarize, we have so far observed two things: first, foreign exchange rates are volatile, with their volatility being influenced primarily by shorter run movements. Second, that there is very little systematic evidence that central bank intervention on foreign exchange markets lowers exchange rate volatility.

What can central bankers do in the face of this volatility to help protect the potentially large sector of their economies which are exposed to exchange rate fluctuations? An unfortunate solution that has been often tried is that of capital and exchange controls. Capital controls are a poor approach to reducing exchange rate volatility; historically they have seemed rather ineffectual. Controls distort the allocation of capital by reducing access to global financial markets and raising the cost of capital. They create opportunities for political "rent seeking" and "rent selling", possibly altering competition and innovation in domestic markets for international financial services. By slowing capital movements, controls eliminate a barometer of the performance of domestic monetary policy, since typically poor policies hasten capital outflows. Furthermore, Barro and Sala-i-Martin (1995) provide evidence that the black market premia for exchange rates, a direct consequence of exchange and capital controls, reduces a country's long-term rate of growth.

An alternative solution is for central banks largely to ignore high frequency exchange rate volatility (barring situations of extreme financial distress such as has occurred in East Asia). This recommendation is supported by the vast empirical evidence that exchange rate volatility does not have a negative impact on trade flows between countries or patterns of foreign direct investment (see Bacchetta and van Wincoop (1998) and the references therein). Rather, central banks would do better by advocating and implementing sound long-term policies, which lie at the heart of the fundamentals that drive exchange rate changes. An example of such a policy is to maintain an environment of low inflation.

Table 3.1 ● Variance-covariance matrix of daily exchange rate growth (correlation coefficients above the diagonal) 1 June 1973 – 6 January 1999

Currency	Pound/Dollar	Mark/Dollar	Yen/Dollar	Dollar index
Pound/Dollar	0.391	0.669	0.430	0.619
Mark/Dollar	0.275	0.432	0.581	0.755
Yen/Dollar	0.174	0.248	0.422	0.717
Dollar index	0.149	0.191	0.179	0.148

Table 3.2 ● Standard deviations of exchange rate growth at alternative horizons expressed at a daily rate

Currency	Pound/Dollar	Mark/Dollar	Yen/Dollar	Dollar index
Daily	0.623	0.659	0.651	0.384
Monthly	0.147	0.151	0.162	0.077
Quarterly	0.083	0.094	0.098	0.047
Annual	0.050	0.048	0.051	0.025

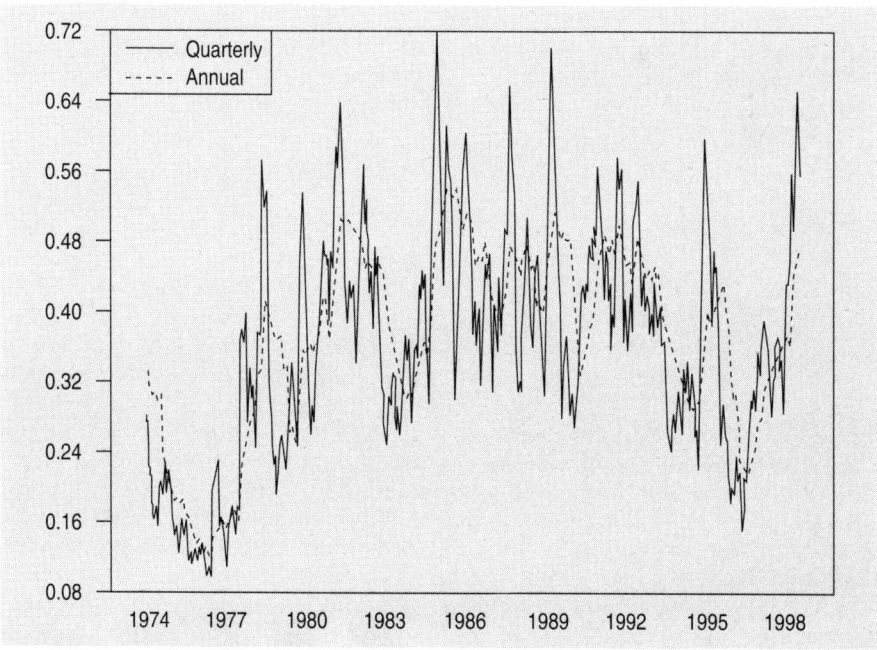

Fig 3.1 ● US dollar exchange rate index growth volatility
Moving standard deviations: 1 June 1974–6 January 1999

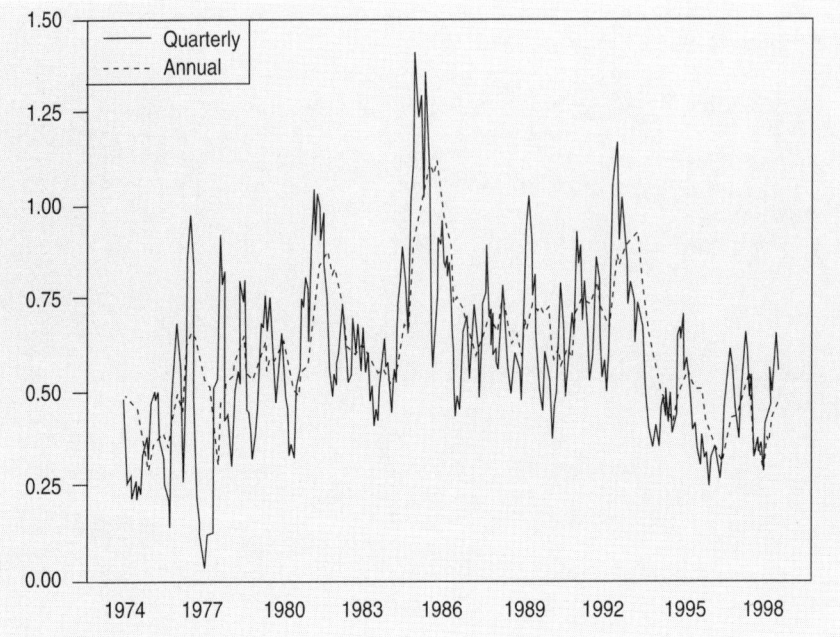

Fig 3.2 ● UK/US bilateral exchange rate growth volatility
Moving standard deviations: 1 June 1974–6 January 1999

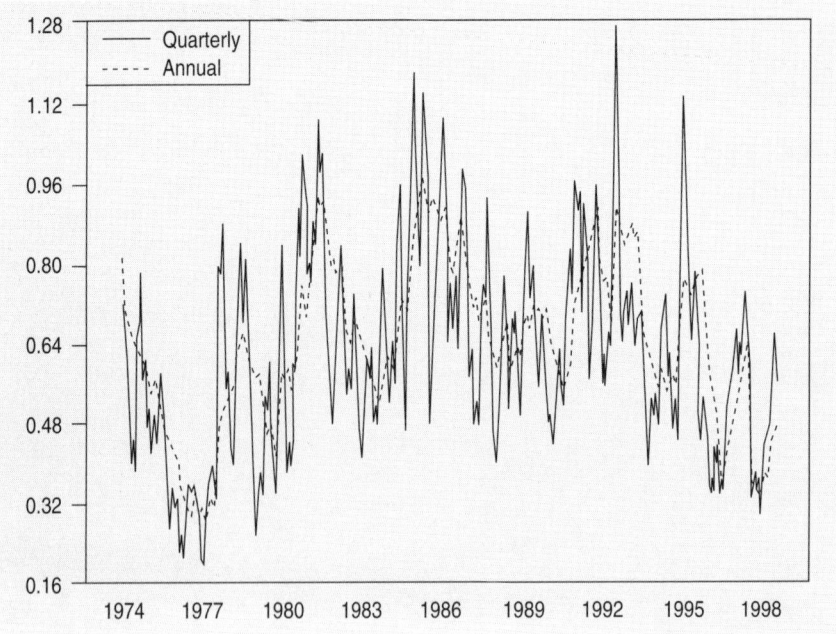

Fig 3.3 ● German/US bilateral exchange rate growth volatility
Moving standard deviations: 1 June 1974–6 January 1999

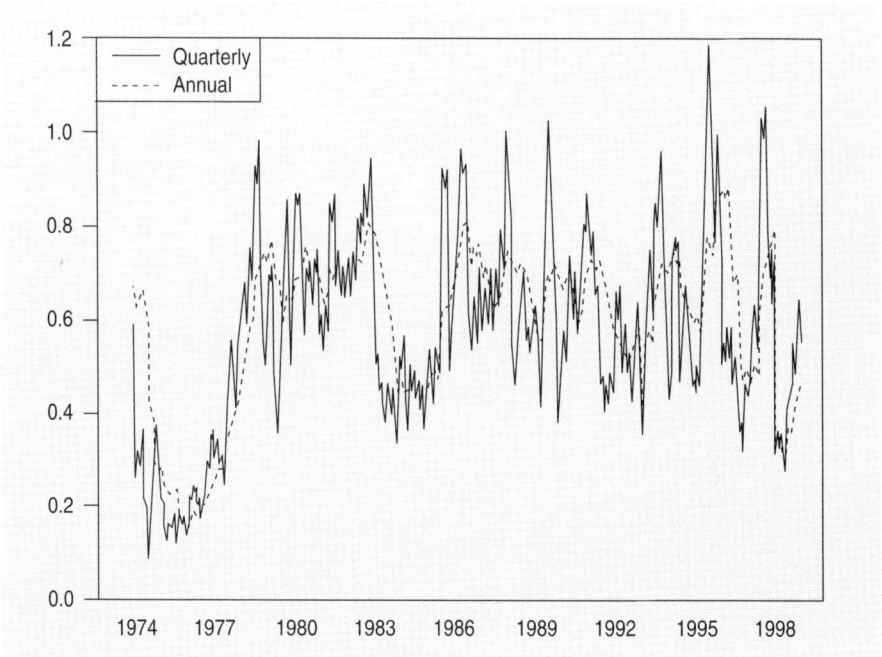

Fig 3.4 ● Japan/US bilateral exchange rate growth volatility
Moving standard deviations: 1 June 1974–6 January 1999

References

Bacchetta, Phillippe and van Wincoop, Eric (1998) "Does Exchange Rate Stability Increase Trade and Capital Flows?" *Federal Reserve Bank of New York*, Research Paper No. 9818.

Baillie, Richard and Osterberg, William P. (1997) "Why Do Central Banks Intervene?" *Journal of International Money and Finance,* vol. 16, no. 6 (December), pp. 909–19.

Barro, Robert J. and Sala-I-Martin, Xavier (1995) *Economic Growth.* New York: McGraw-Hill, Inc., pp. 434–5.

Dominguez, Kathryn M. (1998) "Central Bank Intervention and Exchange Rate Volatility," *Journal of International Money and Finance*, vol. 17, no. 1 (February), pp. 161–90.

Frankel, Jeffrey A. and Rose, Andrew K. (1995) "Empirical Research on Nominal Exchange Rates," in Gene M. Grossman and Kenneth Rogoff (eds), *Handbook of International Economics*, vol. 3, part 2, Amsterdam: North-Holland, pp. 1689–729.

Hali, Edison (1993) "The Effectiveness of Central Bank Intervention: A Survey of the Literature after 1982," *Special Papers in International Economics*, Princeton University, No. 18, July.

Hooper, Gregory P. (1997) "What Determines the Exchange Rate: Economic Factors or Market Sentiment?" in *Business Review,* Federal Reserve Bank of Philadelphia (September/October), pp. 17–29.

Humpage, Owen F. (1998) "The Federal Reserve as an Informed Foreign-Exchange Trader", Working Paper 9815, Federal Reserve Bank of Cleveland, September.

Humpage, Owen F. (1999) "U.S. Intervention: Assessing the Probability of Success," *Journal of Money, Credit and Banking*.

Meese, Richard A. and Rogoff, Kenneth (1983) "Empirical Exchange Rate Models of the Seventies: Do They Fit Out of Sample?" *Journal of International Economics*, 14 February, pp. 3–24.

Mussa, Michael (1981) *The Role of Official Intervention*. New York: Group of Thirty.

CHAPTER 4

The determination of exchange rates in the long and short run:

The fundamental approach and the asset market approach

- Introduction
- The fundamental approach
- Determination of exchange rates in the short run: the asset market approach
- Why do exchange rates change?
- Why are exchange rates so volatile?
- The equity market: a new factor influencing the currency markets

INTRODUCTION

Broadly speaking, there are four approaches to forecasting exchange rates. The first and simplest approach says: assume the exchange rate a year from now will be the same as it is today. This is known as the random walk hypothesis: the probability of a rise in the exchange rate is the same as the probability of a fall. In practice this turns out to be a poor forecasting technique.

The second approach starts from the idea that financial markets are efficient. Suppose a safe dollar-denominated bond is paying 5 per cent a year, and that a safe sterling-denominated bond is paying 7 per cent a year. The market evidently assumes that the total dollar (or sterling) return on these bonds will be the same: otherwise, the interest rate on the bond which is expected to earn less, after allowing for changes in exchange rates, would rise to compensate. Implicitly then, the market is expecting the dollar to appreciate against sterling by 2 per cent a year – sufficient to equalize the total returns, or, in the jargon, to achieve uncovered interest parity (UIP). This also turns out to be a poor predictor of exchange rates.

A third approach asks what change in the exchange rate will be required to move the economy closer to equilibrium, defined mainly in terms of achieving a sustainable balance of payments. The fourth approach is to look at an even more fundamental concept of equilibrium, based on the idea that exchange rates should move to equalize prices in different currency areas. This method is concerned with parity in purchasing power (PPP). You would expect it to work in the long run rather than the short run, and in that case it would be consistent with UIP. In practice it works tolerably well in the long run but not at all in the short run.

As will be evident from this discussion the time period and economic framework within which one attempts to predict currency movements is critical. This chapter examines both the short-term and long-term determinants of exchange rates.

THE FUNDAMENTAL APPROACH

The fundamental approach to the determination of exchange rates refers to those factors which render a given path for exchange rate as being sustainable over long time periods. It can be seen as providing a viewpoint as to whether the current exchange rate can be expected to be maintained when looking further ahead. It is useful to break down these long run factors into various categories:

- international competitiveness
- macroeconomic balance
- tariffs and quotas
- preference for domestic versus foreign goods
- productivity.

The law of one price

The starting point for understanding how exchange rates are determined is a simple idea known as the law of one price, which states that if two countries produce an identical good, the price of the good should be the same throughout the world, no matter which country produces it. Suppose American steel costs $100 per ton and Japanese steel costs 10,000 yen per ton, and that the steel is identical. The law of one price suggests that the exchange rate between the yen and the dollar must be 100 yen per dollar ($0.01 per yen) in order for one ton of American steel to sell for 10,000 yen in Japan (the price of Japanese steel) and one ton of Japanese steel to sell for $100 in the US. If the exchange rate were 200 yen/$, then Japanese steel would sell for $50 per ton in the US or $50 less than the American steel, while American steel would sell for 20,000 yen per ton in Japan (10,000 yen more than Japanese steel). Because American steel would be more expensive than Japancse stccl in both countries and, as it is identical to Japanese steel, the demand for American steel would go to zero. Given a fixed dollar price for the American steel, the resulting excess supply of American steel will be eliminated only if the exchange rate falls to 100 yen/$, making the price of American steel equal to Japanese steel in both countries.

International competitiveness

This is the Purchasing Power Parity (PPP) approach, which focuses on the analysis of the real exchange rate. In line with PPP theory, when prices of American goods rise (holding prices of foreign goods constant), the demand for American goods falls and the dollar tends to depreciate so that American goods can still sell well. On the other hand, if prices of Japanese goods rise so that the relative prices of American goods fall, the demand for American goods increases and the dollar tends to appreciate, because American goods will continue to sell well even with a higher value of the domestic currency. In the long run, a rise in a country's price level (relative to the foreign price level) causes its currency to depreciate, while a fall in the country's relative price level causes its currency to appreciate.

The attraction of PPP lies in its relative simplicity; once the relevant indicators and basket of goods have been identified, the principle can be applied. While providing useful inputs to any assessment of the fundamentals, PPP, however, suffers from a number of drawbacks that reduces its value when measuring a currency's fundamentals. Two of the most significant drawbacks are as follows.

1. The need for careful choice of the base period for comparison. Not only does the external account of the economy in question have to be in equilibrium but it also needs to be a good base period for partner countries – a condition which is seldom fulfilled.

2. The approach is also based on an unchanging equilibrium exchange rate, which may in fact alter through time to reflect a myriad of factors, from changing technologies to changes in the propensity to save and invest. Hence while the signals from PPP are an important part of the fundamentals, a more comprehensive approach is required to get a full assessment of the appropriate level of the exchange rate.

Macroeconomic balance

Sustainability lies at the heart of this approach, which focuses on both the internal and external balance within an economy.

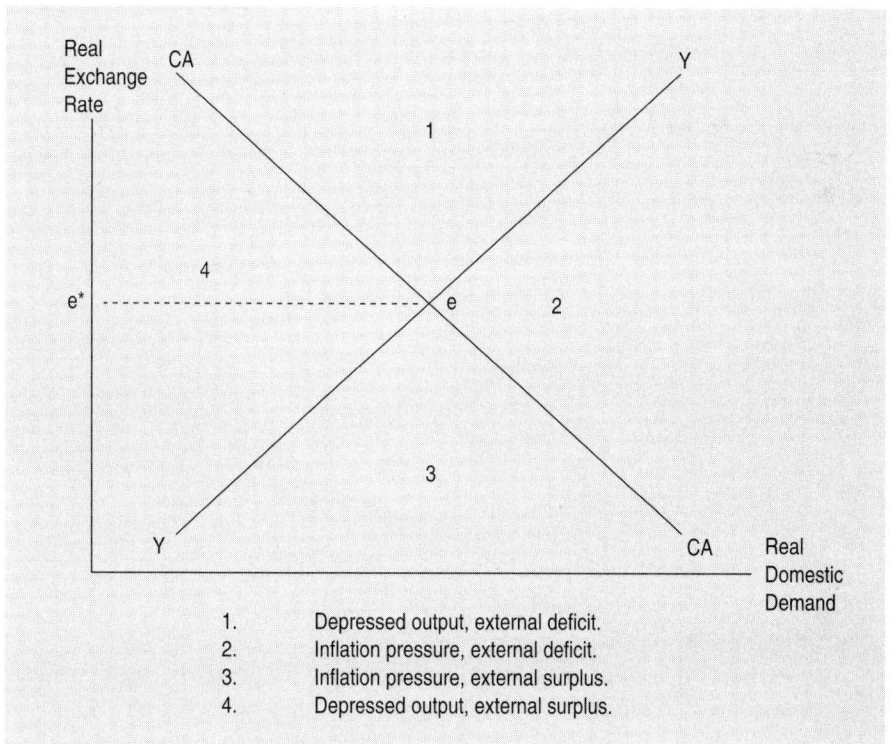

Fig 4.1 ● Macroeconomic balance and the real exchange rate

Internal balance is inextricably linked with the concepts of productive potential and the natural rate of unemployment. An economy can be said to be in internal balance when, against a background of full employment, it is expanding at the fastest rate possible without threatening a rise in inflation over the medium term. In Figure 4.1, internal balance is represented by YY, which slopes upward because as the real exchange rate rises more domestic demand is diverted to imports, the foreign demand for exports falls, and this then necessitates an increase in domestic demand in order to sustain the same level of output. The area to the right of YY shows an economy above its long run productive potential with inflation pressure building. To the left of YY, an economy is operating below productive capacity with spare resources.

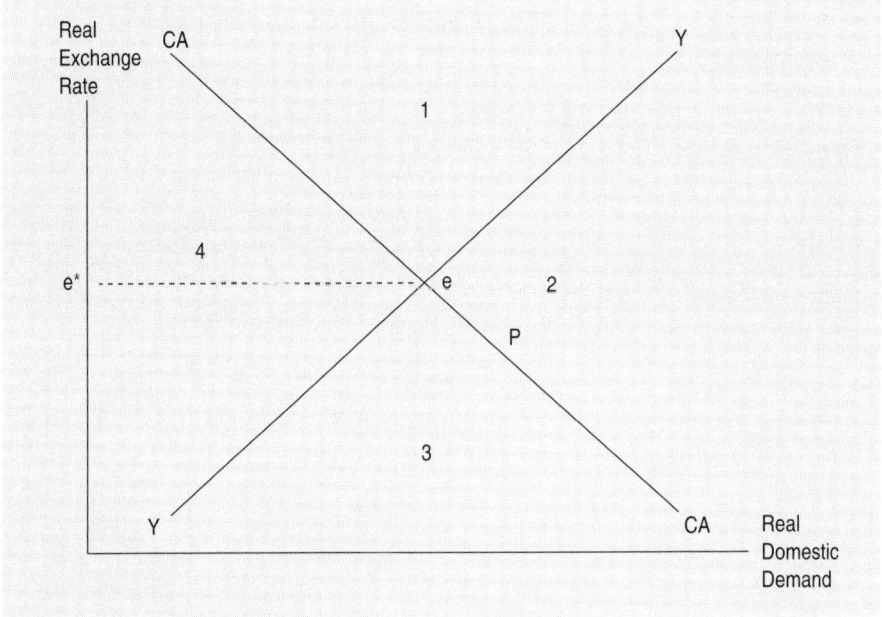

Fig 4.2 ● Inflation risk requires rise in real exchange rate

An economy which is operating with a high level of capacity utilization and with a very low level of unemployment will run an inflation risk if it continues to grow at a rate faster than its productive potential. This would be characterized by point *P* on Figure 4.2.

External balance can be broadly defined as the net flow of international capital that corresponds to the equilibrium levels of national savings and investment over the longer term. Assessing external balance will therefore not only necessitate a view on the structural state of a country's current account of the balance of payments but also on its ability to attract sufficient capital to finance the deficit on a sustainable basis. This will depend, to some extent, on currently existing debt levels, as well as rates of return in the domestic economy relative to those available abroad. A country which is a significant net debtor may find it much more difficult to sustain a current account deficit than one which is a substantial creditor. External balance is represented by *CACA* in Figure 4.2. *CACA* slopes downward because the higher domestic demand, the lower the external balance, which then necessitates a lower real exchange rate to offset this deterioration. The area to the left of *CACA* signifies a current account surplus and to the right a current account deficit.

The equilibrium real exchange rate e^* which sustains both internal and external balance, is determined by the intersection *YY* and *CACA* at point e. Hence, at P in Figure 4.2 the economy is not only above full capacity and therefore in inflation territory it is also running a current account deficit because P is above *CACA*. Internal and external balance are restored at e by the real exchange rate rising, reducing the demand for exports and hence domestic employment. As unemployment slows, domestic demand will slow faster than exports and output will slow sufficiently quickly to relieve the inflation pressure thus restoring internal balance. The slowing in domestic demand will also reduce the demand for imports and external balance will also be re-established at e, and with it the equilibrium exchange rate.

The equilibrium real exchange rate in this approach may well vary over time and with structural changes to the domestic economy. For example, German reunification led to a large transfer of resources from West Germany to rebuild the economy of the east, and thus a redirection of German savings from abroad to the domestic economy. The implicit reduction in the equilibrium current account moved the *CACA* line to the right which points to a higher equilibrium exchange rate at e^{**} (see Figure 4.3).

It is fairly easy to identify episodes from recent economic history that correspond to the four different quadrants in these diagrams. Some examples, applied to Figure 4.2, are as follows.

Point 1. Depressed output, external deficit – UK and Sweden, 1987–92.

Point 2. Inflation pressure, external deficit – US, 1985.

Point 3. Inflation pressure, external surplus – Italy 1995.

Point 4. Depressed output, external surplus – Japan 1993.

The macroeconomic balance approach has significant advantages over the PPP approach by providing a framework in which to assess whether movements in

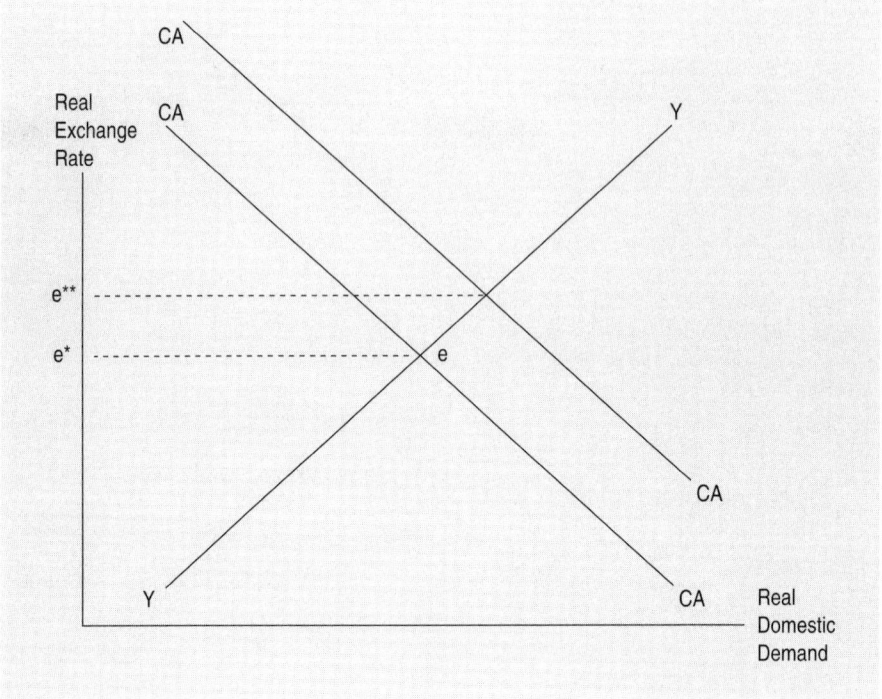

Fig 4.3 ● Equilibrium exchange rate may shift

the exchange rate are in line with the fundamentals. However, it should be pointed out from the outset that while the framework may be used to identify long-term currency misalignment other shorter-term factors, discussed below, may determine actual movements in the currency. In addition, while providing an analytical framework, the macroeconomic balance approach inevitably involves a high degree of judgment. Nonetheless, it provides a particularly useful means of assessing whether significant shifts in exchange rates are in line with the fundamentals or represent a potentially damaging misalignment.

Tariffs and quotas

Barriers to free trade such as tariffs (taxes on imported goods) and quotas (restrictions on the quantity of foreign goods than can be imported) can affect the exchange rate. Suppose that the US imposes a tariff or a quota on Japanese steel. These trade barriers increase the demand for American steel, and the dollar would tend to appreciate because American steel will still sell well even with a higher value of the dollar. Tariffs and quotas cause a country's currency to appreciate in the long run.

Preferences for domestic versus foreign goods

If the Japanese develop an appetite for American goods, say for Florida oranges and American movies, then the increased demand for American goods (exports) tends to make the dollar appreciate, because the American goods will continue to sell well even with a higher value of the dollar. Likewise, if Americans decide that they prefer Japanese cars to American cars, the increased demand for Japanese goods (imports) tends to depreciate the dollar. Increased demand for a country's exports causes its currency to appreciate in the long run, while increased demand for imports causes its currency to depreciate.

Productivity

If one country becomes more productive than other countries, businesses in that country can lower the prices of domestic goods relative to foreign goods and still earn a profit. As a result, the demand for domestic goods rises and the domestic currency tends to appreciate because domestic goods will continue to sell well with a higher value of the currency. If its productivity lags behind other countries, on the other hand, its goods become relatively more expensive and the currency tends to depreciate. In the long run, as a country becomes more productive relative to other countries, its currency appreciates.

The factors that affect exchange rates in the long run are summarized in Table 4.1.

Table 4.1 ● Summary: factors that affect exchange rates in the long run

Factor		Response of the exchange rate (E)[b]	
Domestic price level[a]	↑	E	↓
Tariffs and quotas[a]	↑	E	↑
Import demand	↑	E	↓
Export demand	↑	E	↑
Productivity[a]	↑	E	↑

Note: Only increases (↑) in the factors are shown; the effects of decreases in the variables on the exchange rate are the opposite of those indicated in the second column.
[a] relative to foreign countries
[b] E is defined so that E ↑ means that the currency has appreciated. For the US, this means that E represents units of foreign currency per dollar.

Source: Mishkin, F.S., and Eakins, S.G., *Financial Markets and Institutions*, 1998. Addison Wesley

DETERMINATION OF EXCHANGE RATES IN THE SHORT RUN: THE ASSET MARKET APPROACH*

Central to understanding the short-run behaviour of exchange rates is to recognize that an exchange rate is the price of domestic bank deposits (those denominated in the domestic currency) in terms of foreign bank deposits (those denominated in the foreign currency). The modern asset approach to explaining exchange rate determination does not emphasize the flows of purchases of exports and imports over short periods, because these transactions are quite small relative to the amount of domestic and foreign bank deposits at any given time. Foreign exchange transactions are very large as compared with flows associated with trading, as was illustrated in Chapters 1 and 2. The effect of this is that over short time periods, decisions to hold domestic versus foreign assets play a much greater role in exchange rate determination than do the foreign currency flows associated with exporting and importing.

Assumptions in the asset market approach

To grasp the central role that the asset market approach makes to understanding short-term currency movements, it is necessary to make several assumptions. First, assume that the US is the domestic or home country with the implication that domestic bank deposits are denominated in dollars. Also assume that the foreign country is France and that foreign bank deposits are denominated in euros, although they will in fact be denominated in francs until 2002. The theory of asset demand suggests that the most important factor affecting the demand for domestic (dollar) deposits and foreign (euro) deposits is the expected return on these assets relative to one another. When Americans or foreigners expect the return on dollar deposits to be high relative to the return on foreign deposits (euros), there is a higher demand for dollar deposits and a correspondingly lower demand for euro deposits.

To understand how the demands for dollar and foreign deposits change, we need to compare the expected returns on dollar deposits and foreign deposits (euros).

---

* This section draws on Krugman, P.R. and Obstfeld, M. (1997), *International Economics: Theory and Policy*. Addison Wesley.

Make the following assumption :

i\$ = Return on dollar deposit

i€ = Return on euro deposit

E_t = Spot exchange rate, dollar/euro

E_{t+1}^e = Expected exchange rate

$\dfrac{(E_{t+1}^e - E_t)}{E_t}$ = Expected rate of appreciation of dollar

How would investment returns be seen from a French perspective?

To compare the expected returns of dollar deposits and foreign deposits (euros), investors must convert the expected return from one currency into the currency they use. Therefore, a French investor would see the returns in terms of euros and would go through the following reasoning.

Question: What is the return on a dollar deposit in terms of euros by a French investor (RET\$)?

Answer: $RET\$ = i\$ + \dfrac{(E_{t+1}^e - E_t)}{E_t}$

Question: What is the return to a French investor of investing in euros (RET€)?

Answer: (RET€) = i€
This is simply the return in the investor's local currency.

Question: What is the relative return to a French investor in euros of investing in dollars (relative RET\$)?

Answer: Relative RET\$ = i\$ – i€ + $\dfrac{(E_{t+1}^e - E_t)}{E_t}$

So as the relative expected return on dollars increases (decreases), investors will seek to hold more (fewer) dollar deposits and fewer (more) euro deposits.

How would investment returns be seen from an American perspective?

An American investor would see any investment return in terms of dollars, so any expected returns in euros would have to be converted into dollars. The American investor will be aware that:

$$\text{RET} \euro = i\euro - \frac{(E^e_{t+1} - E_t)}{E_t}$$

Now assume $i\euro = 5\%$
Also assume that the dollar is expected to appreciate by 4%
Insert this into the above formula: $5\% - 4\% = 1\%$
RET\$ = i\$

So relative return on dollars = RET\$ = i\$ $-\left[i\euro - \frac{(E^e_{t+1} - E_t)}{E_t} \right]$

$$= i\$ - i\euro + \frac{(E^e_{t+1} - E_t)}{E_t}$$

This is the same as the earlier result. So the relative expected return on dollar deposits is the same whether calculated in terms of euros or in terms of dollars. As the relative expected return on dollar deposits increases (decreases), both foreigners and domestic residents respond in exactly the same way – both will want to hold more (fewer) dollar deposits and fewer (more) euro deposits. Where does this now take us?

The interest parity condition

Assume, as is the case, that capital is highly mobile and that bank deposits are perfect substitutes. Under these circumstances, if US dollar returns rise, both American and French investors will demand dollars (and vice versa). Under the asset market approach, in order for the demand for assets (domestic and foreign) to equal the supply of asset (domestic and foreign) there must be no difference in their expected returns. This can be restated in that their relative expected returns must equal zero. This condition is known as the interest parity condition and is restated below:

$$i\$ = i\euro - \frac{(E^e_{t+1} - E_t)}{E_t}$$

The interest parity condition states that the domestic interest rate equals the foreign interest rate minus the expected appreciation of the domestic currency. In other words, this also means that the domestic interest rate equals the foreign interest rate plus the expected appreciation of the foreign currency. For the interest parity condition to hold, it must be the case that if the domestic interest rate is above the foreign interest rate then there must be a positive expected appreciation of the foreign currency which thereby compensates for the lower foreign interest rate.

Assume: domestic interest rate (dollars) = 15%
foreign interest rate (euros) = 10%

then the domestic currency (foreign currency) is expected to depreciate (appreciate) by 5 per cent.

The importance of the interest parity condition is that only when the exchange rate is such that expected returns on domestic and foreign deposits are equal (ie interest parity holds), will the outstanding domestic and foreign deposits be willingly held. Otherwise something must give. Exactly what gives is discussed in the next section.

How does the interest parity condition affect the foreign exchange market?

To illustrate how the interest parity condition affects the foreign exchange market, we need to describe how the expected returns on euro and dollar deposits change as the current exchange rate changes.

Expected return on the euro deposit

Earlier we demonstrated that the expected return in terms of dollars on a foreign deposit is:

$$\text{RET} \, \euro \; = i\euro \; - \frac{(E^e_{t+1} - E_t)}{E_t}$$

Assume that: $i\euro$ = 10%
E^e_{t+1} = 10 euros/$
E_t = 9.5 euros/$

Then the expected appreciation of the dollar

$$= \frac{10 - 9.5}{9.5} = 0.052 = 5.2\%$$

$\text{RET} \euro \; = 10\% - 5.2\% = 4.8\%$ (Point A) (Figure 4.4)

Now assume that: E_t = 10 euros/$, then the expected dollar appreciation

$$= \frac{10 - 10}{10} = 0\%$$

$\text{RET} \euro \; = 10\%$ (Point B) (Figure 4.4)

Now assume that: E_t = 10.5 then the expected dollar appreciation

$$= \frac{10 - 10.5}{10.5} = 0.048\% = -14.8\%$$ (Point C) (Figure 4.4)

$\text{RET} \euro \; = 10\% - (-4.8\%) = 14.8\%$

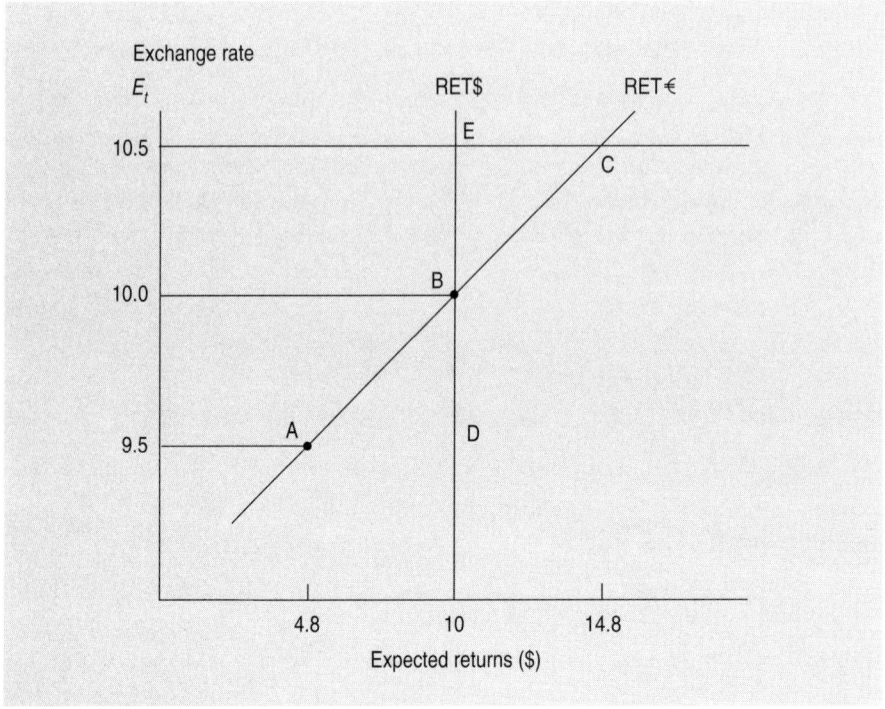

Fig 4.4 ● Expected return on euro deposit

Source: Mishkin, F.S., and Eakins, S.G. (1998) *Financial Markets and Institutions*, Addison Wesley

A change in the current exchange rate results in a movement along the expected return schedule for euro deposits (RET€).

RET€ is positively sloped. As E_t rises the expected return on franc deposits rises. The reasoning behind this is that as the current exchange rate of the dollar rises there is less expected appreciation of the dollar. Thus a higher current exchange rate means a greater expected appreciation of the foreign currency (euro) in the future which increases the expected return on foreign currency deposits in dollars. This is summarized in Figures 4.5 and 4.6.

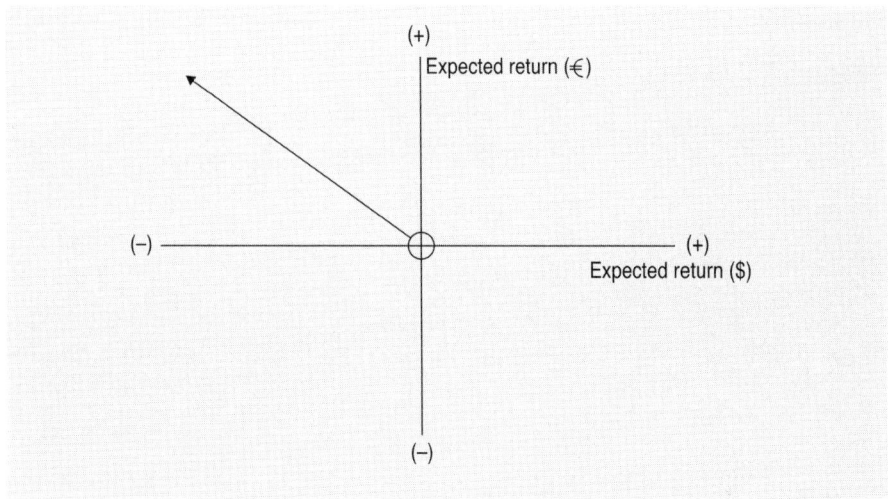

Fig 4.5 ● Spot dollar high, expected to fall: spot euro low, expected to rise

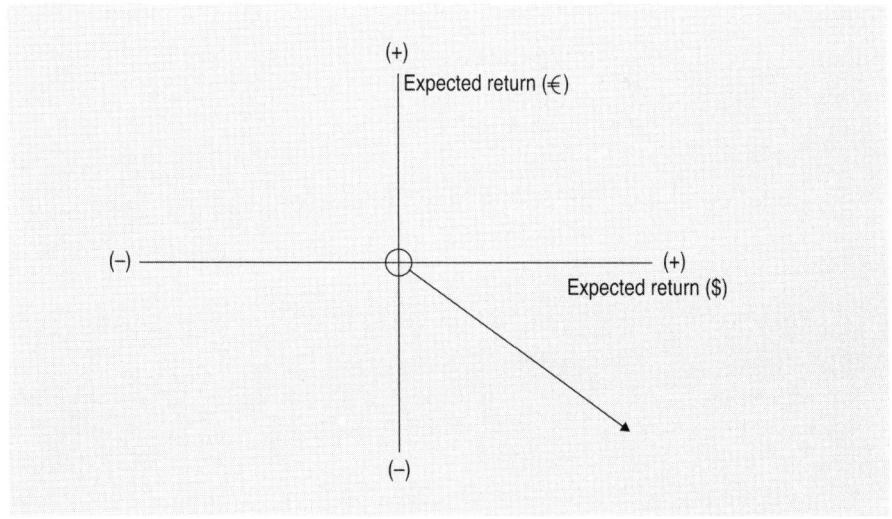

Fig 4.6 ● Spot dollar low, expected to rise: spot euro high, expected to fall

Expected return on dollar deposits

The expected return on dollar deposits in terms of dollars must be RET^s.

Say	RET$	=	i$	=	10%			
If E_t	=	9.5	then	RET$	=	10%	(Point D) (Figure 4.4)
If E_t	=	10.0	then	RET$	=	10%	(Point B) (Figure 4.4)
If E_t	=	10.5	then	RET$	=	10%	(Point E) (Figure 4.4)

But where is the spot rate?

Say   RET$ =   RET€   =   (Point B) = 10.0

Say   RET$ <   RET€   =   (Point E) = 10.5

        Market will sell $/buy euros
          Dollar falls/euro rises

Say   RET$ >   RET€   =   (Point D) =   9.5

        Market will buy $/sell euros
          Dollar rises/euro falls

WHY DO EXCHANGE RATES CHANGE?

As discussed above, the exchange rate settles at the intersection of RET€ and RET$. Naturally, if either of these expected return schedules shift then so will the exchange rate. Let us examine these in turn.

Shifts in the expected return schedule for foreign deposits

Earlier in the chapter, we established that:

$$RET€ = i€ - \frac{(E^e_{t+1} - E_t)}{E_t}$$

A change in E_t will result in a movement along the expected return schedule for euros.

Factors that shift the whole schedule will be the remaining terms in this formula, namely the foreign interest rate i€ and the expected future exchange rate.

Changes in the foreign interest rate (i€)

If i€ rises, the RET€ also rises. In Figure 4.7 $RET_1€$ moves to $RET_2€$. The dollar falls from E_1 to E_2 as investors buy euros and sell dollars. Naturally if i€ falls, RET€ moves to the left, the domestic currency, the dollar, appreciates and the euro depreciates.

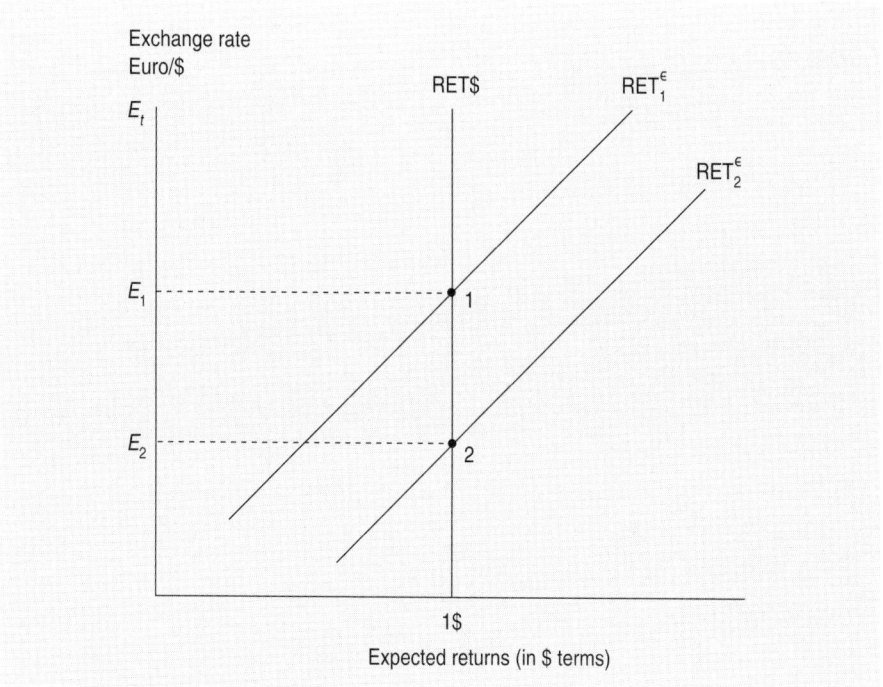

Fig 4.7 ● Effect of changes in the foreign interest rate

Changes in the expected future exchange rate E^e_{t+1}

If the future exchange rate of the dollar is expected to fall, this decreases the expected appreciation of the dollar and hence raises the expected return in euros, moving from $RET_1€$ to $RET_2€$ in Figure 4.7. The dollar falls from E_1 to E_2.

On the other hand, a rise in E^e_{t+1} raises the expected appreciation of the dollar, lowers the expected return on euro deposits, shifts the RET€ schedule to the left, and raises the dollar.

To summarize: a rise in the expected future exchange rate shifts the expected return on foreign (euro) deposits schedule to the left and causes an appreciation of the domestic currency (dollar). A fall in the expected future exchange rate shifts the RET€ schedule to the right and causes a depreciation of the domestic currency (dollar).

Shifts in the expected return schedule for domestic deposits

Since the expected return on domestic (dollar) deposits is just the interest rate on these deposits, $i\$$, this interest rate is the only factor that shifts the expected return on the dollar deposits schedule. This can be seen from Figure 4.8.

Shifts in the expected return on domestic deposits schedule (RET$). An increase in the expected return on dollar deposits ($i\$$) shifts the expected return on domestic (dollar) deposits from $RET_1\$$ to $RET_2\$$ and the exchange rate rises from E_1 to E_2.

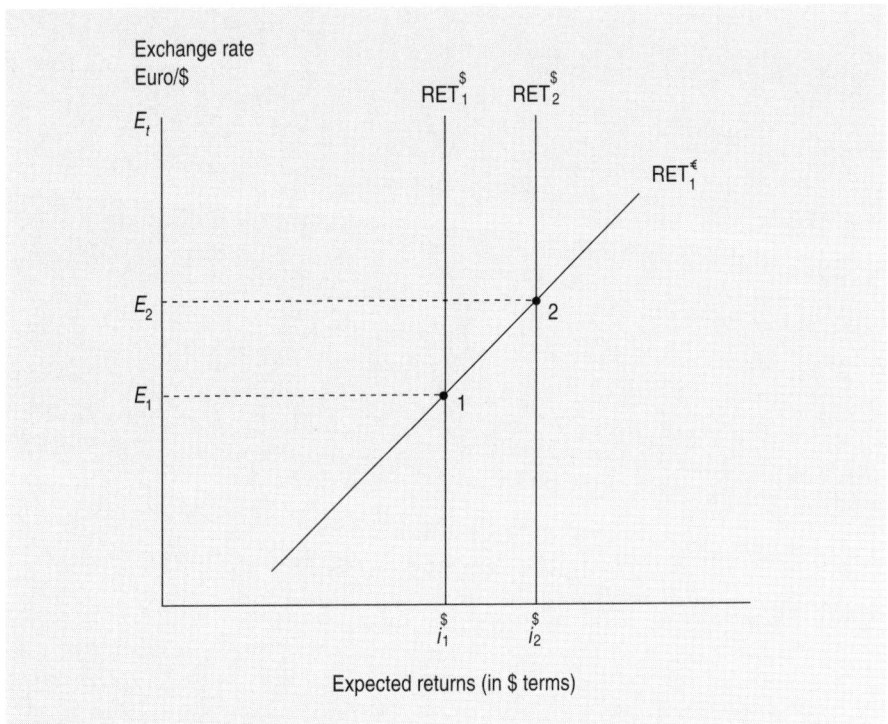

Fig 4.8 ● Effect of changes in the expected return on domestic deposits

Changes in the domestic interest rate (i$)

A rise in $i\$$ raises the expected return on dollar deposits, shifts the RET$ schedule to the right, and leads to a rise in the exchange rate, as shown in Figure 4.8. Another way of seeing this is to recognize that a rise in $i\$$, which raises the expected return on dollar deposits, creates an excess demand for dollar deposits at the original equilibrium exchange rate, and the resulting purchases of dollar deposits causes an appreciation of the dollar. A rise in the domestic interest rate ($i\$$) shifts the expected return on domestic deposits to the right and causes an appreciation of the domestic (dollar) currency: a fall in i$ shifts the RET$ schedule to the left and causes a depreciation of the dollar.

Our earlier analysis of the long-run determinants of the exchange rate indicated that the factors that influence the expected future exchange rate are:

● the relative price level
● relative tariffs and quotas
● import demand
● export demand
● relative productivity.

The theory of purchasing power parity suggest that if a higher American price level relative to the foreign price level is expected to persist, the dollar will depreciate in the long run. A higher expected relative American price level should thus have a tendency to raise the expected return on euro deposits, shift the RET€ schedule to the right, and lower the current exchange rate.

The following long run determinants of the exchange rate will increase the expected return on euro deposits, shift the RET€ schedule to the right, and cause a depreciation of the domestic currency, the dollar.

1. Expectations of a rise in the American price level relative to the foreign price level.

2. Expectations of lower American tariffs and quotas relative to foreign tariffs and quotas.

3. Expectations of higher American import demand.

4. Expectations of lower foreign demand for American exports.

5. Expectations of lower American productivity relative to foreign productivity.

See also Table 4.2.

Table 4.2 ● Factors that shift the RET€ and RET$ schedules and cause exchange rates to change

Factor	Change in factor	Response of exchange rate, E_t
Domestic interest rate, i$	↑	↑
Foreign interest rate, i€	↑	↓
Expected domestic price level*	↑	↓
Expected tariffs and quotas*	↑	↑

Factor	Change in factor	Response of exchange rate, E_t

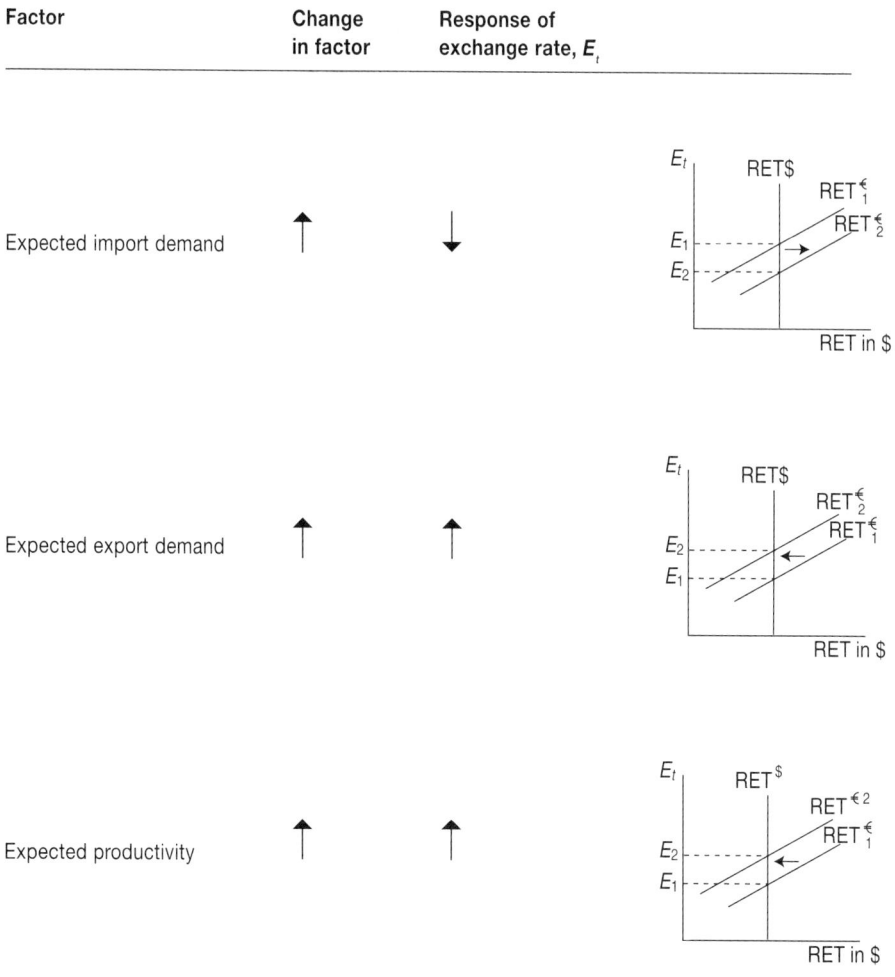

Source: Adapted from Mishkin, F.S. and Eakins, S.G. (1998) *Financial Markets and Institutions,* Addison Wesley.

Note: Only increases (↑) in the factors are shown; the effects of decreases in the variables on the exchange rate are the opposite of those indicated in the third column.

WHY ARE EXCHANGE RATES SO VOLATILE?

The answer to the question, "Why are exchange rates so volatile?", is provided by the asset market approach to exchange rate determination outlined above. Because an expected appreciation of the domestic currency affects the expected return on foreign deposits, then expectations about the price level, inflation, tariffs and quotas, productivity, import demand, export demand, and the money supply play an important role in determining the exchange rate.

When expectations about any of these variables change, there will be an immediate effect on the expected return of foreign deposits and therefore on the exchange rate. Since expectations on all these variables change with just about every bit of news that appears it is not surprising that exchange rates are so volatile. Chapter 5 provides details of the types of economic news that significantly influence the short run behaviour of the dollar.

An illustration of the effect of changing the assumptions about the factors applied in the asset market approach is given in Table 4.3.

Table 4.3 ● Comparing dollar and euro rates of return

Case	Dollar interest rate (%) $i\$$	Euro interest rate (%) $i\euro$	Expected rate of dollar depreciation against euro (%) $\dfrac{E^e_{t+1} - E_t}{E_t}$	Rate of return difference between dollar and euro deposits (%) $i\$ - i\euro + \dfrac{E^e_{t+1} - E}{E_t}$
1	0.10	0.06	0.00	0.04
2	0.10	0.06	0.04	0.00
3	0.10	0.06	0.08	−0.04
4	0.10	0.12	−0.04	0.02

From Table 4.3, it can be seen that in case 1, the interest differential in favour of dollar deposits is 4 per cent per year (i$ – i€ = 0.10 – 0.06 = 0.04) and no change in the exchange rate is expected [$(E^e_{t+1} – E_t)/E_t$ = 0.00]. This means that the expected annual real rate of return on dollar deposits is 4 per cent higher than that on euros so that, other things being equal, investors would prefer dollars rather than euro deposits.

In case 2, the interest differential is the same (4 per cent), but it is just offset by an expected depreciation of the dollar of 4 per cent. The two assets therefore have the same expected rate of return.

In case 3, a 4 per cent interest differential in favour of dollar deposits is more than offset by an 8 per cent expected depreciation of the dollar, so euro deposits are preferred by market participants.

In case 4, there is a 2 per cent interest differential in favour of euro deposits, but the dollar is expected to appreciate against the euro by 4 per cent over the year. The expected rate of return on dollar deposits is therefore 2 per cent per year higher than that on euros, so dollar deposits are preferred by market participants.

THE EQUITY MARKET: A NEW FACTOR INFLUENCING THE CURRENCY MARKETS

As discussed in this chapter, the traditional long-term factors influencing the foreign exchange market would be a country's external trade balance, its rate of monetary growth, inflation and interest rates. Foreign exchange rates, it is argued, are largely determined by capital flows into or out of national bond markets on the basis of real interest rate differentials.

But this has changed dramatically over the past five years as the equity culture has spread. From 1982 to 1995, for instance, the market capitalization of all companies listed on the New York Stock Exchange remained roughly 1.5 times the size of outstanding publicly held US Treasury Bonds. Since then, that ratio has shot up to four to one, without even counting Nasdaq's technology giants, and both asset managers and households are continuing to expand their holdings of stocks, including international stocks.

This means that international equity investment now makes up a substantial amount of global capital flows, even before taking account of cross-border mergers and foreign direct investment.

In the early 1990s, foreigners' transactions in US government bonds were ten times the size of their dealings in the stock market. By the end of 1999 that ratio had shrunk to less than two.

All this is clearly having an influence on the currency markets. Evidence for this is provided by the twin strengths of the US stock market and the dollar (against the euro) during 1999 and their increasingly close, and statistically significant, correlation.

As a result, the models for predicting exchange rates that are used by banks and investors, designed in an era when bonds were the asset of choice for global investors, need to be modified to incorporate the growing impact of equities.

CHAPTER 5

Exactly which economic news affects exchange rates?

- Expected versus unexpected news
- The components of Gross National Product
- Consumer expenditure
- Investment
- Government spending
- Foreign trade and the balance of payments
- The effect of consumer confidence on financial markets
- Is the reaction of the foreign exchange market to "news" supported by empirical research?

EXPECTED VERSUS UNEXPECTED NEWS

The critical judgment to be made when analyzing the effect of economic news on currency market behaviour is to know what the market is expecting and why. In financial market language this is referred to as knowing what has been "discounted" by the market. The relationship between financial markets and news is straightforward. Expected news does not move markets. Unexpected news does move markets, particularly if it could provoke a monetary response on the part of the Central Bank. In this chapter, we are assuming that the news coming into the foreign exchange market is unexpected. In addition we concentrate on news about the US economy given the central role played by the US dollar in the world economy. In each case, we define the key market-sensitive indicator, illustrate how to interpret it and then describe its impact on the currency markets.

THE COMPONENTS OF GROSS NATIONAL PRODUCT (GNP)

It is essential in appreciating the reaction of currency markets to economic news to be able to break down the components of nominal GNP, defined below. The key indicators affecting nominal GNP are shown in Figure 5.1. An understanding of the way the economy is evolving is best seen by applying what economists refer to as the standard macroeconomic model. This breaks the economy down into those factors affecting, in turn, consumer spending, investment, government spending and taxation and the effect of the balance of payments. These together add up to what is referred to as Gross National Product.

Gross national product and gross domestic product

Definition

Gross domestic product (GDP) measures the total value of US output. It is the total of all economic activity in the US, regardless of whether the owners of the means of production reside in the US.

For a more detailed description of the impact of US economic indicators on financial markets, see *What Drives Financial Markets*, by Brian Kettell, in this series.

How should you interpret it?

The currency markets focus on the seasonally adjusted annualized percentage change in real-expenditure based GDP in the current quarter compared to the previous quarter. The markets concentrate on annualized growth in seasonally adjusted, real expenditure-based GDP for the latest quarter compared to the previous quarters.

It is important to calculate Nominal GNP. This consists of two parts – real (or inflation adjusted GNP), and the inflation rate. The growth rate of Nominal GNP equals the sum of the growth rates of real GNP and of the inflation rate. The Federal Reserve follows the behaviour of Nominal GNP very closely.

What is its impact on currency markets?

Currency market behaviour to this economic indicator is often restrained since it is usually expected news, with many of its key components having already been published. However, shocks do occur and an unexpected movement in the GNP figure would be very market sensitive.

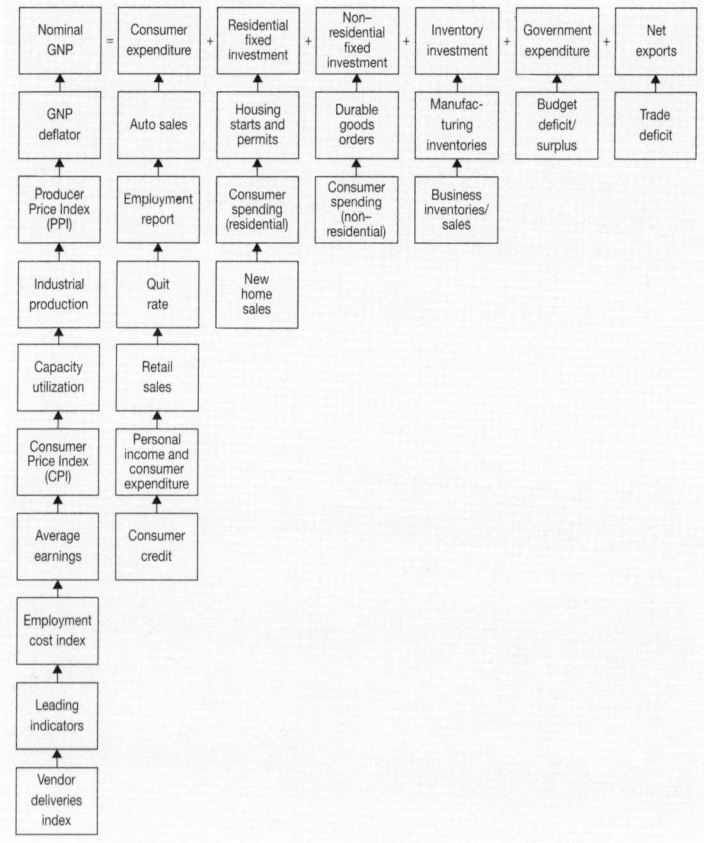

Fig 5.1 ● Economic indicators and financial markets

GDP deflator

Definition

The GDP deflators are comprehensive measures of inflation since they encompass changes in prices in all sectors of the economy – consumer products, capital goods, the foreign sector and the government.

There are actually three GDP deflators:

- the implicit deflator
- the fixed weight deflator
- the chain-price index.

The implicit deflator measures changes in prices as well as changes in the composition of output. The fixed weight deflator works on the same principle as the consumer and producer price indexes since it measures prices for a composition of GDP chosen in a certain time-period. The chain-price index combines the variable and fixed weight baskets.

How do you interpret it?

The fixed weight GDP deflator is a more meaningful measure of inflation and therefore more market sensitive than the implicit price deflator.

What is its impact on currency markets?

Currency market participants closely follow the GDP deflators. In the past few years, more attention has been focused on the fixed weight deflator than on the implicit price deflator. An increase in the deflator tends to force up the value of the dollar on the back of expected interest rate increases. A moderation in this inflation measure will lead to the opposite effect.

Producer price index (PPI)

Definition

The PPI measures the prices that manufacturers and farmers charge to the shops.

How do you interpret it?

Currency market attention is focused on the percentage change in the monthly finished goods PPI. However, because food prices tend to be seasonal, and energy prices are frequently volatile, analysts prefer to watch the "core" rate of producer price inflation which strips out food and energy prices.

The markets concentrate on the seasonally adjusted finished goods PPI and look at how this has behaved on a month-to-month, quarter-on-quarter, six-monthly and year-on-year basis.

What is its impact on currency markets?

Currency market participants anxiously await the producer price index figures. The value of the dollar will probably rise when producer price increases are large and accelerating and if they expect the Federal Reserve to respond by raising interest rates, and vice versa.

Index of industrial production

Definition

The industrial production figures are a set of index numbers which measure the monthly physical output of US factories, mines and gas and electric utilities. The index is broken down by type of industry (manufacturing, mining or utilities) and by type of market (consumer, equipment, intermediate or materials). The currency markets tend to focus on the seasonally adjusted monthly change in the aggregate figure.

How do you interpret it?

The US Index of Industrial Production is a derivative statistic, based in a large part on the Bureau of Labor Statistics (BLS) employment report which comes out two to three weeks earlier and, consequently, normally is expected news.

What is its impact on currency markets?

A rise in industrial production signals economic growth, whereas a decline in production indicates contraction. Participants in the foreign exchange markets would see gains in industrial production and the capacity utilization rate, discussed below, as being good news for the dollar, and vice versa. Foreign exchange dealers will look towards the effects of higher interest rates. High interest rates in the US relative to other countries increase the demand for US securities and therefore US dollars.

Capacity utilization rate

Definition

Capacity utilization measures the extent to which the capital stock of the nation is being employed in the production of goods.

How do you interpret it?

Once capacity reaches a certain point, it is expected that excess demand pressures will result in inflation. At certain times, the market has used this indicator as a good leading indicator of inflation although its value has become limited recently as it has risen without inflationary pressures also rising.

What is its impact on currency markets?

A rise in capacity utilization has the same effect on financial markets as a rise in industrial production as the two indicators are inextricably linked. Industrial production will signal economic growth. The capacity utilization rate reflects the extent of resources utilization and the point at which inflationary pressures set in. Hence, rising capacity utilization will signal inflationary pressures and with them the possibility of interest rate increases and a rise in the dollar, and vice versa.

Consumer price index (CPI)

Definition

The consumer price index (CPI) is a measure of the prices of a fixed basket of consumer goods and, as such, is a measure of inflation.

How do you interpret it?

Reluctantly, many economists exclude parts of the index for analytical purposes: "reluctantly", because those excluded prices affect inflation. Food and energy prices are the usual candidates for exclusion owing to their extreme volatility. The CPI-U minus food and energy is commonly referred to as the "core" rate of inflation.

What is its impact on currency markets?

Currency market participants anxiously await the consumer price index because it drives much activity in the marketplace. Interest rates tend to be altered in line with expected inflationary trends. So rising inflation with the possibility of rising interest rates are good news for the dollar, and vice versa.

Average hourly earnings

Definition

Average hourly and weekly earnings measure the level of wages and salaries for workers on private non-farm payrolls.

How do you interpret them?

The hourly earnings figures reflect changes in basic hourly rates as well as increases in premium pay because of overtime hours worked. The currency markets concentrate on the monthly and year-on-year percentage changes in seasonally adjusted average hourly and weekly earnings.

What is their impact on currency markets?

Average hourly earnings are the earliest available indicator of underlying trends in industry's wage and salary costs. They are closely monitored by the Federal Reserve and have recently received the acclaim of being mentioned by Fed Chairman Alan Greenspan as being an indicator he closely follows.

Their main disadvantage from the point of view of currency markets is that they exclude non-wage costs such as insurance, retirement, savings and other benefits. The employment cost index (ECI), described below, includes these items and is a better measure of total labour costs. Despite its volatility and limitations, currency market participants pounce on the average hourly earnings data – it is the first inflation news for the month. A rapid rise in hourly wages is good news for the dollar if it is expected to provoke a rise in interest rates, and vice versa.

Employment cost index (ECI)

Definition

Wage pressures can be measured in two ways: average wages and the employment cost index. Average earnings measure the level of wages and salaries for employees on non-farm payrolls. The employment cost index (ECI) tracks all civilian employee compensation. Apart from wages and salaries, it also includes many of the other benefits that employees receive.

How do you interpret it?

The advantage of ECI over average earnings is that it includes non-wage costs, which can add 30 per cent to total labour costs. The employment cost index is not, however, a measure of change in the total cost of employing labour. For example, it does not include training costs, nor does it report retroactive pay. The index does not cover all employers and employees in the US, although it does cover nearly all workers in the civilian non-farm economy. The main group not covered is the self-employed.

What is its impact on currency markets?

Currency market participants react to the employment cost index as they would to any other inflation measure. Because it is a quarterly release, and a more stable series than most, the market impact is often muted. It is known to be watched closely by Alan Greenspan, the Chairman of the Federal Reserve, giving it extra impetus should the outcome be significantly different from market expectations.

Index of leading indicators (LEI)

Definition

The index of leading indicators is a weighted average of the economic variables that lead the business cycle. It is part of the family of indicators designed to provide information on the current stage of the business cycle.

The ten variables that make up the index are listed below. They were chosen because each has a tendency to predict (lead) economic activity and because data on them are frequently and promptly reported. This second characteristic is essential because a variable cannot be of much help in forecasting if accurate data on the variable arrive only after a long delay.

The leading economic indicators in the index are as follows.

1. Average work week in manufacturing, measured by hours worked.
2. Average weekly initial jobless, measured by claims for unemployment insurance.
3. Manufacturers' new orders for consumer goods and materials.
4. Vendor performance – percentage experiencing slower deliveries to their factories.
5. Plant and equipment contracts and orders.
6. New private sector building permits.
7. M2.
8. S&P 500 and dividend yields. S&P Corporate Composite.
9. Michigan Index of Consumer Sentiment. This consists of two parts:
   (a) consumers assessment of current economic conditions – not included in the LEI
   (b) expected economic changes, included in the LEI.
10. Yield spread.

How do you interpret it?

Although the components of the index are varied, there are good economic reasons why each component helps predict economic activity. For example, new orders for plant and equipment, and new building permits are all direct measures of the amount of future production being planned in the economy. The index of stock prices reflects the optimism or pessimism of stock market participants about the economy's prospects. It is essential to determine whether increases or decreases in the index are broadly based. If six indicators rise and four indicators fall, it is difficult to generalize about the trend.

What is its impact on currency markets?

The percentage change in the index of leading indicators is reported monthly, with two or three consecutive monthly declines being regarded by currency markets as a warning sign that a recession is on the way. On the whole, the index is a valuable and much-watched forecasting device, correctly predicting a large majority of economic turning points during the post-World War II period. Consequently, the currency markets will certainly react violently to large shifts in the index. Large rises in the LEI will boost the dollar. The dollar will react in the opposite direction given large falls in the LEI.

Vendor deliveries index

Definition

The National Association of Purchasing Managers is asked how the overall delivery performance from vendors compared with the month before is changing.

How do you interpret it?

The index is benchmarked at 50. An index greater than 50 indicates that more manufacturers are reporting slower deliveries rather than faster deliveries. So if, to take an example, the index was 65 then this can be interpreted that 65 per cent are reporting slower deliveries with 35 per cent reporting faster deliveries. The financial markets would see this as evidence of an acceleration of economic activity and with it the possibility of price increases and consequently higher interest rates.

What is its impact on currency markets?

If manufacturers are reporting prompter deliveries, this is seen as evidence of slackness in the economy, taking pressures off price increases. Slower deliveries

provide evidence that capacity constraints are being hit, provoking fears of inflationary pressure, and, with it, both higher interest rates and a higher dollar.
Again this is an index that Alan Greenspan has, at times, drawn attention to,
making it at those times very market sensitive.

A major limitation of the index is that it is centred on the manufacturing
sector, which represents only 20 per cent of the economy and gives no information about pressures to raise wages in the service sector.

CONSUMER EXPENDITURE

Consumer expenditure accounts for two-thirds of GDP. Consequently, it is the
major component of nominal GNP and its behaviour is of great interest to the
currency markets. A strong consumer sector signals a healthy economy, which
can lead to inflation and higher interest rates. The key indicators of consumer
expenditure are auto sales, the Employment Report, the quit rate, retail sales and
consumer instalment credit.

Auto sales

Definition

The most frequently reported indicator of consumer spending is ten-day unit
auto sales. Unit auto sales tell us the number of autos that were sold during that
particular ten-day period.

How do you interpret them?

Most importantly, they provide the very first piece of information concerning the
strength or weakness of the economy in the monthly cycle. No other indicator is
as timely because none is released during the course of that current month, which
also gives exact data about that month.

Auto sales have a second great strength. They can provide analysts with an
important clue concerning the retail sales and personal consumption expenditures (PCE) data to be released later in the month, both of which can be big
market movers. Auto sales represent about 25 per cent of retail sales and about
8 per cent of consumption.

Auto sales have a third important feature. They can give analysts an early
warning signal of an impending recession, and also tell them when they can begin
to expect a recovery.

What is their impact on currency markets?

The foreign exchange markets will react positively to a rise in auto sales. A strong economy followed by rising interest rates increases the demand for dollars, and vice versa.

The Employment Report

Definition

The Employment Report consists of employment-related data, which in turn comes from two separate surveys, the Establishment Survey and the Household Survey. The Establishment Survey provides information on non-farm payroll employment, the average hourly workweek and the aggregate hours index. The Household Survey provides information on the labour force, household employment and the unemployment rate. Non-farm payroll employment measures the number of people in gainful employment in all non-farm industries, such as manufacturing and services.

How do you interpret it?

It is essential to concentrate on the seasonally adjusted monthly unemployment rate and the change in non-farm payrolls. The currency markets focus on the seasonally adjusted monthly change in the number of payroll jobs.

What is its impact on currency markets?

The Employment Report has frequently been referred to as the "jewel in the crown" of all the economic indicators to which financial markets will react. It is the most market-sensitive monthly economic indicator. Financial market participants can extract a wealth of market-sensitive information from the fine details of this report. Economic weakness usually signals lower interest rates. Conversely, robust increases in non-farm payrolls could indicate a healthy economy and signal higher interest rates. The potential for higher interest rates makes foreign exchange market participants push up the value of the dollar, and vice versa.

Quit rate

Definition

The quit rate is officially defined as job leavers as a percentage of the total unemployed. It is essentially the share of unemployed people who have chosen to leave their jobs. Job leavers are not workers who were fired or laid off. They are those who leave voluntarily, ie they quit.

How do you interpret it?

Presumably most people who quit their jobs do so because they have better, higher-paying jobs lined up, suggesting the possibility of increased economic activity and with it the potential for higher interest rates.

What is its impact on currency markets?

The quit rate acquired the status from 1997–2000 of being one of the indicators that the Federal Reserve Chairman, Alan Greenspan, follows when setting the course of monetary policy. The empirical evidence shows that if the quit rate rises above 12 per cent pressure for wages and prices to rise takes place, and with it pressures for rising interest rates and the US dollar, and vice versa.

Retail sales

Definition

Retail sales include all merchandise sold for cash or credit by establishments primarily engaged in retail trade.

How do you interpret them?

Retail sales are reported in current, or nominal, dollars. Auto sales constitute the largest single component of retail sales, about 25 per cent of the total. Many currency market analysts focus on the year-on-year change in retail sales. Analysts believe that when the Federal Reserve looks at the retail sales data it is not so much concerned with the trend in the total but in that of discretionary spending which is taken to be retail sales minus energy, food and drug store sales. This represents a better picture of consumer confidence.

What is their impact on currency markets?

Foreign exchange participants would interpret a rise in retail sales as a factor pointing to a strong US economy suggesting that the Federal Reserve may force up interest rates. Rising interest rates relative to the rest of the world leads to a rise in demand for the dollar. If retail sales decline, however, interest rates are likely to drop, and the softer demand will then cause the dollar to fall, on the back of falling interest rates.

Personal income and consumer expenditure

Definition

Personal income represents the compensation that individuals receive from all sources. That includes wages and salaries, proprietor's income, income from rents, dividends and transfer payments such as social security, unemployment and welfare benefits. Personal income is important for financial markets as it clearly holds the key to future spending and hence economic activity.

What is its impact on currency markets?

In practice, the currency markets rarely find this indicator very market sensitive. Increases in personal income generally point to increases in consumer spending and gains in economic activity overall. Rising personal income growth augurs well for the economy, pointing to higher interest rates and therefore an increase in the demand for dollars. This will raise the value of the dollar, and vice versa.

Consumer instalment credit

Definition

Consumer instalment credit covers loans to households, scheduled to be repaid in two or more monthly payments, for purchases of goods and services.

How do you interpret it?

The currency markets focus on the seasonally adjusted net credit advanced. For the most part, when consumer credit increases, it suggests gains in consumer spending and a sense of optimism about the economy. This will happen during economic expansions. When consumer credit decreases, it suggests decreased consumer spending, possibly coupled with a sense of pessimism about future economic activity.

What is its impact on currency markets?

Consumer credit data is difficult to interpret on its own. In practice, currency market participants do not usually react strongly to consumer credit data.

INVESTMENT

Investment spending refers to the creation of capital: the purchase or putting into place of buildings, equipment, roads, houses and the like. There are fewer indicators of investment spending than there are of consumer spending because investment spending accounts for only about one-fifth of GDP. Despite its smaller contribution to GDP, investment spending is significant because the volatility inherent in investment spending exacerbates the business cycle. It is useful to break down investment spending into its major components, these being residential fixed investment, non-residential fixed investment and inventory investment, and then to examine the individual sub-components.

Residential fixed investment: housing starts and permits

Definition

The level of activity in the US housing market is measured monthly at each stage of construction; the number of permits issued authorizing a new house to be built; the number of houses actually started; the number of houses completed; and the number of houses sold.

How do you interpret them?

Housing construction plays a critical role in the economy. Increases in housing starts raise construction employment, and recent homebuyers often purchase other consumer durables leading, through a multiplier effect, to increased employment. Construction is especially important for the business cycle, because changes in residential construction tend to lead recessions and recoveries.

What is their impact on currency markets?

An increase in housing starts is a positive factor for the foreign exchange markets because they increase the likelihood of interest rates rising and thus the potential value of the dollar. A drop in housing starts has negative implications for the dollar because it signals weak domestic growth, and with it lower interest rates.

Residential fixed investment: construction spending

Definition

The definition of "construction spending" includes residential buildings and new housing. New housing is broken down into single units and new units.

How do you interpret it?

Residential construction provides information about the residential component of investment. Together with non-residential construction and state and local government spending on construction they account for around 20 per cent of GNP, a number too large to be ignored. Residential spending accounts for around 5 per cent of GDP.

Construction industries, together with automobiles, are typically the first two sectors to go into recession when the bad times arrive and the first two sectors to recover when conditions improve, and consequently can be very market sensitive.

What is its impact on currency markets?

Unfortunately, there are two problems with the monthly report on construction spending which reduce its market sensitivity. First, it is not very timely. It is released on the first business day of the month with the data for two months prior. That makes it one of the last pieces of information received about the state of the economy for any given month. Second, the report tends to be quite volatile and revisions can be sizeable.

Residential fixed investment: new home sales

Definition

Sales of new and existing single family houses are another indicator of housing demand. Figures are issued on the number of houses sold, homes for sale, and the month's supply of unsold homes.

How do you interpret them?

New home sales are an important indicator of the degree of strength of the housing market. As discussed earlier, large changes in consumer spending first appear in housing and automobiles. A problem with the home sales data is that they tend to be quite volatile.

What is their impact on currency markets?

Despite their volatility, if home sales rise unexpectedly and currency market participants conclude that this is the beginning of a new trend, the participants react adversely and push interest rates higher, which is good for the dollar. An unanticipated decline prompts the opposite response. In practice, the foreign exchange market does not normally attach a great deal of importance to this report.

Non-residential fixed investment: advance durable goods orders – manufacturers' shipments, inventories and orders release

Definition

Durable goods are goods designed to last for three years or more. The report when published is referred to as "advance" because it is an early release of the Manufacturers' Shipments, Inventories and Orders data. New orders are leading indicators of production three to six months in the future. Shipments, which are the same as sales, are indicators of current production and sales of manufactured goods.

The durable goods report is divided into broad categories such as defence and non-defence capital goods, including such diverse items as blast furnaces and computers. They are an indicator of capital spending. Non-capital goods are generally of the household variety, such as automobiles, refrigerators and other appliances.

How do you interpret them?

Durable goods orders are generally believed to be a front runner for activity in the manufacturing sector because a manufacturer must have an order before contemplating an increase in production. Conversely, a drop-off in orders eventually causes production to be scaled back; otherwise the manufacturer accumulates inventories which must be financed.

Unfortunately, the orders report has two major drawbacks. The first problem with the orders data is that they are extremely volatile. This is because they include civilian aircraft and defence orders. The second problem with the orders data is that they are notable for sizeable revisions once more data becomes available, one week later.

What is their impact on currency markets?

Economic strength indicated by strong durable goods orders would push up the value of the dollar, based on rising interest rates, and vice versa.

Non-residential fixed investment: construction spending

Definition

Non-residential construction spending includes spending on buildings, industrial premises, offices, hotels/motels, religious buildings, educational buildings and hospitals.

How do you interpret it?

The statistics are incorporated directly into the GDP numbers by the Bureau of Economic Analysis and consequently do not receive a great deal of financial market attention.

What is its impact on currency markets?

As with residential construction spending, these statistics contain little new information on the state of the economy and are largely ignored.

Inventory investment: manufacturing inventories, business inventories and sales

Definition

Total business inventories can be broken down into:

- manufacturing inventories
- wholesale inventories
- retail inventories.

How do you interpret them?

Inventories are stocks of goods on hand which may be raw materials, goods in process or finished products. They are generally thought of as being a necessary evil, providing a cushion against unexpected orders. If inventories are produced in order to meet an expected increase in demand then this is a signal that economic growth is happening and that prices are rising with the possibility that interest rates may also be rising. Similarly, an expected drop in sales and a consequent reduction in inventories will be a natural forerunner to falling prices and a reduction in interest rates. Consequently, falls in desired inventories suggest interest rate falls. Rises in desired inventories indicate pressures for interest rate rises.

In order to know whether inventories are desired or not, it is essential to compare them with sales. If the ratio of inventories to sales rises then there are pressures for interest rates to fall, and vice versa.

Manufacturing inventories represent about half of total business inventories. To this manufacturing inventory figure it is necessary to add inventories at the wholesale and retail levels to obtain overall business inventories, which are available about two weeks later.

What is their impact on currency markets?

At business cycle turning points, the markets will react to business inventories data. Undesired inventory accumulation during a sluggish economic period suggests producers will have to unload unwanted inventories and production will suffer. Production declines are not favourable news to foreign exchange players looking for a strong dollar. Low interest rates indicate capital flows to the US will be reduced and a drop in demand for the dollar will ensue, and vice versa.

GOVERNMENT SPENDING

In January of each year, the President of the US sends his budget message to Congress. Government purchases of goods and services (G) are a direct component of total spending. As we discussed earlier they are to be added to Investment (I), Consumption (C) and Net Exports (X – IM) if we are to foresee the likely trend in GNP.

Fiscal position – deficit or surplus

How do you interpret the fiscal position?

The reaction of currency markets will vary greatly depending on whether government expenditures exceed receipts, a budget deficit, or whether government receipts exceed government revenues, a budget surplus.

What is its impact on currency markets?

Currency markets distrust budget deficits under most circumstances, as they fear that they are inflationary. The reasoning behind this is that when government spending pushes up aggregate demand, firms may find themselves unwilling or unable to produce the higher quantities that are being demanded at the going prices. Prices will therefore have to rise.

In 1992, the year of Bill Clinton's election as US President, the deficit in the $1.3 trillion budget was $290 billion. By 1998, the budget deficit had been replaced by a budget surplus, with many analysts forecasting that all government debt could be repaid by 2013. This has largely taken the US budget deficit out of the picture as a factor influencing currency markets, for the first time in 40 years.

FOREIGN TRADE AND THE BALANCE OF PAYMENTS

Definition

The balance of payments is the collective term for the accounts of US transactions with the rest of the world.

How do you interpret it?

The current account is the balance of trade plus services (passenger and freight transportation, insurance, telecommunications, construction, engineering and income from royalties, patents, etc) plus defence transactions (transfers under foreign military sales programmes, defence purchases) plus remittances and Government grants.

How do you interpret it?

Focus on the seasonally adjusted trade numbers. A single month's trade figure is not regarded as a reliable guide to the underlying trend, so it is important to take a three-month moving average at the very least.

What is its impact on currency markets?

The impact of the trade deficit on financial markets has been subject to violent changes of fashion. Currently its impact is less significant than it was in the 1970s and 1980s, a situation that, given the size of the current deficit, could easily change. A decline in the trade deficit is usually good news for the US dollar, as one must buy dollars to purchase US exports and sell dollars to buy imports. However, in general, if the dollar has been trading within a well-defined range, the monthly trade figures tend to be ignored beyond a few hours. Conversely if the dollar has just broken out of its recent trading range, data on trade flows have a greater impact. The current account deficit in 2000 reached 4 per cent of GDP, a figure that could easily trigger foreign holders of US dollars to sell them abruptly if confidence in the US economy was, for whatever reason, undermined.

THE EFFECT OF CONSUMER CONFIDENCE ON FINANCIAL MARKETS

As well as relying on "hard" economic data, currency analysts also pay a great deal of attention to non-economic factors such as consumer attitudes towards spending. While such data is, by its nature, more qualitative than quantitative, it is no less important in providing valuable information as to the likely future behaviour of the economy and with it the currency. Household sentiment, which turned adverse in early 1990, has frequently been cited as a major cause of the US 1990–91 recession.

Attitudes, expectations and sentiment are terms that are frequently used when people refer to the psychological mood of consumers. These are distinct concepts. Attitudes reflect the feelings that consumers have about current conditions, and expectations are attitudes, which have been projected to some point in the future. Both attitudes and expectations are subsumed into the larger category called consumer sentiment or consumer confidence.

Definition

Two organizations provide indicators of US consumer attitudes. They focus on consumer perceptions of general business conditions and of their personal financial well-being, plus their attitudes toward purchasing big-ticket items, purchases that last a relatively long time – homes, autos, furniture and major household appliances.

These attitude indicators are the Consumer Sentiment Index of the University of Michigan and the Consumer Confidence Index of the Conference Board. Both indexes measure similar phenomena but, because the methodologies differ and the concepts are not identical, there are periods when their movements differ.

Michigan Index of Consumer Sentiment (ICS)

Each month, the University of Michigan conducts a representative cross-section sampling of 700 respondent households by telephone.

Conference Board Consumer Confidence Index

The Conference Board survey is ten times larger than the University of Michigan's Survey, covering a representative sample of 5,000 households.

How do you interpret the sentiment and confidence indicators?

While both indices measure consumer confidence, it is important to understand the respective methodologies in order to interpret them properly. On the Conference Board Index, it is useful to examine the present and expectations components separately – the former as a proxy for economic activity, the latter as a proxy for growth. On the Michigan Index, this distinction is less clear, as both components mix level and growth measures.

What is their impact on currency markets?

Consumer confidence is a coincident indicator of the economy, telling analysts what stage the economy is currently at in the business cycle. Typically, consumers feel confident about the economy during an expansion and pessimistic about the economy during a recession.

Economic pessimism signals a weak economy and low interest rates, leading to a drop in the value of the dollar. An optimistic consumer is favourable for the prospects for the dollar in that interest rates have a tendency to rise forcing up the demand for dollars, pushing up the value of the dollar, and vice versa.

National Association of Purchasing Managers Index (PMI)

Definition

The National Association of Purchasing Managers Index (PMI) is a composite index of five series:

- new orders
- production
- supplier deliveries (also known as vendor deliveries)
- inventories
- employment.

The PMI is derived from the Report on Business. This is based on data compiled from monthly replies to questions asked of purchasing executives in more than 300 industrial companies. The Report on Business survey is designed to measure the change (ie whether there has been an improvement or deterioration), if any, in the current month compared to the previous month for the answers to a series of questions which produce the indexes.

How do you interpret it?

The NAPM indexes are different from most other indexes. Instead of setting a base year equal to 100, and measuring growth from there, the NAPM series are set at a trigger rate of 50 per cent. According to the NAPM, an index level of 50 per cent or more indicates that the economy as well as the manufacturing sector is expanding; an index level less than 50 per cent but greater than 45 per cent suggests that the manufacturing sector has stopped growing, but the economy is still expanding; a level less than 45 per cent signals a recession both in the economy and in the manufacturing sector.

What is its impact on currency markets?

Financial market participants have anxiously anticipated the PMI ever since Federal Reserve Chairman, Alan Greenspan, once claimed that he placed great emphasis on this report. Foreign exchange market players would regard a high number (ie one well above 50) as one likely to trigger interest rate increases which would boost the dollar, and vice versa.

IS THE REACTION OF THE FOREIGN EXCHANGE MARKET TO "NEWS" SUPPORTED BY EMPIRICAL RESEARCH?

A considerable amount of academic research has recently been employed to ascertain whether the expected reaction in the foreign exchange market to "news" can be supported by academic research. Naturally, if the market view that the currency markets do react in line with market expectations can be substantiated by research, the credibility of the market view is substantially reinforced.

Almeida, Goodhart and Payne[1] examine the effect of macroeconomic "news" on exchange rate behaviour. Their research analyzes the impact of "news" on the level and volatility of exchange rates, focusing on macroeconomic news releases from the US and Germany and using data on the Deutsche mark/US dollar exchange rates sampled at a five-minute frequency. "News" is extracted from the announcement data via a set of market expectation series provided by Money Market Services International. This permits a distinction to be made between "expected" and "unexpected" news. The main result of their research, discussed in detail below, is that macroeconomic "news" has significant effects both on exchange rate levels and volatility. The direction of the impact of news on the exchange rate movements is consistent with the view that the monetary authorities react to "news" by varying short-term interest rates in order to control future inflation. This is very much in line with the view held within the foreign exchange market itself.

The authors first found that the expected reaction of news on the dollar/mark exchange rate moved in the correct way. For example, unexpected retail sales growth resulted in an appreciation of the dollar/mark whereas unexpected unemployment shocks had the opposite effect, and similarly for the other indicators listed in Table 5.1. Tests as to whether the actual dollar/mark reaction to the news was statistically significant were then undertaken. For the statistically minded these were undertaken using "t" statistics, with a significance levels of both 5 and 10 per cent. A large "t" statistic, in absolute value, implies that one should be more confident that the true value of the coefficient is non zero. Basically the higher the "t" statistic, the more the reaction of the dollar/mark to the indicator concerned.

The reaction of the payroll employment data, which had the highest "t" statistic, corresponds with the view in the market that this is the key indicator to watch. There is then a group of other statistically significant indicators which, in ranked order, are:

- durable goods orders
- the PMI
- retail sales

- trade deficit
- consumer confidence
- unemployment rate.

Table 5.1 ● The impact of US announcements on DM/USD returns

US economic indicator		Coefficient	T-stat	R^2
Non-farm payrolls	(pay)	0.00004	5.77	0.44
Durable goods orders	(DG)	0.00090	5.39	0.44
National Association of Purchasing				
Managers index	(NAPM)	0.00087	4.94	0.35
Retail sales	(RS)	0.00385	3.48	0.23
Merchandise trade deficits	(trade)	0.00110	3.41	0.24
Consumer confidence	(CC)	0.00030	2.74	0.20
Unemployment rate	(U)	−0.00730	−1.77	0.44
Consumer price index	(CPI)	0.00450	1.48	0.06
Producer price index	(PPI)	0.00290	1.29	0.04
Industrial production	(IP)	0.00280	0.76	0.03
Capacity utilization	(CU)	0.00046	0.28	0.03
Index of Leading Indicators	(LEI)	0.00060	0.25	0.01

Source: adapted from Almeida, Goodhart and Payne[2]

Note: The second column displays the estimated coefficient on the forecast error series. The next column gives the t-statistics relating to the hypothesis that the coefficients are zero. The critical values for the t-statistics are 2.04 at 5 per cent and 1.70 at 10 per cent.

More surprisingly the authors found that the results for the price series, namely, the Producer Price Index and the Consumer Price Index were not found to be market sensitive, a view definitely not shared by dealers working in the market. It was thought that this was due to the relative inadequacy of the forecast series for these announcements. Other indicators which were found to be relatively market insensitive include the Index of Leading Economic Indicators, Industrial Production and Capacity Utilization.

The long-term importance of news

In the section above the findings were reported for the effect of information revealed by announcement on the DM/USD in the 15 minutes after the release of the data. The authors then went on to test the persistence of the effect of "news" on the exchange rate by examining the impact of the unanticipated information on exchange rate returns measured over various intervals post announcement.

Table 5.2 ● The persistence of the effect of "news" on the DM/USD

US economic indicator		5min	15min	30min	45min	1h	1.5h	2h	2.5h	3h	6h	12h
Consumer confidence	(CC)	0.00008*	0.00029*	0.00027*	0.00029*	0.00036*	0.00034*	0.00042*	0.00041*	0.00041*	0.00031*	0.00044*
Consumer Price Index	(CPI)	0.00290*	0.00450	-0.00160	-0.00240	-0.00088	-0.00200	-0.00510	-0.00660	-0.00580	0.00320	0.00280
Capacity utilization	(CU)	0.00016	0.00046	0.00028	0.00160	0.00110	-0.00021	-0.00190	-0.00240	-0.00210	-0.00300	-0.00120
Durable goods orders	(DG)	0.00065*	0.00091*	0.00083*	0.00075*	0.00077*	0.00089*	0.00053	0.00043	0.00068	0.00043	0.00060
Industrial production	(IP)	0.00058	0.00290	-0.00021	-0.00180	-0.00147	-0.00015	-0.00023	0.00340	0.00430	0.01235	0.01783*
Index of Leading Indicators	(LI)	0.00240*	0.00058*	0.00049	-0.00048	0.00510	0.00150	0.00020	0.01000*	0.01270*	0.00597	0.01350*
NAPM		0.00044*	0.00087*	0.00087*	0.00056*	0.00080*	0.00048	0.00025	-0.00006	0.00029	0.00012	0.00008
Non-farm payrolls	(pay)	0.00001*	0.00004*	0.00005*	0.00005*	0.00005*	0.00005*	0.00005*	0.00006*	0.00006*	0.00006*	0.00005*
Produce Price Index	(PPI)	0.00042	0.00290	0.00210	0.00120	0.00210	-0.00043	-0.00220	-0.00320	-0.00360	-0.00290	-0.00088
Retail sales	(RS)	0.00110	0.00390*	0.00280*	0.00220	0.00220	0.00240	0.00240	0.00330	0.00210	0.00100	0.00340
Trade deficit	(trade)	0.00078*	0.00110*	0.00097*	0.00120*	0.00140*	0.00120*	0.00130*	0.00048	0.00055	0.00018	-0.00022
Unemployment rate	(U)	-0.00260	-0.00730*	-0.00850*	-0.00570	-0.00580	-0.00270	-0.00100	0.00290	0.00120	-0.00010	-0.00300

Source: Almeida, Goodhart and Payne[3]

Note: Each cell gives the slope coefficient from a linear regression of the return over the period displayed in the first row of the given column on the series of forecast errors from the series in the first cell of the given row. An asterisk denotes that the coefficient is significantly different from zero at a 5 per cent level.

Table 5.3 ● The impact of non-farm payroll, employment and consumer confidence on the DM/USD

US economic indicator		5min	15min	30min	45min	1h	1.5h	2h	2.5h	3h	6h	12h
Non-farm payroll	(pay)	0.00001*	0.00004*	0.00005*	0.00005*	0.00005*	0.00005*	0.00005*	0.00006*	0.00006*	0.00006*	0.00005*
Consumer confidence	(CC)	0.00008*	0.00029*	0.00027*	0.00029*	0.00036*	0.00034*	0.00042*	0.00041*	0.00041*	0.00031*	0.00044*

Note: An asterisk denotes that the coefficient is significantly different from zero at a 5 per cent level.

Table 5.2 summarizes the author's findings. The general picture that emerges is that the impact of these macroeconomic releases on the DM/USD is a very short run phenomenon. The authors examined first the group of seven announcements that were found to be fairly influential in the 15 minutes after their announcement, namely, non-farm payroll employment, durable goods, PMI, retail sales, trade deficit, consumer confidence and the unemployment figures. Of the 77 regressions over differing horizons, the authors found that 73 yielded the correct sign for the coefficient, ie that if the exchange rate was supposed to rise following the news it did, and vice versa. The pattern of significance however, was not strong. In general, the impacts are significant only up to around two hours after release, after which it seems, the effect of unanticipated macroeconomic information is drowned in the subsequent random fluctuations of the exchange rate.

Watch for non-farm payroll employment and consumer confidence figures

The key exceptions to this drowning-out effect are the patterns for the non-farm payroll employment and consumer confidence figures (see Table 5.3). These retain their significance until the 12-hour horizon, in line with the earlier results. This thereby confirms the market view that these economic indicators are extremely market sensitive indicators in the foreign exchange market.

References

1.   Alvaro Almeida, Charles Goodhart and Richard Payne, "The Effect of Macroeconomic 'News' on High Frequency Exchange Rate Behaviour". LSE Financial Markets Group Discussion Paper No. 258.

2.   Ibid.

3.   Ibid.

CHAPTER 6

What makes a great currency?

How does the euro compare with the dollar?[1]

- Roles of an international currency
- Great currencies and great powers
- How does the euro compare with the US dollar?

ROLES OF AN INTERNATIONAL CURRENCY

The introduction of the euro on 1 January 1999, which will inevitably go down as the greatest monetary experiment in history, provokes the question, What are the attributes that a currency needs to possess for it to succeed?

Elementary monetary economics teaches us that money serves three functions: it is a medium of exchange, a unit of account, and a store of value. International money does the same. It is used to settle international payments, it is used to fix prices, and it is held as a liquid asset for international transactions. An added dimension is provided by the distinction between private investment behaviour and by the decisions of central banks. Until recently there were no serious threats to the US dollar remaining as the world's dominant currency and consequently discussion of the role of international money tended to revolve around the US dollar. Six roles of the US dollar are stressed in the literature. The dollar is used as a medium of exchange in private transactions, or "vehicle", and is also bought and sold by central banks, thus making it an "intervention" currency. Trade contracts are sometimes denominated in dollars, making it an "invoice" currency, and the par values for exchange rates are sometimes stated in terms of the dollar, which makes it serve as a "peg". Finally, private agents hold liquid dollar-denominated assets – the "banking" role – and central banks hold the dollar as a reserve currency. These principles are summarized in Table 6.1.

Table 6.1 ● **Roles of an international currency**

	Private role	Official role
Medium of exchange	Vehicle currency	Intervention currency
Unit of account	Invoice currency	Peg currency
Store of value	Banking currency	Reserve currency

Source: European Central Bank, *Monthly Report,* August 1999

In principle, and to some extent in practice, these roles are separable. The separation of roles can be either horizontal or vertical. Thus under the gold standard the official roles were filled by gold, yet sterling played the private roles. In the European currency snake in the mid-1970s, the currencies were pegged to one another, yet the dollar was used as a reserve and as an intervention currency. One can even separate the medium of exchange and unit of account functions. The most famous example here is the small Persian Gulf nations, Bahrain, Oman, Kuwait and the United Arab Emirates which, until 1974, set their oil prices in dollars but required payment in sterling. But the roles are not independent. The more the dollar, or any one currency, is used in one role, the more incentive there is to use it in the others.

The US dollar

It is useful to review the extent to which the dollar plays these different roles:

Vehicle currency

It is important to distinguish three types of transaction here. First is the settlement of payments between non-bank firms, which is closely tied to invoicing. The dollar plays a special but not exclusive role here. Second is the "retail" foreign exchange market in which firms deal with banks. Here, the dollar plays no special role. A Swedish bank will sell, say, kronor for euros, and a French bank will buy kronor for euros, with the dollar not being central to the transaction. Finally, there is the interbank market. Here the dollar is *the* medium of exchange.

Intervention currency

Central banks often intervene in the existing private interbank market. Here the dollar is *the* intervention currency. This was true even for some of the interventions which maintained parities within the European Monetary System.

Invoice currency

In the trading of manufactured goods between countries there is usually a preference for invoicing in the exporter's currency but also often a preference for invoicing in the currency of the larger country. This in itself gives the US, as the world's largest economy, a disproportionate share of the invoicing role. In addition, much of the world's raw materials trade, even if it does not involve the US, is also invoiced in dollars. In financial transactions the dollar is the dominant currency for international borrowing and lending, though this dominance has diminished over time and can be expected to be further diminished by the introduction of the euro.

Pegging currency

In 1970, most of the world's currencies were pegged to the dollar. Now, as discussed in Chapter 2, only a limited number of small countries still follow this arrangement. This does not, however, represent the rise of a new currency but more the abandonment of fixed rates altogether.

Banking currency

Dollars in New York and Eurodollars in London constitute the main liquid international asset, although there has been some recent diversification into other currencies, especially euros.

Reserve currency

The dollar accounts for the bulk of non-gold reserves. Again, there is now some trend toward diversification into euros.

Benefits and costs for the issuing country of its currency being used internationally

International use of a currency provides several major benefits to the issuing country. The first benefit is that it derives seigniorage, defined below, because the non-interest-bearing claims on it are denominated in its own currency. Seigniorage accrues whenever this happens, given that paper money can be produced at very low cost. Thus, if the US Board of Governors of the Federal Reserve prints dollars at very little cost and the dollars are used either to buy real resources or exchanged for another currency and invested, then the US Government benefits. The Board of Governors of the US Federal Reserve System estimates that this seigniorage revenue for the US amounts to between $11 billion and $15 billion per year. Additionally, because the nominal interest rate on debt comprises a real component and an expected-inflation component, a country with an international currency can create extra seigniorage by unexpectedly inflating its currency, although repeatedly doing so would ultimately jeopardize the currency's international use.

The second benefit to the issuing country is that as the international use of a currency expands, loans, investments and purchases of goods and services will increasingly be executed through the financial institutions of the issuing country. Thus, the earnings of its financial sector are likely to increase. The third benefit has been the tendency of world trade in general to be denominated in US dollars. This means that the US economy is less vulnerable to changes in the value of its currency than are other economies.

The main costs of having a currency that is used internationally are twofold. First, under pegged exchange rates, a shift in preferences by foreigners can lead to large capital flows and undermine the capacity of the monetary authorities to control the monetary base and influence domestic economic activity. Second, under floating rates, such a shift can lead to large variations in the exchange rate, which could also limit the degree of influence exerted by the authorities over the domestic economy. Concern about the effects of changes in portfolio preferences on the domestic economy caused both the German and Japanese Governments to take measures to restrict the international use of their respective currencies during the 1970s and early 1980s.

GREAT CURRENCIES AND GREAT POWERS

As Mundell illustrates[2] the international monetary system is at any time composed of a multiplicity of currencies and in history, tens of thousands of currencies have existed. Theory provides us with the ability to simplify which currencies dominated in which historical time frame The simplification in the field of money arises from the fact that important currencies can be typically identified with great powers. See Table 6.2 for a historical summary. Sterling in the 19th century and the dollar in the 20th century have been dominant currencies partly because the British Empire and the US were and are top powers in their heyday.

Table 6.2 ● Great powers and great international currencies

Era	Power	Currency		
		Silver	Gold	Paper
Pre-7th C BC	Babylonia	shekel		
7th–6th C BC	Persia	shekel	daric	
5th–4th C BC	Greece	drachma	stater	
4th–3rd C BC	Macedonia	drachma	stater	
3rd BC–4th AD	Rome	denarius, sesterec	solidus, aureus	
4th–13th C AD	Byzantium	siliqua	solidus, besant	
7th–13th C AD	Islamic	dirham	dinar	
8th–12th C AD	Carolingian	denier		
9th–13th C AD	China	tael		cheun
13th–16th C AD	Italy	grosso	florin, sequin, ducal	
16th–17th C AD	Spain	real	escudos	
17th–18th C AD	France	denier, sol	louis d'or	
18th C AD	India	rupee	mohur	
19th C AD	France	franc	10, 20, 40, 100 franc	
19th–20th C AD	Britain	shilling	pound	paper £
19th–20th C AD	US	dollar	eagle, double eagle	
20th C AD	US	dollar		paper $

Source: Mundell[3]

Mundell stresses the role that stability plays in identifying what makes a currency important internationally. Stability in turn depends on five factors:

- size of transactions domain
- stability of monetary policy
- freedom from controls: broad and deep financial markets
- security of the issuing state
- fallback value.

Each of these factors is explained below.

Size of transactions domain

Size (in the sense of depth and breadth of the market) is a measure of the degree to which a currency can exploit the economies of scale and scope inherent in money as a public good. Size feeds on itself. The larger the transactions domain, the more liquid the currency. The simplest surrogate for transactions domain is GDP. An alternative measure is the size of the capital market. The size of a single-currency area determines its liquidity. Obviously, a currency that is money for 100 million people is much more liquid than a currency that is money for 1 million.

Size is also important for a different reason. The larger the single-currency area, the better it can act as a cushion against shocks. An excellent example of this is German unification in 1990. The transfers east of more than DM150 billion came close to destabilizing the German economy. Imagine the effect of a similar event on a smaller economy.

Monetary policy

The importance of monetary policy can hardly be overestimated. No currency has ever survived as an international currency with a high rate of inflation or with a recurring risk of debasement or devaluation. The lower and more stable the rate of inflation, the lower the cost of holding money balances, and the more of them that will be held.

Additional considerations are predictability and consistency in monetary policy. In a democracy, both are abetted by *transparency*. If the monetary authorities openly state their economic targets and their strategies for achieving them, the market and the critical public will be able to make its own judgment about potential inflation outcomes.

Freedom from controls

Exchange controls are frequently a symptom of a currency's weakness, anathema to the prospects of a currency being successful internationally. But controls are often imposed for political reasons, to enforce sanctions or to carry out other objectives of foreign policy. As Mundell[4] points out, gone are the days when George Washington in the midst of revolutions could draw on his account at the Bank of England!

The security factor

Monetary stability of course depends on monetary policy. But monetary policy is in turn affected by its *sine qua non*; political stability. Strong international currencies have always been linked to strong central states. The reason for this is not difficult to see. When a state cannot maintain both internal economic stability and/or defend itself from an external threat, the prospects are not good for the currency. Examples here include the hyperinflation of Germany and a few other countries after World War I, the collapse of the rouble after the October 1917 revolution; the hyperinflation of Kuomintang China after the Communist forces of Mao-Tse-Tung crossed the Yang-Tse; and the hyperinflation in the former Yugoslavia in the 1990s.

Fall-back value factor

Modern currencies differ from the great currencies of the past in that holders always had a fall-back in the sense that they could convert the currencies into a precious metal, normally silver or gold. Until the advent of the dollar, there is no historical record of a "fiat" currency, ie money that has value solely because the general public has "faith" that it will be accepted as legal tender, achieving great international significance. Before the 20th century, all the great international currencies were metallic. The predecessor of the dollar, the pound sterling, achieved its great distinction as a metallic currency and came to be phased out, many argue, when it ceased to be freely convertible into gold.

HOW DOES THE EURO COMPARE WITH THE US DOLLAR?

Size of transactions domain

Size is relative. How the euro will evolve depends on the competition. Its principal rival is clearly the dollar. The 11 EU Member States adopting the euro have a population of 292 million, somewhat larger than that of the US. At early 2000 exchange rates, the EU 11 GDP stands at $6.6 trillion compared with US GDP of around $8.5 trillion.

In addition, the criteria listed in Table 6.3 below all indicate that using the size criteria the euro compares favourably with the dollar.

Table 6.3 ● US and EU: relative economic size and use of currencies

	US	EU
Economic size		
Share of world GDP 1996	20.7	20.4
Share of world exports, 1996*	15.2	14.7
Use of currencies		
World trade, 1995	51.0	31.0
International bond offerings, September 1997	45.1	41.9
Developing country debt, end of 1996	50.2	15.8
Global foreign exchange reserves, end of 1996	63.7	19.5
Foreign exchange transactions, April 1995	11.5	35.0

Sources: International Monetary Fund; World Economic Outlook database; *Annual Report*, 1997

* Excluding Intra-European Union trade transactions

Stability of monetary policy

High and variable inflation generates expectations of nominal exchange rate depreciation and in turn uncertainty. In this connection, the inflation perform-ance of the US has compared favorably with the performances of the other major industrial countries since the move to managed floating exchange rates in 1973.

However, from the standpoint of sound monetary policy, the outlook for the euro is favourable. The Maastricht Treaty is unambiguous in making price stability the target of monetary policy. While the European System of Central Banks (ESCB) can and should assist the monetary union in carrying out its other objectives, it is forbidden to do so if such assistance would conflict with price stability. Monetary policy cannot be used to reduce unemployment by "surprise inflation" or to inflate away embarrassing public debts.

Freedom from controls: broad and deep financial markets

As discussed earlier, a necessary condition for a successful international currency is freedom from controls. The financial markets must be substantially free of controls, broad (that is, containing a wide variety of financial instruments) and deep (that is, having well-developed secondary markets). Well-developed financial markets contribute to the international demand for a country's currency, given the preference of investors for safe, liquid financial instruments.

The US has the world's largest and deepest financial markets. As an example, domestic debt outstanding in the US capital market is larger than the combined total of domestic debt outstanding in the capital markets of all the other Group of Seven economies. In addition, the US stock market's capitalization is almost as large as the combined total of the stock market capitalization of all the other Group of Seven countries.

As Table 6.3 indicates, however, in terms of bond market size and foreign exchange transactions, the EU is either the same size or larger than the US. The introduction of the euro is also resulting in the integration of the EU financial sectors which should increase the long-term demand for the euro.

Security of the issuing state

Monetary union is a fact of life in the US. Monetary union in Europe is supposed to be irrevocable. However, the potential for asymmetric shocks is always possible. As we discuss in Chapter 10, these could come from different directions and until the euro has survived the terms-of-trade type of shock that was experienced in the 1970s, when the oil price quadrupled, the jury must remain out on this aspect of the competition between the euro and the dollar.

The ending of the Cold War and the EU link with NATO and the military alliance with the US should protect the EU from military threat, although recent events in the Balkans would indicate that one should not remain complacent on these issues.

Fall-back value factor

The dollar achieved its international importance as a gold backed currency. When it was selected as the unofficial anchor at Bretton Woods, it had ceased to be internally redeemable against gold, but was still externally convertible to gold, the only such currency apart from the Swiss franc. As Mundell illustrates,[5] if the dollar is now a fiat currency, as a "ghost of gold", it is the exception that makes the rule.

In any great political emergency, and especially one that threatened the durability of the EU, there would be a run on the euro. That would not be helped by the lack of a fallback value.

Such an emergency of course might also weaken the dollar. Total political and military security can never be assumed. Nevertheless, the US situation, many argue, differs in that the dollar has an established reputation. The US, though a federation, has a strong central government, and it is unquestionably *the* military superpower.

Will the euro become a great currency?

The euro, Mundell stresses, has two great strengths: a large and expanding transactions size; and a culture of stability surrounding the European Central Bank (ECB) in Frankfurt. Initially, the EU-11 is smaller than the dollar area, but as other members enter, as the EU expands, and as the poorer countries catch up, the euro area should eventually be larger than the dollar area. From the standpoint of monetary policies, there is also not much to choose between the two areas. Information is globally mobile and there is no reason why the European Central Bank should not become as efficient as the Federal Reserve System in the US.

Mundel stresses that the euro however, also has two weaknesses. It is not backed by a central state, and it has no fallback value. In an unstable world, these weaknesses are potentially fatal. But the present environment is far from unstable, despite events in the Balkans in the late 1990s. If, as one should expect, NATO survives in a post-euro world, the stability of the coming decades should be as assured as have been the decades following the ending of World War II.

References

1. The author wishes to acknowledge many of the ideas in this chapter to Mundell, R.A. (1998) *What makes a great currency? Central Banking*, Volume IX.
2. Ibid.
3. Ibid.
4. Ibid.
5. Ibid.

CHAPTER 7

Covered and uncovered interest arbitrage in the foreign exchange market

A puzzle in international finance

- Interest rate parity
- Covered interest arbitrage: the textbook view
- Covered interest arbitrage: the academic literature view

INTEREST RATE PARITY

Interest rate parity theory asserts that the discount or premium on a currency, the percentage difference between the spot and forward rates, is equal to the difference in the interest rates between the two currencies. This relationship – known as covered interest arbitrage – is what brings about interest rate parity. When there is a disequilibrium between interest rate differentials and the forward discount or premium on a currency, the covered interest arbitrageur can make a profit by borrowing in one currency, investing in high-quality securities, possibly government or other high-quality instruments in the other currency and simultaneously entering into a forward contract.

The assumption of interest rate parity is a key ingredient to many of the models used in international macroeconomics and finance. When a theory such as this is seemingly so central to an understanding of international finance and when it is explained and discussed in such an authoritative and similar way, one would reasonably expect it to describe the real world of international finance. But does it? First, let us review the theory as set out in the textbooks and then in the academic literature. Chapter 8 turns to the realities of the foreign exchange dealing room.

The formal textbook statement of interest rate parity or, as it is often called, covered interest rate parity, comes with differing degrees of sophistication, all of which are suitably modified and empirically tested in the academic literature. The outcome of one well known survey of the literature is that there remains, following econometric tests, a "puzzle".[1] According to the interest rate parity condition, the expected returns in one country should be equalized through speculation to the returns in another country once converted to the same currency. Despite this theoretical prediction, the behaviour of domestic relative to foreign returns has decisively rejected this assumption over the floating rate period. The "puzzle" concerns explanations for deviations from uncovered interest parity, or equivalently, excess returns on foreign relative to domestic deposits. Chapter 8 looks at this puzzle taking into account both the mechanics of arbitrage as seen from inside a foreign exchange dealing room and of recent innovations in financial markets.

Readers are advised that some of the issues in this chapter are technically demanding and can be skipped without losing the thread of the book.

COVERED INTEREST ARBITRAGE: THE TEXTBOOK VIEW

The standard textbook explanation for the equilibrating forces in the foreign exchange market goes along the following lines. See O'Connnor and Bueso.[2]

Consider a situation in which the direct spot quote on the British pound is £1 = $1.00, while the 1-year forward rate is £1 = $1.10. This means that the pound is selling at a forward premium of 10 per cent. We will assume that the annual interest rate is 25 per cent in the US and 10 per cent in the UK. Interest rate parity does not exist, since the forward premium (10%) is not equal to the difference in interest rates.

In this situation, the covered interest arbitrageur would make a profit by borrowing pounds at the lower interest rate and investing the funds in dollars at the higher interest rate. In effect, the arbitrageur can earn 15 per cent more interest than would have to be paid (25 per cent –10 per cent). At this point in the interest arbitrage transaction, the person executing the deal is at risk (speculating), since he or she has a liability in pounds (a loan repayment) and an asset in dollars (an interest and principal receipt). Fluctuations in the value of the British pound could result in the speculator incurring a substantial loss. The risk associated with the interest rate arbitrage activity can be eliminated if the transaction is "covered" with a forward contract. Specifically, the future dollar receipts could be sold forward, locking in an exchange rate and, in this case, a sure profit. Covered interest arbitrage, involves borrowing in one currency, investing in another, and covering the foreign exchange risk with a forward contract.

Let us work through the illustration and see exactly how the profit is earned and how the risk is avoided. We will assume that the arbitrageur borrows £1 million.

Step 1   The arbitrageur borrows £1 million at an interest rate of 10 per cent. This means that at the end of one year, a principal and interest payment of £1.1 million is due.

Step 2   The pounds are immediately converted to dollars and invested at 25 per cent. The £1 million is converted to dollars at the spot rate of £1 = $1.00. Thus, there is $1 million to invest at 25 per cent. At the end of one year, the arbitrageur has $1.25 million.

Step 3   At exactly the same time that the arbitrageur borrows and invests, she or he enters into a forward contract that commits a bank to deliver pounds for the dollar inflow expected by the arbitrageur. The arbitrageur agrees to deliver $1.25 million. The bank agrees to a 1-year forward rate of £1 = $1.10, which means that the bank is obligated to deliver £1,136,364 ($1,250,000/$1.10).

Step 4   At the end of the year, the arbitrageur liquidates the dollar investment and delivers the $1.25 million to the bank. The bank pays the arbitrageur £1,136,364. The £1.1 million loan repayment is then made. The arbitrageur makes a profit of £36,364.

The profitability of this transaction can also be determined using internal rates of return. The investor invests £1 million and will receive £1,136,364 in one year. This is a rate of return of 13.64 per cent. The investment offers a higher rate of return than its 10 per cent cost. Thus, the investment is profitable. It is important to note that the covered interest arbitrage transaction is riskless. The exchange rate, the amount to be received, and the amount to be paid are all known. Unfortunately for arbitrageurs, situations similar to the one just described cannot persist for any length of time in free currency markets. The conditions of interest rate parity are the rule.

If interest rate parity did not exist, arbitrageurs would quickly bring it about. In the preceding illustration, for example, there would be a tremendous demand for British pound borrowings, since everyone would want to get into the act. This would drive up British interest rates. At the same time, interest rates in the US would fall, since investment funds would rush into the country. The difference between the interest rates in the two countries [i(home) – i(foreign)] would narrow.

The rush to covered interest arbitrage investments would also alter both the spot and the forward exchange rates for the pound. The spot rate on the pound would fall as more and more people requested that their pound borrowings be converted to dollars. The forward rate on the pound would rise because many investors would be requesting that dollars be converted into pounds at the future date. A falling spot rate and a rising forward rate mean that the premium on the pound would increase.

The simultaneous increase in the premium on the pound and the reduction in the difference in interest rates would eventually result in a situation in which the premium would be equal to the differences in interest rates. In other words, interest rate parity would be established. Once interest rate parity existed, covered interest arbitrage opportunities would cease to exist. In effect, the feasibility of conducting covered interest arbitrage more or less ensures that interest rate parity does exist.

The formal mathematical statement of interest rate parity, as already suggested comes with differing degrees of sophistication. Textbooks – by their nature – cannot claim to be excessively detailed nor unnecessarily complex. Nevertheless, the textbook explanations are remarkably different from how the markets really work, particularly with reference to the true equilibrating forces at work, as will be seen in Chapter 8.

The explanation in Madura,[3] comes along the following lines.

"The relationship between the forward premium (or discount) and the interest rate differential according to interest rate parity is simplified in an approximated form as formula (1):

$$(1) \qquad p = \frac{F_j - S_j}{S_j} \cong i_h - i_j$$

where

p = forward premium (or discount)
F_j = forward rate
S_j = spot rate
i_h = home interest rate
i_j = foreign interest rate"

Pilbeam,[4] in a similar vein, puts it in the following way.

"The presence of arbitrageurs ensures that what is known as the covered interest parity (CIP) condition holds continually – this is the formula used by banks to calculate their forward exchange quotation and is given by formula (2):

$$(2) \quad F = \frac{(r^* - r)\, S}{(1+r)} + S$$

where F is the one-year forward exchange rate quotation in foreign currency per unit of domestic currency, S is the spot exchange rate quotation in foreign currency per unit of domestic currency, r is the one year domestic interest rate, and r* is the one year foreign interest rate.

Formula (2) has to be amended by dividing the 3-month interest rates by 4 to calculate the 3-month forward exchange rate quotation, and dividing the 6-month interest rates by 2 to calculate the 6-month forward exchange rate."

O'Connor and Bueso⁵ explain interest rate parity as follows.

"This relationship, called *interest rate parity*, asserts that the discount or premium on a currency (the percentage difference between the spot and forward rates) is equal to the difference in the interest rates between the two countries. Algebraically, the relationship can be expressed as follows (where *i* is the interest rate):

$$\% \; \frac{discount}{premium} = i(home) - i(foreign)$$

For example, assume that the annual 90 day interest rate in the US (home) stands at 10 per cent and the annual rate in France is 15 per cent. This means that the French franc should be selling at a 5 per cent discount. That is, if the spot rate on the French franc is FF1 = $0.1600, then the 90 day forward rate on the franc would be 5 per cent lower, or $0.1580."

This oversimplification is however, to their credit, further developed in two footnotes (see pages 31 and 33)

"The preceding equation is a convenient and easy-to-understand approximation. A more precise expression of the relationship between interest rates and the discount/premium is provided by formula (3):

$$(3) \; \% \; \frac{discount}{premium} = \left(\frac{1 + i(home)}{1 + i(foreign)} - 1 \right) \times 100$$

On an annualized basis, the forward discount will be

$$\% \; discount = \frac{0.1580 - 0.1600}{0.1600} \times \frac{360}{90} \times 100 = -5\%$$

(Page 31)

In actual practice, there may be slight discrepancies between interest rate differentials and the forward discount or premium. A more precise estimate of the relationship would require that the more accurate equation be used. In addition, the existence of transaction costs, government restrictions on capital flows, and taxes may result in situations in which profits are unobtainable even though the principle of interest rate parity appears to be violated. For this illustration the interest rate differential is not 15 per cent but

$$\% \; \frac{discount}{premium} = \left(\frac{1 + 0.25}{1 + 0.10} - 1 \right) \times 100 = 13.64\%"$$

(Page 33)

Again in a similar exercise Eitemann, Stonehill and Moffett[6] put it:

"The theory of interest rate parity (IRP) provides the linkage between the foreign exchange markets and the international money markets: *The difference in the national interest rates for securities of similar risk and maturity should be equal to, but opposite in sign to, the forward rate discount or premium for the foreign currency, except for transaction costs.* Unlike the international Fisher effect, the theory is applicable only to securities with maturities of one year or less, as forward contracts are not routinely available for periods longer than one year."

(Page 122)

"Ignoring transaction costs, if the returns in dollars are equal between the two alternative money market investments, the spot and forward rates are considered to be at *interest rate parity* (IRP). The transaction is 'covered' because the exchange rate back to dollars is guaranteed at the end of the 90-day period. Therefore, in order for the two alternatives to be equal, any differences in interest rates must be offset by the difference between the spot and forward exchange rates (in approximate form) as given by formula (4):

$$(4) \quad \frac{F}{S} = \frac{(1 + i^{SF})}{(1 + i^{\$})} \quad or \quad \frac{SF1.4655/\$}{SF1.4800/\$} = \frac{1.01}{1.02} = 0.9902 \approx 1\%$$

(Page 123)

Where

F = Forward rate of exchange, Swiss franc/dollar
S = Spot rate of exchange, Swiss franc/dollar
i^{SF} = Interest rate on Swiss francs
$i^{\$}$ = Interest rate on US dollars"

Grabbe[7] puts it similarly:

"To summarize, in economic equilibrium we must have equality between the rate of return on domestic assets and covered foreign assets:

$$1+i(T/360) = [1/S(t)][1+i^*(T/360)]F(t,T)$$

Or, rearranging this equation gives us formula (5):

$$(5) \quad F(t, T) = S(t) \frac{[1+i(T/360)]}{[1+i^*(T/360)]}$$

The last equation is the famous interest parity theorem. It relates the forward exchange rate to the spot exchange rate and the interest rates on eurodeposits denominated in the domestic(i) and foreign(i^*) currencies. Notice that if i is greater than i^* (ie the domestic interest rate is higher than the foreign interest rate), then the domestic currency price of forward exchange $F(t,T)$ will be higher than the domestic currency price of spot exchange $S(t)$. Foreign currency would be at a forward premium and domestic currency at a forward discount."

Solnik[8] again has a similar interpretation.

"The interest rate parity relation states that the interest rate differential must equal the forward discount (or premium). The exact mathematical relation, can be written as:

$$\frac{F}{S^0} = \frac{1+r_F}{1+r_D}$$

or, with the first-order linear approximation as formula (6):

$$(6) \quad s = \frac{F-S^0}{S^0} = \frac{r_F - r_D}{1+r_D} \cong r_F - r_D$$

The linear approximation might be quite wrong when interest rates are high. Interest rate parity is not an economic theory but rather a technical arbitrage condition. It must hold; otherwise, riskless arbitrage would take place to exploit this situation."

Shapiro[9] puts it almost identically to Solnik.

"The covered interest arbitrage relationship can be stated formally. Let e_0 be the current spot rate (dollar value of one unit of foreign currency), and f_1 the end-of-period forward rate. If r_h and r_f are the prevailing interest rates in New York and, say, London, respectively, then one dollar invested in New York will yield $1 + r_h$ at the end of the period. The same dollar invested in London will be worth $(1+r_f)f_1/e_0$ dollars at maturity. This latter result can be seen as follows: One dollar will convert into $1/e_0$ pounds that, when invested at r_f, will yield $(1+r_f)f_1/e_0$ dollars when the investment matures.

Funds will flow from New York to London if and only if

$$1+r_h < \frac{(1+r_f)f_1}{e_0}$$

Conversely, funds will flow from London to New York if and only if

$$1+r_h > \frac{(1+r_f)f_1}{e_0}$$

Interest rate parity holds when there are no covered interest arbitrage opportunities. This no-arbitrage condition can be stated as formula (7):

$$(7) \quad \frac{1+r_h}{1+r_f} = \frac{f_1}{e_0}$$

Interest rate parity is often approximated by the equation below

$$r_h - r_f = \frac{f_1 - e_0}{e_0}$$

In effect, interest rate parity says that *high interest rates on a currency are offset by forward discounts and that low interest rates are offset by forward premiums.*

Transaction costs in the form of bid-ask spreads make the computations more difficult, but the principle is the same: compute the covered interest differential to see whether there is an arbitrage opportunity."

To finish off what I would consider to be a reasonable representation of popular international finance textbooks we have Giddy.[10]

"The *interest rate parity theorem* results from arbitrage between the spot and forward markets and the Eurocurrency deposit markets. *Covered-interest arbitrage*, undertaken by large international banks, involves the rapid movement of funds between securities denominated in different currencies in order to profit from different *effective* rates of interest in different currencies after taking hedging costs into account:

Effective interest rate on a foreign currency deposit
= nominal interest rate + cost of forward cover
= interest rate + forward premium (positive) or discount (negative)

This interest rate parity theorem says that covered-interest arbitrage equalizes the return (adjusted for the cost of eliminating exchange risk by means of a forward contract) in different currencies. For example, the interest rate on a dollar deposit must equal the interest rate on a German mark deposit covered in the forward market. More specifically, the following relationships hold true. Here I_{ES} and I_{EDM} represent the Eurodollar and Eurodeutschemark interest rates, respectively.

Value at (t + n) of   value at (t+n) of $1 converted into foreign currency and
$1 earning dollar = earning foreign currency interest rate I_{EDM}, until (t + n)
interest rate I_{ES} when foreign currency is converted back into dollars at
the prearranged forward rate, F_t^n. This gives us formula (8):

$$(8) \quad \$1(1+I_{ES}) = \$1 \left(\frac{1+I_{EDM}}{S_t} \right) F_t^n$$

where S_t is the spot exchange rate (dollars per German mark) and F_t^n is the forward rate.

$$\frac{1+I_{ES}}{1+I_{DM}} = \frac{F_t^n}{S_t}$$

Subtracting 1 from each side gives the interest-rate parity relationship in formula (9):

$$(9) \quad \frac{I_{ES} - I_{EDM}}{1+I_{EDM}} = \frac{F_t^n - S_t}{S_t}$$

For a period of n days, the right-hand side must be converted to an annualized percentage:

$$\frac{I_{ES} - I_{EDM}}{1+I_{EDM}} = \left(\frac{F_t^n - S_t}{S_t} \right) \left(\frac{365}{n} \right)$$

$$= \text{Forward premium or discount}$$

and if I_{EDM} is small, then to a close approximation, gives us formula (10):

$$(10) \quad (I_{ES} - I_{EDM}) = \left(\frac{F_t^n - S_t}{S_t} \right) \left(\frac{365}{n} \right) 100$$

That is, *the interest-rate differential equals the forward premium or discount.*"

COVERED INTEREST ARBITRAGE: THE ACADEMIC LITERATURE VIEW

As discussed above, the assumption of uncovered interest parity lies at the core of many of the models used in international finance. According to the Fisher[11] interest parity condition, the expected returns in one country should be equalized through speculation to the returns in another country once converted to the same currency. Thus the *ex ante* expected home currency returns on foreign deposits in excess of domestic deposits should be zero.

The covered interest parity (CIP) relationship has a long history in financial economics. One of the earliest statements is due to Keynes:[12]

> Forward quotations for the purchase of the currency on the dearer money market tend to be cheaper than spot quotations by a percentage per month equal to the excess of the interest which can be earned in a month in the dearer market over what can be earned in the cheaper.

There now exists a large literature on empirical tests of CIP. For an early survey see Officer and Willett.[13] The sustained interest in CIP is due to several factors. First, in so far as profitable deviations from covered interest rate parity represent riskless arbitrage opportunities, the existence of such deviations is indicative of market inefficiency. Tests of CIP thus form part of an ongoing research programme into the efficiency of international financial markets. Second, CIP provides an important link between spot and forward rates so that, for example, tests of the forward rate as an optimal spot rate predictor can be viewed as tests of *uncovered* interest rate parity, conditional on the maintained hypothesis of CIP. See Boothe and Longworth.[14]

A number of studies exist which report deviations from covered interest parity. These attempt to rationalize deviations from CIP in terms of optimizing behaviour. This approach views deviations from CIP as a response to real world frictions such as transactions costs, see Frenkel and Levich,[15, 16] capital controls, see Dooley and Isard,[17] and capital market imperfections, see Otari and Tiwari.[18] Such frictions create a neutral band around the theoretical parity condition within which it would be unprofitable to engage in arbitrage activities.

A feature of such studies, however, is that the empirical models are developed using published data, often averages of some kind, which can introduce imperfections into the data and in doing so may bias results. See Agmon and Bronfeld.[19] Taylor[20] argues that as a true deviation from CIP:

> represents a profitable arbitrage opportunity at a particular point in time to a market trader, . . . it is important to have data on the appropriate exchange rates and interest rates recorded at the same instant in time and at which a trader could have dealt.

Hence an unbiased test of covered interest parity should be conducted, using data that market traders actually faced at particular points in time, ie contemporaneous trading data.

Taylor and Fraser[21] tested the efficiency of foreign exchange and international capital markets by carrying out an analysis of covered interest arbitrage using high-frequency, high-quality data sampled around the release of economic figures during the period 7 August to 1 September 1988. Their empirical findings revealed support for covered interest arbitrage when institutional details were incorporated into the model. Their findings support the conclusion that data imperfections can explain persistent deviations from covered interest parity. This implies that tests of arbitrage opportunities should pay meticulous attention to institutional details and use prices, markets and formulae that market traders use at a particular moment in time. This is discussed in greater detail in Chapter 8.

Explanations for deviations from uncovered interest parity are equivalently stated, in the literature, as excess returns on foreign relative to domestic deposits.

Explaining this "puzzle" has been made more difficult by an important observation made by Fama.[22] In a simple regression test, he showed that, not only are excess returns predictable *ex ante*, but the variance of these predictable returns is greater than the variance of the expected change in the exchange rate itself. Thus theoretical models of the excess returns across countries must explain, not only their presence, but also their high variation. This behaviour has been labelled by Lewis[23] as the "predictable excess return puzzle".

Note that "covered interest parity CIP" is defined as in formula (11):

(11) $i_t - i_t^* = f_t - s_t$

where i_t and i_t^* are the interest rates on domestic and foreign deposits, respectively, s_t is the logarithm of the domestic currency price of foreign currency at time t, and f_t is the logarithm of the forward rate, the time t domestic currency price of foreign currency delivered at time $t + 1$.

Holding a foreign deposit will give the investor the foreign interest rate return plus the capital gain on foreign currency, $i_t^* + s_{t+1} - s_t$. Lewis[24] illustrates that if the investor borrowed in dollars to obtain the funds for this investment, the excess return on foreign currency would be given by formula (12):

(12) $er_{t+1} = i_t^* + s_{t+1} - s_t - i_t$

Substituting covered interest parity (11) into (12) gives formula (13):

(13) $er_{t+1} \equiv s_{t+1} - f_t$

Both forms of excess returns are used by Lewis below.

Since the excess return is not known at the time of taking out the contract, t, analyzing any behavioural aspects of these returns depends upon measures of expected excess returns. One such measure is the statistically predicted value of the excess return based upon time t information given by formula (14):

(14) $per_t \equiv E_t\left(er_{t+1}\right) = E_t \Delta s_{t+1} - \left(f_t - s_t\right),$

where $E_t (\cdot)$ is the statistical expectations operator conditional on time t information. Thus,

$er_{t+1} = per_t + \epsilon_{t+1}$

where the last term is the statistical forecast error, $\epsilon_{t+1} \equiv s_{t+1} - E_t s_{t+1}$.

Much of the early research on excess returns questioned whether the predictable component of these returns were equal to zero. Under the assumption that the market forms expectations by linear statistical prediction, then predicted excess returns will equal zero if uncovered interest parity holds. To see why, note that uncovered interest parity is given here by formula (15):

(15) $i_t - i_t^* = E_t^m s_{t+1} - s_t$

where $E_t^m (\cdot)$ is the market's expectation conditional upon current information. Note that this expectation is not necessarily the statistical expectation, $E_t (\cdot)$. If the market's expectation does not equal the statistical expectation, conditional upon current information, then $E_t (\cdot) \neq E_t^m$.

Thus, uncovered interest parity in (15) says that the returns on a unit of domestic currency invested in a domestic deposit equals the expected returns from converting the domestic currency into the foreign currency, investing it in a foreign deposit and then converting the proceeds back into domestic currency at the future realized exchange rate. If uncovered interest parity holds and furthermore the market's expectation equals the statistical prediction of the exchange rate, then predictable excess returns must be equal to 0, since in this case, $per_t \equiv i_t^* + E_t^m s_{t+1} - s_t - i_t = 0$.

Lewis[25] estimates the predictable excess annualized monthly returns for the dollar/DM and dollar/yen rate from the beginning of 1975 to the end of 1989. Three features stand out from Lewis's findings. First, the predicted returns are significantly different from zero over some periods in the sample. Second, the returns change sign during the sample. The predictable excess returns on holding DM or yen deposits was significantly negative during part of the early 1980s and was significantly positive in the late 1980s. Therefore, explanations of excess foreign bond returns must explain not only why these returns are not zero, but also why they are sometimes negative and at other times positive. Third, the predictable returns display considerable variability. The DM returns range from 20 per cent to –30 per cent per annum, while the yen returns vary from over 32 per cent to –30 per cent.

How can these results be explained? Generally the explanation can be classified into two groups: (a) the presence of a foreign exchange risk premium or (b) expectational errors. One explanation for predictable excess returns is that domestic investors who are willing to hold foreign bonds and then convert the returns back into domestic currency at the future prevailing exchange rate must be compensated for the foreign exchange risk.

Lewis[26] finds no empirical explanation for the foreign exchange premium concluding that unless risk aversion is extremely high, neither the static Capital Asset Pricing Model nor general equilibrium relationships can explain the risk premium.

Since excess returns cannot be explained by foreign exchange risk, perhaps they can be due to systematic expectational errors. In this case, expectational errors may contribute to the high degree of variability in predictable excess returns.

There are two basic groups of explanations for these expectational errors. First, forecast errors may be systematic because some agents in the market are not rational. The "market's forecast" is really a composite of a heterogeneous group of traders. Since some of these traders are irrational, measures of the market's expectations will not be rational. The second explanation for systematic expectational errors arises from statistical problems with measuring expectations. However Lewis[27] was unable to explain the excess returns by modelling expectations and concludes by emphasizing that all the different expectational assumptions, when judged separately, lead to the conclusion that predictable excess returns remain a complete mystery! Chapter 8 attempts to throw some light on this mystery.

References

1. Lewis, K.K. (1995) "Puzzles in International Financial Markets", in Grosman, G. and Rogoff, K. (eds) *Handbook of International Economics*, vol. III. North-Holland.

2. O'Connor, D.J. and Bueso, A.J. (1990) *International Dimensions of Financial Management*. Maxwell Macmillan International Editions.

3. Madura, J. (1992) *International Financial Management*. West Publishing Company.

4. Pilbeam, K. (1998) *International Finance*. Macmillan Business.

5. O'Connor, D.J. and Bueso, A.J. (1990) *International Dimensions of Financial Management*. Maxwell Macmillan International Editions.

6. Eitemann, D.K., Stonehill, A.I. and Moffett, M.H. (1998) *Multinational Business Finance*. Addison Wesley.

7. Grabbe, O.J. (1996) *International Financial Markets*. Prentice Hall.

8. Solnik, B. (1996) *International Investment*. Addison Wesley.

9. Shapiro, A.C. (1999) *Multinational Financial Management*. Prentice Hall.

10. Giddy, I. (1994) *Global Financial Markets*. DC Heath and Company.

11. Fisher, I. (1930), *The Theory of Interest*. New York: Macmillan.

12. Keynes, J.M. (1923), *A Tract on Monetary Reform*, London and Basingstoke: Macmillan.

13 Officer, L.H. and Willett, T.D. (1970) "The covered arbitrage schedule: a critical survey of recent developments", *Journal of Money, Credit and Banking*. 2, 247–57.

14. Boothe, P. and Longworth, D. (1986) "Foreign exchange market efficiency tests: implications of recent empirical findings", *Journal of International Money and Finance*, 5, 135–52.

15. Frenkel, J.A. and Levich, R.M. (1975) "Covered interest arbitrage: unexploited profits?" *Journal of Political Economy*, 83, 325–38.

16. Frenkel, J.A. and Levich, R.M. (1977) "Transactions costs and interest arbitrage: tranquil versus turbulent periods", *Journal of Political Economy*, 85(6), 1209–25.

17. Dooley, M.P. and Isard, P. (1980) "Capital controls, political risk and deviations from interest-rate parity", *Journal of Political Economy,* 88(2), 370–83.

18. Otari, I. and Tiwari, S. (1981) "Capital controls and interest rate parity: the Japanese experience, 1978–81", *International Monetary Fund Staff Papers*, 28, 793–815.

19. Agmon, T. and Bronfeld, S. (1975) "The international mobility of short-term arbitrage capital", *Journal of Business Finance and Accounting,* 2, 269–79.

20 Taylor, M.P. (1989) "Covered interest arbitrage and market turbulence: an empirical analysis", *Economic Journal*, 99, 376–91.

21. Taylor, M.P. and Fraser, P. (1991) "Some News on Covered Interest Arbitrage", *Money and Financial Markets*. Basil Blackwell. Chapter 9.

22. Fama, E. (1984) "Forward and spot exchange rates", *Journal of Monetary Economics,* 14, 319–38.

23. Lewis, K.K. (1995) "Puzzles in International Financial Markets", in Grosman, G. and Rogoff, K. (eds) *Handbook of International Economics*, vol. III, p. 1914. North-Holland.

24. Lewis, Ibid. p. 1917.

25. Lewis, Ibid. p. 1918.

26. Lewis, Ibid. p. 1939.

27. Lewis, Ibid. p. 1950.

CHAPTER **8**

The foreign exchange market

The view from inside the dealing room

- A review of the theory
- Inside the dealing room
- Interest rate futures: short-term deposits
- Forward rate agreements

A REVIEW OF THE THEORY

As was discussed in detail in Chapter 7, interest rate parity theory asserts that the discount or premium on a currency, the percentage difference between the spot and forward rates, is equal to the difference in the interest rates between the two currencies. The process, known as covered interest arbitrage, is what brings about interest rate parity. When there is a disequilibrium between interest rate differentials and the forward discount or premium on a currency, the covered interest arbitrageur can make a profit by borrowing in one currency, investing in high-quality securities, possibly government or other high quality instruments in the other currency and simultaneously entering into a forward contract.

Textbooks play an educational informative role not necessarily connected with realities. However, when a theory, such as interest rate parity, is seemingly so central to an understanding of international finance and when it is explained and discussed in such an authoritative and similar way one would reasonably expect it to describe the real world of international finance. But does it? The answer is both yes and no. Without quibbling about assumptions about transactions costs, bid ask spreads, dealing room profits, short-term interest rates versus long-term interest rates, all of which are important, the real world dealing room would recognize the textbook principles described above, and in more detail in Chapter 7, but would have difficulty in accepting that in practice they were directly connected with what actually takes place. To see the reasoning behind this, let us consider the real world of what goes on inside the foreign exchange dealing room.

INSIDE THE DEALING ROOM

The formula used

First, the exact formula used by foreign exchange dealers in deriving the forward rates is in fact different from the one employed in the textbooks. A dealer would derive the forward rates, more accurately forward points where one point is 0.0001 or one ten-thousandth expressed as a fraction, using formula (1) below:

The author would like to gratefully acknowledge the assistance, in writing this chapter, of Gavin Wells, Foreign Exchange Dealer and Vice-President, Citibank, London.

$$
(1) \quad F = S^* \left[\frac{1 + \left(RT \times \dfrac{D}{BT} \right)}{1 + \left(RC \times \dfrac{D}{BC} \right)} - 1 \right]
$$

where:

F	=	Forward points
S	=	Spot rate
RT	=	Interest rate of term currency expressed as a fraction
RC	=	Interest rate of commodity currency expressed as a fraction
D	=	Number of days in the period
BT	=	Basis of the terms currency
BC	=	Basis of the commodity currency

Converting interest rate differentials into true forward points involves ensuring that the above definitions are rigorously adhered to.

Example

Assume that spot sterling/dollar, more commonly referred to as cable, is $1.6200. The British Pound (GBP) is based on 365 days. Assume the 1-year deposit rate is 5.06 per cent. The United States Dollar (USD) is based on 360 days. Assume the 1-year deposit rate is 4.95 per cent. From the dealing room point of view the length of the year varies from 365 to 370 days, depending on whether the one-year value date falls on a holiday. The 1-year here is 366 calendar days. Using formula (1) 1-year forward points can be derived as –6.3. With a spot rate of 1.6200 this gives a 1-year forward outright rate of 1.61937 (1.62–0.00063).

However for dealing room purposes, interest rates are derived from the interest rate futures market, and not, as the academic literature assumes, from the deposit markets. But first of all let us be clear about the role futures markets play in the interest parity exercise.

INTEREST RATE FUTURES: SHORT-TERM DEPOSITS

The most actively traded futures contracts in the world are interest rate futures, such as Eurodollar or US Treasury bonds contracts. Commercial banks and money managers use these futures to hedge their interest rate exposure, ie to protect their portfolios of loans, investments, or borrowing against adverse movements in interest rates. They are also used by speculators as leveraged investments, based on their forecasts of movements in interest rates.

Organized markets for interest rate futures exist for instruments in several currencies. Following the US and the UK, most countries with a major bond market have either already developed, or are in the process of developing, a futures market for long-term bonds and sometimes short-term paper.

Interest rate futures create a deposit loan commencing several months hence. Their valuation is somewhat difficult, because the futures are written on a security that has not yet been issued and therefore has no spot price. For example, the September Eurodollar futures price indicated in July quotations relates to a three-month deposit that will start in September. Even if three-month deposits are traded in July, they are not the ones that will be issued in September. This is a marked difference from other financial contracts for which the underlying security is simultaneously traded in the cash market.

The short-term interest rate futures are often referred to as *forward/forward rates*; the valuation of such a contract is usually obtained by observing two interest rates currently quoted in the market.

How does it work?

Assume that we want to determine the futures interest rate on the September Eurodollar contract. As of, say, 14 July the contract is deliverable in about two months. Since the contract is written on a three-month deposit, the final maturity takes place in five months (two plus three). Buying the futures contract in July is equivalent to a contract to lend Eurodollars for three months in September (two months from now) at the futures interest rate. This is similar to lending in July for five months and simultaneously borrowing for two months. Therefore, the futures interest rate r_F, is given by formula (2):

$$(2) \quad 1+r_F = \frac{1+r_m}{1+r_d}$$

where

r_F is the futures interest rate

r_m is the current interest rate to maturity (five months, in the example), and

r_d is the current interest rate to delivery (two months, in the example).

Since interest rates are usually quoted on an annual basis, they should be multiplied by the time to maturity: r is equal to the annual interest rate multiplied by (period = days/360). Annual interest rates are calculated over 365 days, rather than 360, in a few countries, eg the UK.

Example

Let's assume that the five-month annual interest rate is equal to 6.3 per cent and that the two-month annual interest rate is equal to 6.068 per cent. The interest rate over the periods are

$$r_m = 6.3\% \ \frac{5}{12} = 2.6259\% \text{ and}$$

$$r_d = 6.068\% \ \frac{2}{12} = 1.0113\%$$

So, by formula (2) we find that:

$$1+r_F = \frac{1.02650}{1.010113} = 1.015975$$

Hence $r_F = 1.5975$ per cent, and the annual interest rate is

$$1.5975 \ \frac{12}{3} = 6.39\%$$

Therefore the futures price should be equal to 100 per cent minus the interest rate of 6.39 per cent, which is 93.61.

Returning to the dealing room

As already discussed, interest rates for dealing room purposes are derived from the interest rate futures market. In practice, it is the futures markets which drive the Forward Rate Agreements, described below, rather than the other way around. Taking a real world example, Short Sterling has three-month contracts which expire on the third Wednesday of March, June, September and December (the International Money Market dates).

These are traded out to ten years with different colours being assigned to each year for clarity. The terminology needs to be explained at this point. As at May 1999, the term "Front Four" refers to the expiration dates of June 1999, September 1999, December 1999 and March 2000. The next four contracts are June 2000, September 2000, December 2000 and March 2001. The years are Front 4, Red, Green, Blue, Gold, Purple, Orange, Pink, Silver, Copper. Thus the December 1999 Short Sterling contract would be referred to as the "front Dec" and the June 2001 Short Sterling contract would be referred to as "Green Jun".

These contracts show the market's expectation for three-month cash as at that date. Thus, December 2000 at the time of writing was 94.5 implying that three-month cash will be at 5.5 per cent in December 2000. In a moving market, mistakes are avoided when trading these instruments so, for example, Green March cannot be confused with any other contract. This principle applies to all futures markets.

FORWARD RATE AGREEMENTS
Another divergence from the textbooks

Under a forward rate agreement (FRA), two parties – one the buyer and the other the seller – contract whereby the seller will pay the buyer the increased interest cost on a nominal sum of money if interest rates rise above the agreed rate, but the buyer will pay the seller the increased cost if interest rates fall below the agreed rate. For example, it might be an agreement on a three-month interest rate for a three-month period beginning six months from the present and terminating nine months from the present. Such an agreement, if made today, would be called "six against nine" or 6 * 9.

Before illustrating how FRAs and forward interest rates interrelate, it is essential to highlight how the financial market form views or expectations about future interest rates. Forecasting interest rate begins with the markets own implied forecast, known in the dealing room as the series, or strip, of forward interest rates.

Forward interest rates, also called forward spot rates, are interest rates for specified time periods beginning at future dates. Forwards are useful for a number of instruments used in obtaining contractual or hedge commitments for interest rate obligations of the firm (debts or investments) that begin at future dates. Forwards are calculated from yield curves. Any currency that possesses interest-bearing instruments of varying maturities at the same level of risk can be used as a base for forward interest rates.

Example

A US investor has $1 million to invest for six months. The investor considers two alternatives:
- invest for the entire six months at current Eurodollar rates of 5.0625 per cent (per annum)
- invest the funds for three months at 4.8750 per cent (per annum), and then roll the funds over at the end of the three-month period for a second three months.

Case1. Invest for six months at 5.0625% p.a.

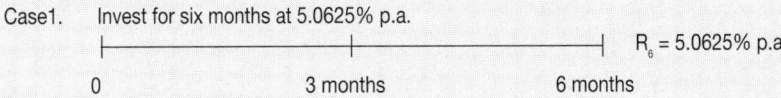

Case 2. Invest for three months at 4.8750 per cent, then reinvest for a second three-month period.

The problem is the investor does not know at time t = 0 the second three month interest rate, the one starting three months from time 0.

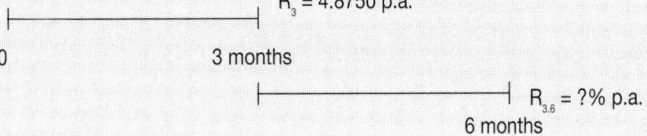

Because financial markets are generally efficient, the two investments should actually have the same rate of return (in the absence of a liquidity premium or risk premium for the second rollover alternative). If it is assumed the same rate of return should be achieved by either path, the two alternatives can be set equal to solve for the implied forward spot interest rate, as in formula (3):

$$(3) \quad \left[1 + \left(0.48750 \times \frac{90}{360} \right) \right] \times (1 + R_{3,6}) = \left[1 + \left(.050625 \times \frac{180}{360} \right) \right]$$

This relationship creates a "3 against 6 forward spot rate" of

$$R_{3,6} = \left[\frac{1.0253125}{1.0121875} - 1 \right] = .012967$$

This rate is 1.2967 per cent for three months, or 5.1868 per cent per annum for the second three-month period.

The market already has knowledge of the yield curve for individual money markets. From this yield curve an entire "strip" of implied forward rates can be derived. These implied forward rates can be considered the markets implied forecasts of future short term interest rates. See Figure 8.1, for an example of a Eurodollar yield curve.

As already indicated a forward rate agreement is an interbank traded contract to buy or sell interest rate payments on a notional principal. These contracts are settled in cash. The buyer of an FRA obtains the right to effectively lock in an interest rate for a desired term that begins at a future date. The contract specifies that the seller of the FRA will pay the buyer the increased interest expense on a

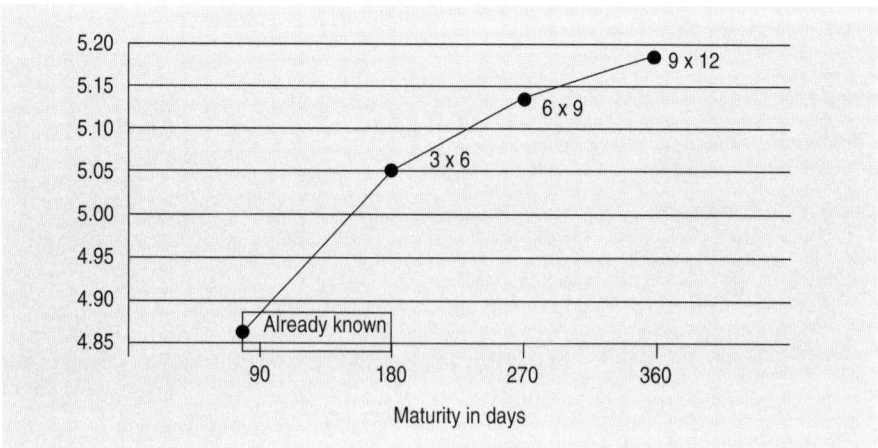

Fig 8.1 ● The Eurodollar yield curve

nominal sum (notional principal) of money if interest rates rise above the agreed rate, but the buyer will pay the seller the differential interest expense if interest rates fall below the agreed rate. Maturities are typically 1, 3, 6, 9 and 12 months.

The contract is priced on the basis of the strip of forward interest rates that are calculated from yield curves for the interest rate, as described earlier. For example, a firm buys a "three against six" FRA for a notional principal of $2 million. Such an FRA applies to the three-month period beginning three months from now. An example of this is given below.

Example

Assume the agreed rate is 7.50 per cent per annum with 91 days in the three-month period. Three months from now, at the beginning of the FRA period, the actual three-month rate is 9.00 per cent. Because the actual rate of 9.00 per cent is above the agreed rate of 7.50 per cent, the firm that purchased the FRA (the holder) will receive from the seller of the FRA (the writer) the difference in the interest expenses. This payment would amount to

$$\$2,000,000 \times \left[(.0900 - .0750) \times \left(\frac{91}{360}\right)\right] = \$7,583.33$$

Because the differential cash flow of the FRA is settled at the beginning of the three-month period (and not at the end as in a normal interest payment), the cash flow must be discounted back to the three months of the FRA period. The actual rate of 9.00 per cent is used here as the discount factor:

$$\frac{\$7,583.33}{\left[1 + \left(.0900 \times \frac{91}{360}\right)\right]} = \$7,414.65$$

The actual payment to the buyer of the FRA is therefore $7,414.65.

The impact of the firm's borrowing costs can be seen by isolating the various actual interest and FRA cash flows. The interest expense, independent of the FRA, payable at the end of the six-month period, is

$$\$2,000,000 \times 0.900 \times \frac{91}{360} = \$45,500.00$$

The end-of-period value (six months) of the FRA compensation payment then serves as a cash inflow of $7,583.33. The final net borrowing cost to the firm for the $2 million optional principal is $37,916.67.

Interest payment	($45,500.00)
FRA inflow	7,583.33
Net payment	(37,916.67)

The firm has locked in a borrowing rate of 7.50 per cent per annum, $37,916.67 on $2 million.

Forward rate agreements are purchased when a firm intends to borrow in the future or faces a variable rate interest payment in the future, but expects interest rates to rise. If the firm expects interest rates to fall by the date interest is due, it could either remain uncovered or sell (write) the FRA to profit from the expected fall in rates. Similarly, a firm planning to invest funds at a future date, but fearing a fall in market interest rates, can purchase an FRA to lock in an investment (or reinvestment) rate. As mentioned earlier the futures markets drive the FRAs rather than the other way around.

Example: Deriving the forward euro/dollar rate

Assume that the spot rate for the dollar/euro rate is $1.0700. The euro is based on 360 days. Assume that the one-year deposit rate is 2.68 per cent. The US dollar contract is based on 360 days.

Assume that the one year deposit rate is 5.15. The one-year, has 366 calendar days. Using formula (1) the one-year forward points can be derived as 261.5.With a spot rate of 1.0700 this gives a one-year forward outright rate of 1.09615 (1.0700 + 0.02615).

For dealing room purposes, as discussed earlier, interest rate are derived from the futures markets. The relevant interest rate for the euro is EURIBOR. (See Chapter 12 for a description of the new money market conventions adopted since the introduction of the euro on 1 January 1999.) EURIBOR has three-month contracts which expire on the third Wednesday of March, June, September and December, these being the IMM dates. Using the convention mentioned earlier, the December 1999 EURIBOR contract would be referred to as the "front December" and the June 2001 contract EURIBOR contract would be referred to as "Green June". These contracts show the markets expectations for three-month cash as at that date. At the time of writing, the December 2000 is 96.835, implying that three-month cash will be at 3.165 per cent in December 2000.

It is then necessary to extrapolate interest rates for the forwards from the futures. We discussed the mechanism for doing this earlier. From the futures we calculate the 3*6 FRA, 6*9 FRA and the 9*12 FRA. Using the three-month cash rate from EURIBOR and the above run of FRAs we compound the rates to produce a one-year interest rate. A similar exercise is carried out for the US dollar using the Eurodollar contract on SIMEX or the CME.

As an example at the time of writing the one-year rate for the euro is 2.725 per cent and for the US dollar it is 5.23 per cent. Putting these into formula (1) with the same spot rate gives us a forward outright rate of 1.09657.

To extrapolate interest rates for our forward rates from the futures the following calculations now take place. From the futures calculate the 3 * 6 FRA, 6 * 9 FRA, and 9 * 12 FRA. We are still missing the three-month rate. So using the three-month cash from LIBOR and the above run of FRAs, we compound the rates to produce a one-year sterling interest rate. A similar exercise is carried out for the US dollar using the Eurodollar futures contracts on the Singapore Monetary Exchange (SIMEX) or on the Chicago Mercantile Exchange (CME). To take an example using the one-year forward rates extrapolated using the above method, at the time of writing gives rates of 5.325 per cent for sterling and 5.185 per cent for the dollar. Putting these into formula (1) gives us the forward points of −10.5 giving us a forward outright rate of $1.61895 (1.62 − 0.00105), somewhat different from the earlier rate of $1.61937 (see page 174).

The difference can be explained by two factors. First of all the spread. Mid points were used for the second set of calculations. More importantly from a dealing room point of view is what is known as basis point adjustment. This takes into account the adjustments necessary to allow for the fact the actual calculations have ranged through three separate although connected markets, the money markets, the futures markets and the foreign exchange market.

Forward traders in the foreign exchange markets use spreadsheet software to automate the above process, taking live feeds for spot and futures, and adding in "sentiment" as they see fit. This type of tool is typically known as a strip, as mentioned earlier, as it strips out rates from the implied interest rates shown by the futures contracts.

The answers produced by the strip are only a guide – the trader uses these as an indication of the price, but does not know whether it is the bid, the offer, the mid or even outside the range. Sentiment can push market prices well away from implied prices, although arbitrage activity will usually bring the two back into line fairly quickly. So the mechanism of interest rate parity moves through the money markets, interest rate futures markets and through FRAs rather than the simplistic illustrations of the textbooks.

In conclusion, the mechanics of deriving forward exchange rates and money market rates are far different from the crude assumptions used in the textbooks. Tests for interest rate parity does confirm its existence, assuming that interest rates are derived via futures, FRAs and money markets.[1] In conclusion interest rate parity does hold but not through the equilibrating adjustments that the traditional textbook writers would have us believe.

Reference

1.   International Monetary Fund (1997) "A Survey by the Staff of the International Monetary Fund", *World Economic Outlook*, May 1997. World Economic and Financial Surveys (Washington).

CHAPTER 9

Currency board versus dollarization

Radical solutions for radical problems?

INTRODUCTION

Brazil's devaluation of the Real on 13 January 1999 strengthened the conviction of those who argue that, when it comes to the choice of an exchange rate regime, there is no longer any feasible middle way. This view is reinforced by the earlier experience with the 1997 Asian currency collapse. It argues that countries must either fix their currencies permanently and irrevocably, ideally through the introduction of a currency board, let them float freely or abolish their own currency completely and adopt the currency of another country. Attempts to peg the exchange rate, it is argued – leaving open the possibility of occasional changes in the parity – are doomed to fail given the integrated nature of today's capital markets. In this chapter, we review the ideas behind currency fixing either through the introduction of a currency board, or, alternatively, abolishing your own currency altogether and replacing it with the currency of another country (normally, but not necessarily, the US dollar). This latter exchange rate system is known as "dollarization".

A currency board combines three elements: an exchange rate that is fixed to an "anchor currency", automatic convertibility (that is, the right to exchange domestic currency at this fixed rate whenever desired), and a long-term commitment to the system, which is often set out directly in a central bank law. The main reason for countries to contemplate a currency board is to pursue a visible anti-inflationary policy.

CURRENCY BOARDS[1]

Currency board arrangements (CBAs) have been adopted in a number of countries as a means of enforcing financial discipline and stabilizing economies, especially from initial circumstances of financial instability. Their ability to help restore confidence in financial markets and withstand subsequent financial market pressures has long been demonstrated. Djibouti has had a currency board since 1949, Brunei Darussalam since 1967, and Hong Kong, China restored its currency board in 1983. Subsequently the Argentine Convertibility Law applied the same principles of monetary control under the fixed exchange rate system it introduced in 1991, showing that CBAs could also be used to halt hyperinflations and maintain low inflation even in relatively large economies. Shortly thereafter, two more CBAs were introduced, in the transition economies of Estonia and Lithuania. Most recently, CBAs have been established in Bulgaria, and in Bosnia and Herzegovina.

Table 9.1 below provides a summary of the currency boards in operation, as of the time of writing.

Table 9.1 ● Currency boards in operation

Country/region	Years in operation (as of 2000)	Peg currency	Special features
Antigua and Barbuda	35	US dollar	Member of East Caribbean Central Bank (ECCB)
Argentina	9	US dollar	One-third of coverage can be in US dollar denominated government bonds
Bosnia and Herzegovina	4	Deutsche mark/euro	
Brunei Darussalam	34	Singapore dollar	
Bulgaria	4	Deutsche mark/euro	Excess coverage in banking department to deal with banking sector weaknesses
Djibouti	51	US dollar	Switched peg currency from French franc to US dollar
Dominica	35	US dollar	Member of ECCB
Estonia	9	Deutsche mark/euro	Excess coverage for domestic monetary interventions
Grenada	35	US dollar	Member of ECCB
Hong Kong SAR	17	US dollar	
Lithuania	7	US dollar	Central bank has the right to appreciate the exchange rate
St Kitts and Nevis	35	US dollar	Member of ECCB
St Lucia	35	US dollar	Member of ECCB
St Vincent and the Grenadines	35	US dollar	Member of ECCB

Sources: Balino *et al.*;[2] Ghosh, Gulde and Wolf[3]

What is a currency board arrangement?

A currency board arrangement (CBA) represents an unequivocal commitment to supply or redeem, without limit, monetary liabilities of the central bank *qua* currency board at a fixed exchange rate. Moreover, these are the *only* terms under which monetary liabilities will be exchanged. This means that currency boards, in their pure form, cannot extend credit to the government, the banking system, or anyone else. Under these conditions, even short-term interest rates are purely market determined, linked to interest rates in the country to whose currency the domestic currency is anchored, and completely independent of the will of the domestic monetary authorities. The commitment to exchange monetary liabilities for foreign currency at a fixed exchange rate requires that the currency board has sufficient foreign exchange to honour this commitment. This ideally means that its foreign reserves at least equal the value of its monetary liabilities. Excess reserves are only necessary in CBA where the central bank wishes to pursue some, albeit limited, policy functions.

The differences between a currency board and a central bank

The differences between a currency board and a central bank are summarized in Table 9.2.

Table 9.2 ● A typical currency board versus a typical central bank

Typical currency board	Typical central bank
Usually supplies notes and coins only	Supplies notes, coins, and deposits
Fixed exchange rate with reserve currency	Pegged or floating exchange rate
Foreign reserves of 100 per cent	Variable foreign reserves
Full convertibility	Limited convertibility
Rule-bound monetary policy	Discretionary monetary policy
Not a lender of last resort	Lender of last resort
Does not regulate commercial banks	Often regulates commercial banks
Transparent	Opaque
Protected from political pressure	Politicized
High credibility	Low credibility
Earns seigniorage only from interest	Earns seigniorage from interest and inflation
Cannot create inflation	Can create inflation
Cannot finance spending by domestic government	Can finance spending by domestic government
Requires no "preconditions" for monetary reform	Requires "preconditions" for monetary reform
Rapid monetary reform	Slow monetary reform
Small staff	Large staff

Source: Hancke, S., Jonung, L. and Schuler, K. (1993) *Russian Currency and Finance*. Routledge

Note: The characteristics listed are those of a typical actual currency board or central bank, especially one in a developing country, not those of a theoretically ideal or exceptionally good currency board or central bank.

Preconditions for the successful introduction of a currency board arrangement

Certain preconditions are essential for a successful currency board arrangement. First, the prohibition on central bank lending to the government requires considerable fiscal discipline. While some financing may be available to the government domestically, and some externally, both sources are subject to powerful constraints. (Crowding out occurs when the public sector "crowds out" the private sector, forcing up domestic interest rates. In addition, there are limits imposed by external lenders who will only accept more foreign debt if they are compensated with higher interest rates.) Given these financing constraints, countries with currency boards must therefore commit themselves to appropriately tight fiscal positions over the medium term. Second, the limited resources available for the currency board to act as lender of last resort means that the banking system must be robust and able to function without routine central bank credits. Third, the commitment to the exchange rate peg must be seen to be durable. This requires that wages and prices are flexible and labour markets relatively free of distortions.

What makes currency board arrangements as robust as they have been in certain countries?

Proponents of CBAs argue that they offer the strongest form of exchange rate peg that is possible short of full currency union. Their strength, it it argued, derives from a number of factors, including the preconditions listed above, but most of all from the free operation of market forces in determining interest rates. In particular, their proponents argue, they avoid the "too little, too late" trap that policy makers can fall into when determining interest rates in a discretionary manner. Their administrative and operational simplicity has also been an important feature in some small open economies. The credibility of CBAs comes from the governments' commitment to the rules of the game in determining the issuance of money, and from the framework they provide that fosters financial discipline and structural reform. It also comes from the fact that a CBA entails a much higher cost of abandoning a fixed parity than is the case for fixed-but-adjustable exchange rate arrangements. In most existing CBAs, the exchange rate is set by law, making changes to the exchange rate very costly for governments.

What are the problems that currency board arrangements can encounter?

The cast iron convertibility of domestic currency into foreign currency comes at the expense of the convertibility of commercial bank deposits into cash that central banks provide as ultimate lenders of last resort. This is because a currency board can serve as a lender of last resort only to the extent that it has external reserves exceeding what is required to back the monetary base. Its capacity to support commercial banks is therefore bounded, so that such support must be on stricter terms than normal. The reliance of CBAs on interest rates to equilibrate financial markets, meanwhile, forces banks to assume an important share of the burden of adjustment, and the absence of central bank monetary operations to smooth out very short-term interest rate volatility implies that banks must be able to weather such volatility. All this means that banking supervision must be even more rigorous than usual. Bank collapses have occurred in some CBAs (Argentina and Lithuania in 1995, Estonia in 1992 and 1994, and Hong Kong in 1986), but all were handled within the constraints established by their respective CBAs.

As already indicated, a currency board system can be credible only if the central bank holds sufficient official foreign exchange reserves to at least cover the entire narrow money supply. In this way, financial markets and the public at large can be assured that every domestic currency bank note is backed by an equivalent amount of foreign currency in the official coffers. Demand for a "currency board currency" will therefore be higher than for currencies without a guarantee, because holders know that "rain or shine", their liquid money can be easily converted into a major foreign currency. In the event of a "testing of the system", a currency board's architects contend, automatic stabilizers will prevent any major outflows of foreign currency. The mechanism works through changes in the money supply within the currency board country – a contraction in the case of a flight into the anchor currency – which will lead to interest rate rises that, in turn, will induce investors to move funds back again. While this is essentially the same mechanism that also operates under a fixed exchange rate, the exchange rate guarantee implied in the currency board rules ensures that the necessary interest rate changes and the attendant cost for the economy will be lower.

The benefits and costs of a currency board are discussed in detail below, but it is useful to review the basic ideas at this stage. Economic credibility, low inflation, and lower interest rates are the immediately obvious advantages of a currency board. But currency boards may prove limiting, especially for countries that have weak banking systems or are prone to economic shocks. With a currency board in place, the central bank can no longer be an unlimited lender of last resort to banks in financial trouble. At most, it may make loans from an emergency fund that is either set aside at the time the currency board is designed or, over time, funded from central bank profits. Another cost could be the national authorities' inability to use financial policies, such as adjustments of domestic interest or exchange rates, to stimulate the economy. Instead, under a currency board, economic adjustment will have to come by way of wage and price adjustments, which can be both slower and more painful.

Benefits and costs of currency boards

Currency board arrangements have become, as already suggested, an increasingly popular system of monetary arrangement in recent years. To date, no currency board has been abandoned as a result of a currency crisis and this has encouraged many countries to consider the benefits and costs of such a system.

CBAs confer considerable credibility on fixed exchange rate regimes. This credibility is most noticeable in the narrowing of interest rate differentials vis-à-vis the anchor currency. Thus, interest rates in Argentina declined from 12.5 per cent a month just before the introduction of the currency board in March 1991 to 1.5 per cent the following month. In Bulgaria, interest rates declined from over 18 per cent a month before the announcement, in March 1997, that a CBA was to be implemented on 1 July, to under 0.5 per cent a month in mid-July. Interest rates on (credit-risk-free) instruments in Estonia have closely tracked those of the peg currency. In Hong Kong, China, interest rates have generally oscillated around those of the peg currency (the US dollar), reflecting their role as automatic stabilizer – high when money demand was high or markets were subject to disturbances (such as after the 1995 Mexico crisis) and low when conditions were softer.

In their role as nominal anchors, CBAs help deliver price stability. Structural changes and other adjustments in the economy, however, can sometimes result in inflation remaining for a time higher than in the country whose currency provides the peg. For example, faster productivity growth in the tradables sector than in the non-tradables sector, which tends to be a feature of an economy that is growing relatively rapidly, may mean faster overall inflation than in the anchor country, and an associated real appreciation of the domestic currency in terms of overall price indices, implying no loss of international competitiveness in terms of traded goods prices. This helps explain why inflation in Hong Kong, China has been persistently higher than in the US, host to the peg currency, without giving rise to difficulties for the former in terms of competitiveness. Inflation in Estonia and Lithuania also remains higher than in Germany and the US, the respective reserve currency countries. This partly reflects the phasing of utility price adjustments, and the initial undervaluation of the Estonian kroon and Lithuanian litas and their subsequent real appreciation through domestic price increases.

Given the stringent preconditions and attendant risks, currency boards are obviously not appropriate for all countries or in all circumstances. CBAs can evolve, with the introduction (or reintroduction) of instruments and facilities more normal for conventional central banking arrangements. Thus, the currency board arrangements of Hong Kong, China and Argentina already allow for limited interest-rate-smoothing open market operations, and the Hong Kong Monetary Authority now effectively applies a band on overnight interest rates. CBAs could evolve to the point where countries could one day choose to exit them in favour of other arrangements, including greater exchange rate flexibility. For CBAs to deliver their promise of credibility and financial stability, however, it is essential that they be seen to represent a durable commitment. Steps toward evolution, or toward exit, it is argued, should therefore be taken only after the CBA has been in force for a sustained period of time and has done its job, on the condition that the authorities enjoy a high degree of credibility in their commitment to financial discipline, and where such steps would clearly represent an advantage to the country concerned.

CURRENCY BOARDS AND INFLATION: A REVIEW OF THE EVIDENCE

Enoch and Gulde[4] stress that ultimately, the relative merits of currency board arrangements and other forms of exchange rate pegs cannot be resolved by theory alone. Ghosh, Gulde and Wolf[5] have undertaken an empirical investigation, extending the existing literature on inflation performance under fixed exchange rates. Given the empirically verified anti-inflationary capability of fixed exchange rate systems, it can be argued that instituting a currency board arrangement makes sense only if the regime delivers even better inflation performance. By using a data set containing all IMF member countries, over more than 25 years, the study attempted to isolate the inherent effects of a currency board arrangement regardless of the many country-specific challenges facing countries where such arrangements are in operation – for example, hyperinflation (Argentina and Bulgaria), transition to a market economy (Bulgaria, Estonia and Lithuania), volatile terms of trade (Eastern Caribbean Currency Board), post-conflict situations (Bosnia), or the presence of an international financial centre (Hong Kong SAR).

Empirical analysis confirms, the authors argue, that, historically, currency board arrangements have done better than even other fixed exchange rate regimes. For example, the presence of a currency board arrangement is found to lower annual inflation by about 3.5 percentage points – the result of a "confidence effect" that essentially arises from the faster growth of money demand made possible by the greater institutional certainty associated with a currency board. In contrast to fears often raised by opponents of currency boards, Ghosh, Gulde and Wolf did not find that existing currency boards had any negative effects on growth.

Hancke,[6] in a similar study examined data from 98 developing countries for the period 1950–93. His results showed that countries with fixed exchange rates, by which he means currency boards, experienced growth rates of per capita GDP that were 54 per cent greater than those of countries with pegged exchange rates. Furthermore, the variability of those growth rates (as measured by their standard deviations) was virtually identical, indicating that the lack of discretionary policy with fixed exchange rates did not result in any greater incidence or vulnerability to external economic shocks. Hancke also found that, with respect to inflation performance, fixed exchange rates have proved far superior to pegged rates, with average inflation rates being 4.9 times higher in countries with pegged rates and 4.2 times more variable. In terms of budget deficits, measured as a percentage of GDP, Hancke found that countries with pegged rates had deficits that were, on average, 65 per cent larger and 1.4 times more variable than those of countries with fixed rates.

HOW WOULD A CURRENCY BOARD BE INTRODUCED?

Appendix 9.1 illustrates the issues involved in making a currency board operational. As Enoch and Gulde[7] show, even if economic arguments favour a currency board arrangement, its operational feasibility will depend on whether the attendant legal and institutional issues are effectively addressed. The importance of the legal and institutional issues should not be underestimated. Although a currency board is a simple monetary arrangement, a range of important decisions are needed to implement the institutional framework for financial management in the economy and, especially, in the legal environment in which central banking is carried out. Unless these adjustments – which tend to be more time-consuming than those involved in carrying out other exchange regime shifts and in many countries will have to be resolved in full public view (for instance, in parliamentary debates) – are completed satisfactorily, a currency board cannot be established in a way that will enable a country to achieve the necessary improvement in the credibility of its monetary policy.

There are several basic decisions that need to be made when a country establishes a currency board arrangement include choosing the peg or anchor currency, setting the level of the peg, and determining whether or not to include a "safety margin" for the financial sector. Changes are also required to the legal system and the government's relations with the central bank.

Choosing the anchor

The obvious criteria to use in choosing an anchor include the strength and international usability of a currency. This generally rules out all but a handful of moneys. In fact, the 14 currency board arrangements currently in operation involve pegs to only three currencies: the US dollar (ten countries), the Deutsche mark/euro (three countries), and the Singapore dollar (one country). In choosing from among this much narrower field, a country should carefully consider its current and prospective trade flows as well as other economic links, with the country issuing the currency to which a country's currency is pegged. A country's choice can get more complicated if its economy is characterized by widespread "currency substitution", where the currency used is not that of its major trading partner. In this case, or where the values of a country's trade with two dominant currency blocs are roughly equal, a currency basket is a theoretical option. In practice, however, all countries that have introduced currency board arrangements so far have opted for the simplicity of a single currency.

Enoch and Gulde indicate that setting the exchange rate would appear straightforward, given that a currency board arrangement by definition has to cover a monetary aggregate, this usually being the full amount of reserve money, but sometimes narrower definitions of money can be applied. Yet the rate at which the central bank's available international reserves cover the monetary aggregate in question varies depending on the exact definition of reserves used. Choosing the appropriate definition most likely involves a trade-off. Although a narrow definition of foreign reserves, such as "net reserves", might signal strong discipline and possibly improve the credibility of the system, it might also require an up-front devaluation that would prove politically and economically unfeasible.

In a "pure" currency board arrangement, the currency board has no margin to intervene as lender of last resort on behalf of a bank in difficulties or to engage in open market operations. A country weighing the option of establishing a currency board may, however, seek a "safety margin" of some excess coverage, holding reserves of say 100–115 per cent of the monetary base. While most operating arrangements do allow for some form of limited intervention, the decision to include this feature is not one to be taken lightly. Room for manoeuvre in case of unexpected difficulties is possible only at a more depreciated exchange rate than would have been necessary under other exchange arrangements. Intervention may also limit transparency – and, thereby, the credibility – of the system.

Changing the legal system

A sound legal basis, Enoch and Gulde, go on to argue, is essential, because a currency board arrangement derives much of its credibility from the changes required in the central bank law concerning exchange rate adjustments. Countries seriously considering establishing a currency board may therefore wish to incorporate some, or all, of the above-mentioned principles into the central bank law. The law must define both the exchange rate and reserves, as well as specify the limited powers of the managing institution under the system.

It is sometimes argued that the rules governing a currency board could be asymmetrical, permitting the central bank to appreciate the exchange rate but requiring legal action before depreciation can be undertaken. For example, the rules governing Lithuania's currency board contain such provisions. The period needed to set up the necessary legal process will obviously differ across countries, depending on the availability of technically skilled lawyers who can draw up a draft bill and the minimum parliamentary requirements for its enactment into law. In most countries, the process will take time owing to parliamentary discussions about the merits of the proposed arrangement, which may itself require the relevant authorities to carry out an intensive information campaign.

Relationship with the central bank and the government

Finally, establishing a currency board arrangement will require the redefinition of the financial relationships within the country's government. More often than not, the initial inflationary impetus that is to be eliminated by moving to a currency board has been created through extensive central bank financing of the government. Rules for a currency board arrangement therefore need to prohibit new central bank loans to the government. Other considerations include the financial links between the central bank and the government, and how these are to function and, most important, how the central bank will handle government deposits. Although the central bank continues to handle government accounts under some currency board arrangements, doing so may decrease the arrangement's transparency.

Further difficulties may arise from the fact that government deposits are callable at short notice, and consistency with currency board arrangement rules can be achieved only if such accounts are fully covered by foreign reserve holdings. For these reasons, some economies with currency boards, most notably Hong Kong SAR, have moved all government accounts to commercial banks. Other economies with currency board arrangements, including some transition economies, have felt that the commercial banking sector was not yet able to handle the government's accounts and have opted to keep them with the monetary authority. In this case, however, interest on these accounts can be paid only to the extent that the currency board has a flow income from its foreign reserve holdings that exceeds its operating costs. In addition, transparency is likely to be enhanced if the public debt management function, an auxiliary service provided by many central banks, is clearly placed outside the domain of the currency board, possibly by creating an independent agency under the ministry of finance.

TRANSITION TO A CURRENCY BOARD

The rules laid down in the new central bank law will serve as guideposts for reorganizing the central bank into a currency board. In a number of countries that have recently adopted currency board arrangements, this has involved setting up separate banking and issue departments, each with distinct functions and coming under the authority of different deputy governors. Other countries with currency board arrangements, such as Argentina, have retained a unified structure for the monetary authority. In either case, a reorganization has to take place to allow easy identification of the central bank's key activities and to ensure that maintenance of the relevant currency cover ratios will be clearly visible. To that end, the currency board arrangement will have to publish a well-defined set of statistics (including, for instance, the balance sheet of the issue department or statistics on selected assets and liabilities included in that balance sheet) in a form, and according to a calendar, that are consistent with the currency board arrangement law.

Establishing a currency board arrangement will also generally involve reviewing how the central bank will carry out its new core functions, the most important of which is reserve management. The added importance of reserve management under a currency board arrangement is obvious, given that the board's earnings from foreign exchange holdings will probably be its major source of income and because even a small violation of the cover requirement, which could arise from technical problems in reserve management, might cause a serious undermining of confidence in the arrangement.

Finally, conducting a review of the banking sector and prudential standards and deciding on the location of banking supervision will generally also be necessary during the transition to a currency board arrangement. The review and, if required, a streamlining of the banking sector are important because of the elimination of, or reduction in, the central bank's ability to function as a lender of last resort under such an arrangement. During this period, the authorities may decide to transfer banking supervision, which has often been carried out by the central bank, to an independent agency to avoid possible circumvention of currency board arrangement rules in case of banking sector difficulties. If, for reasons of timing or organization, banking supervision functions cannot be performed outside the central bank, it has to demonstrate clearly that any support it provides to banks in difficulty will not breach the currency board arrangement rules.

WHAT IS THE SCORECARD ON CURRENCY BOARDS?

Currency boards in many countries have achieved impressive economic results, both in achieving lower inflation than other exchange rate regimes and in stabilizing expectations after prolonged hyperinflation. There have thus been calls for such arrangements to be established in a rather diverse group of other countries, many of which are in crisis. Such calls, Enoch and Gulde[8] stress, should be viewed warily by national governments, for at least three reasons. First, the success stories largely reflect the experiences smaller countries have had with currency boards, whose applicability to larger countries has yet to be fully demonstrated. Second, and equally important, the successful establishment of a currency board arrangement requires time for building consensus, as well as for careful planning and implementation of important legal and institutional changes. Third, countries with one or several weak banks may have to rehabilitate them before changing their monetary regimes. These prerequisites to establishing a currency board may, in many cases, be too involved and take too much time to make it advisable for a country to attempt to do so during a macro-economic crisis.

THE MOVE FROM CURRENCY BOARD TO DOLLARIZATION

At the beginning of this chapter we discussed three options open to countries choosing between different exchange rate regimes, permanent fixing through a currency board, free floating and abolition of the domestic currency and its replacement by another country's currency, a concept known as dollarization. The second option was discussed in detail in Chapter 2. This third option, dollar-ization, is the subject of the remainder of this chapter. Consider the question "Why not eliminate the exchange rate altogether and just use dollars instead of the domestic currency?" As Manuel Hinds, finance minister of El Salvador recently commented "Having a currency is just too expensive."[9] What Hinds was referring to was that loans in the local currency, the colone, cost 7.5 per cent p.a. more than loans in US dollars.

Argentina currently has a currency board. The essence of a currency board, as already discussed, is that the supply of notes and coins is "asset backed" by the central banks' foreign exchange reserves. In Argentina's case, the $24.2 billion of foreign exchange reserves, as of April 1999, are more than enough to back the $14.4 billion of notes and coins – the monetary base is in fact over-collateralized. (See Table 9.3.)

Table 9.3 ● Argentina's currency board

April 1999 ($bn)

Assets		Liabilities	
Liquid foreign exchange reserves	24.2	Money in circulation, notes and coins	14.4
		Banks' liquidity requirements	9.8
Total liquid assets	24.2	Total monetary liabilities	24.2

Source: Banco Central de la República Argentina (BCRA). Please note this is a highly simplified presentation of the BCRA's balance sheet

Some recent Argentine history

Argentina has a long history of high inflation rates fuelled by chronic fiscal deficits. When Menem was elected president in May 1989, the economy was already sliding into hyperinflation. In March 1991, the Congress passed the "convertibility law", establishing the convertibility of the *austral* (the Argentine currency since 1985) at a rate of 10,000 australes per US dollar. In January 1992 the *peso* replaced the austral (1 peso for 10,000 australes).

Under the convertibility law, the central bank stands ready to sell dollars at the rate of $1 per peso. Reserves consisting of gold and foreign currency or deposits and bonds payable in gold and foreign currency, must be maintained at a level no less than 100 per cent of the monetary base. Up to 33 per cent of reserves can be held in bonds of the Argentine Government. But, as of 7 April 1999, only 4 per cent of reserves were actually held in that form. Furthermore, the central bank cannot change the amount of these bonds by more than 10 per cent in any given year.

The convertibility law also forbids the central bank from monetizing Government deficits. Thus, the system cannot be sustained in the long term without sound fiscal discipline. This has forced the Government to privatize many state-owned companies and to carry out other major reforms, including trade liberalization, freeing of international capital flows, and deregulation of the banking industry, with resulting benefits to the economy.

Evidence for these beneficial effects is illustrated by the effect on inflation and output. The average annual rate of inflation, which reached a staggering 600 per cent from 1983–91, maintained a stable pace of 4.6 per cent from 1992–8 under the convertibility plan. After a long period of stagnation, the growth rate of output jumped from 0.4 per cent in 1983–91 to 3.9 per cent in 1992–8. The 1990s expansion was interrupted only twice, coinciding with the Mexican balance of payments crisis (the "Tequila effect", discussed below) in 1995 and the international turmoil in 1998.

Although the Argentine peso has remained pegged at $1 since 1992, currency crises elsewhere in the world have prompted speculation on a possible devaluation of the peso, in spite of limited trade links between the affected countries and Argentina. For example, Mexico's share of Argentine exports was only 1.7 per cent in 1994, and Argentina's exports overall accounted for just 9 per cent of its gross domestic product (GDP). Similarly, although Brazil is Argentina's main trading partner, exports to Brazil represented only 3 per cent of Argentine GDP in 1998. Interest rates rise sharply with each speculative attack. Furthermore, the premium in interest rates on peso-denominated loans over dollar-denominated loans rises as well, suggesting that the perceived risk of devaluation is much higher.

Two days after Brazil devalued the Real, on 13 January 1999, it became known that President Menem had asked his finance minister to study dollarization, and early in 2000 Ecuador instituted policies to replace the sucré with the US dollar.

So what is dollarization?

Dollarization – either in an emergency, or by negotiation – would in principle be a very simple extension of Argentina's currency board mechanism. Dollarization would simply be a process in which the central bank invites holders of notes and coins to exchange their currency for dollars at the central bank. In effect, the central bank closes itself down, except as a repository of commercial banks' liquidity requirements.

So dollarization, in this context, means the elimination of the Argentine currency, the peso, and its complete replacement with the US dollar. At present, the monetary base in Argentina consists of the peso-denominated currency. It would be converted into US Federal Reserve notes. The US dollar would be the sole legal tender and sole unit of account.

The Argentine economy is already partly dollarized. For example, 60 per cent of private non-financial sector deposits are in dollars. The reserve requirements of commercial banks are met with dollar-denominated assets. Argentines are already used to quoting prices and carrying out transactions in dollars. Complete dollarization would not dramatically change their habits and practices.

For Argentina to dollarize unilaterally, the only requirement is to eliminate the peso-denominated monetary base. Since commercial banks presently hold reserves in dollar-denominated assets, the monetary base is just the currency in circulation. To replace the currency, Argentina needs to buy dollars and exchange all outstanding peso notes for dollar notes. Argentina already has enough resources to buy the required amount of dollars.

Official dollarization has a rich history. At least 120 countries have officially used the currency of another country at some time. Today the best-known country that is dollarized is Panama. However, there are 28 other small countries and dependent territories that do not have a national currency and use a foreign one instead. Twelve use the US dollar, five the Australian dollar, and two each use the British pound, New Zealand dollar, Italian lira and French franc. And the Turkish lira is used in northern Cyprus, the Danish krone in Greenland, and the Swiss franc in Liechtenstein. See Table 9.4 for a full list.

The benefits of dollarization

The biggest measurable gain from dollarization would be the elimination of the spread between Argentine peso interest rates and Argentine US dollar interest rates – a spread which purely reflects Argentine currency risk. Between 1997–9 the spread (for three-month money) has averaged around 170 basis points. Since peso loans amount to $25 billion and peso deposits amount to $34 billion, it follows that the benefit of dollarization would roughly equal $1 billion ($0.6 billion for savers and $0.4 billion for borrowers). In addition to this, there is the less quantifiable benefit that Argentine financial system would no longer have to suffer the *volatility* of the peso–dollar spread.

Table 9.4 ● Dollarized economies at the beginning of 1998

Country	Population	Political status	Currency used	Since
Andorra	63,000	Independent	French franc and Spanish peseta	1278
Channel Islands	140,000	British dependencies	Pound sterling	1797
Cocos (Keeling) Islands	600	Australian external territories	Australian dollar	1995
Cyprus, Northern	180,000	De facto independence	Turkish lira	1974
Greenland	56,000	Danish self-governing region	Danish krone	1800
Guam	150,000	US territory	US dollar	1898
Kiribati	80,000	Independent	Australian dollar	1943
Liechtenstein	31,000	Independent	Swiss franc	1921
Marshall Islands	60,000	Independent	US dollar	1944
Micronesia	120,000	Independent	US dollar	1944
Monaco	30,000	Independent	French franc	1865
Nauru	8,000	Independent	Australian dollar	1914
Niue	2,000	New Zealand self-governing territory	New Zealand dollar	1901
Norfolk Island	2,000	Australian external territory	Australian dollar	1900
Northern Mariana Islands	48,000	US Commonwealth	US dollar	1944
Palau	18,000	Independent	US dollar	1944
Panama	2,500,000	Independent	1 balboa=US$1; uses US dollar notes	1904
Pitcairn Island	56	British dependency	New Zealand dollar & US dollar	1900s
Puerto Rico	3,500,000	US commonwealth	US dollar	1899
Saint Helena	6,000	British colony	Pound sterling	1834
Samoa, American	60,000	US territory	US dollar	1899
San Marino	24,000	Independent	Italian lira	1897
Tokelau	1,600	New Zealand territory	New Zealand dollar	1926
Turks and Calcos Islands	14,000	British colony	US dollar	1973
Tuvalu	10,000	Independent	Australian dollar	1892
Vatican City	1,000	Independent	Italian lira	1929
Virgin Islands, British	17,000	British dependency	US dollar	1973
Virgin Islands, US	100,000	US territory	US dollar	1917

Source: Global Finance, January 2000

Discussion about the macroeconomic benefits of dollarization revolve around the elimination of the "Tequila effect". This is the negative effect on economic growth of having to deflate to eliminate the adverse effects of devaluation, a phenomenon common to Latin America. So any economic policy such as dollarization, which eliminates the Tequila effect, avoids the output loss associated with it.

The major benefit of dollarization would be reduced interest rates in Argentina. With no peso-dollar exchange rate, currency risk would be eliminated and the spread in interest rates between pesos and dollars for loans within Argentina would be eliminated. In consequence, it is argued, Argentina's trend rate of growth would be higher with dollarization than with its currency board-like system.

In addition, dollarization would be politically more attractive than devaluation.

The costs of dollarization

The most obvious cost of dollarization is the fact that the government binds itself even more tightly into the straightjacket which is imposed by the currency board – namely the inability to use the exchange rate as a tool of policy. This in turn means that any adjustment the economy needs to go through – to reduce a big current account deficit, say – has to be done by means other than devaluation, which implies either:

- that prices and wages need to be downwardly flexible, or
- that domestic spending needs to shrink.

In other words, dollarization raises the possibility that Argentina, or any other country that dollarizes, will continually be faced with the prospect of recession whenever an external shock occurs.

If Argentina adopts the dollar as its national currency, it will be unable to pursue an independent or active monetary policy. However, Argentina has not had an independent monetary policy since the passage of the convertibility law in 1991. What the repeated speculative attacks on the peso indicate, however, is that retaining the *option* to resume an independent policy has proven expensive for Argentina.

Another consequence of adopting the dollar is that no Argentine institution will be able to act as lender of last resort to the banking sector by issuing currency to financial institutions in distress. Again, Argentina has not had that ability since 1991. But it has devised alternative mechanisms to deal with liquidity crises.

The most obvious cost to Argentina is the lost seigniorage on the peso, because once the peso is replaced by the dollar, that seigniorage will accrue to the US. The benefit is in eliminating the consequences of Tequila effects.

The cost of unilateral dollarization for Argentina stems mainly from the loss of the foreign reserves that it would have to sell in exchange for dollars. These reserves bear interest, and therefore are a source of income for Argentina. This income known as seigniorage, comes from the structure of any central bank's balance sheet: Its liabilities (money) bear no interest, while its assets do. But once Argentina's reserves are replaced by dollar banknotes, this source of income disappears.

Preconditions for a successful dollarization

By eliminating currency risk, dollarization, it is argued by its proponents, would lower interest rates, foster deeper domestic capital markets, boost investment and growth, and reduce government debt service. Dollarization, however, is not a substitute for good policies and is not for everyone. The preconditions for dollarization include the following:

- a period of exchange rate stability with the US dollar
- inflation and productivity growth similar to that in the US
- a strong fiscal position and financial system with no hidden public liabilities
- price and wage flexibility
- as large a ratio of international reserves to currency in circulation as possible, since these reserves will provide the collateral enabling the lender of last resort function to operate efficiently.

HOW WOULD A COUNTRY DOLLARIZE?

Steve Hancke[10] has set out the main features that would be desirable for a law on dollarization. A model statute for Argentina would include the following provisions.

1. The Banco Central de la República Argentina (BCRA) shall cease to issue pesos. It shall withdraw from circulation the Argentine peso monetary base and shall replace it with dollars at the exchange rate of 1 dollar = 1 peso. The BCRA shall preferably accomplish the bulk of this task within 30 days after this law enters into force. Peso notes currently accepted for redemption into dollars shall continue to be accepted by the BCRA or the government for five years after this law enters into force. After five years, all peso notes in circulation may be demonetized by a decree of the executive power.

2. Wages, prices, assets and liabilities shall be converted from pesos to dollars at the exchange rate of 1 dollar = 1 peso. By 30 days after this law enters into force, wages and prices shall cease to be quoted in pesos.

3. Interest rates and other financial ratios shall remain the same in dollars as they were in pesos. The maturities of loans and other financial obligations shall remain unchanged.

4. The executive power may appoint a committee of experts on technical issues connected with this law to recommend changes in regulations that may be necessary.

5. Nothing in this law shall prevent parties to a transaction from using any currency that is mutually agreeable. However, the dollar may be established as the default currency where no other currency is specified.

6. Previously enacted legislation conflicting with this law is repealed.

7. This law becomes effective immediately.

References

1. Many of the discussions on currency boards, in this chapter draw on "A Currency Board: A Cure for all Monetary Problems?" Enoch, C. and Gulde, A. (1998) *Finance and Development*, December, which the author wishes to acknowledge.

2. Balino, T., Enoch, C., Ize, A., Santiprabhob, V. and Stella, P. (1997) *Currency Board Arrangements: Issues and Experiences*, IMF Occasional Paper 151.

3. Ghosh, A.R., Gulde, A. and Wolf, H.C. (1998) "Currency Boards: The Ultimate Fix?" IMF Working Paper 98/8.

4. Enoch, C. and Gulde, A. (1998) *Finance and Development*.

5. Ghosh, A.R., Gulde, A. and Wolf, H.C. (1998) "Currency Boards: The Ultimate Fix?" IMF Working Paper 98/8.

6. Hancke, S.H. (1999) "Some Thoughts about Currency Boards", in Blejer, M.I. and Skreb, M. (eds) *Balance of Payments, Exchange Rates, and Competitiveness in Transition Economies*. Norwell, MA: Kluwer.

7. Enoch, C. and Gulde, A. (1998) *Finance and Development*.

8. Ibid.

9. *Euromoney*, June 1999, p.186.

10. Hancke, S. (1999) "Dollarization: linchpin of the new international financial architecture". *Central Banking*, Volume IX, Number 4, May.

Making a currency board operational*

IMF Paper on Policy Analysis and Assessment

This is a *Paper on Policy Analysis and Assessment* and the author(s) would welcome any comments on the present text. Citations should refer to a *Paper on Policy Analysis and Assessment of the International Monetary Fund*. The views expressed are those of the author(s) and do not necessarily represent those of the Fund.

PPAA/97/10

INTERNATIONAL MONETARY FUND

Monetary and Exchange Affairs Department

Making a Currency Board Operational

Prepared by Charles Enoch and Anne-Marie Gulde[1]

November 1997

Abstract

The past years have witnessed a revival of interest in the adoption of currency board arrangements (CBAs). This paper argues that the successful establishment of a CBA requires that, in addition to adopting appropriate macroeconomic policies, the authorities make careful preparations on the technical aspects of the transition. The range of necessary preparations will vary from country to country, but will generally involve changing the central bank law, reorganizing the central bank, devising appropriate guidelines for reserve management, and adapting the government's cash and debt management activities. Additional measures are required for countries that recently experienced banking sector problems.

JEL Classification Numbers: E58, E61, F31

Keywords: Currency board, monetary arrangement, credibility

Author's e-mail Address: CEnoch@imf.org, AGuldewolf@imf.org

* This appendix was reprinted, with permission, from the International Monetary Fund.

Contents

I. INTRODUCTION

In the last few years there has been a revival of interest in the adoption of Currency Board Arrangements (CBAs), with such arrangements introduced in, for instance, Argentina, Bulgaria, Estonia and Lithuania, and under consideration in a number of countries elsewhere. There has been a growing literature on the advantages and disadvantages of such arrangements, and on the principal considerations as to whether a country should adopt a CBA.[2] This paper leaves to one side the broad policy aspects of this subject: whether to establish a CBA; what should be the appropriate stance of macroeconomic policy to support the CBA; what should be the degree of foreign exchange cover, and how it should be defined; and what should be the scope for monetary operations. It assumes that these questions have been addressed, and that the authorities are now facing the next set of tasks: how to make a CBA operational.

In general, the establishment of a CBA will involve close co-ordination among the authorities, including the highest level of government, the Ministry of Finance, and the central bank. The Ministry of Justice and other agencies may also need to be involved. The process is facilitated if the authorities establish a formal high level committee, possibly backed by a secretariat to conduct day-to-day technical preparations, which will meet on a regular basis, probably several times a week.

II. DESIGNATION OF THE CURRENCY AND LEVEL OF THE PEG

The decision on the peg currency should be guided by three principles.[3] First, to allow the CBA to benefit from the strength and financial depth of the peg currency, it should be selected among stable currencies with reasonably deep financial markets, offering a range of financial instruments, underwritten by domestic and foreign issuers.[4] These considerations suggest that the benefits will be larger if the selection is made from among the currencies of G7 countries or the small set of other widely-held international reserve currencies.

To decide between possible international reserve currencies, a country should take into account the direction of trade flows, the denomination of imports and exports, the denomination of international debt, and the correlation among cyclical movements between its economy and that of the proposed designated currency. Choosing the currency of the predominant trading partner is in most cases advisable, as it reduces exposure to swings in the import value of reserves. In this regard the authorities should be forward looking. It is more important to analyze prospective trade patterns than to assume that existing patterns reflecting the legacy of the past will necessarily continue to dominate in the future.[5]

Finally, the domestic acceptance of a currency may also have to be taken into account in the ultimate selection process. Widespread "dollarization" could, for example, be an argument in favour of the US dollar, even in a country whose trade is not predominately with the US or US dollar-denominated. The benefits of choosing the dollar in such a case, however, might well be offset through the variability likely to derive from receipts and expenditures denominated in non-dollar foreign currencies, although it might be possible to hedge such variability, using the US financial markets.

In addition to the designation of the peg currency, the level at which to peg is one of the initial and crucial decisions that need to be taken.[6] The most appreciated level for the exchange rate that would be feasible would be the rate at which the available foreign exchange reserves would be just covering the specified domestic monetary liabilities. To calculate this rate requires a definition of available foreign exchange reserves and of the specified domestic monetary liabilities. Foreign exchange reserves can be specified net or gross, and can include or exclude borrowings from the IMF and other long term debt items.[7] The specified domestic monetary liabilities can comprise reserve money, or domestic liabilities of the central bank. Although this can be defined, at a minimum, to include currency in circulation plus banks' deposits at the central bank, generally other short-term liabilities of the central bank are also included. The appropriate definition of reserves needs to be decided on a case-by-case basis, with the final choice also depending on the liquidity of the liability and whether or not the government or the central bank will ultimately be responsible for servicing it. There is in general a trade-off for the authorities to consider, since on the one hand greater restrictiveness – in the sense that a narrower set of foreign reserves has to cover a broader set of domestic liabilities – should ensure strong discipline on the system and improve the credibility of the system, while on the other hand it would put increased strains on the system and thus instead jeopardize its credibility. It should also be kept in mind that a net reserve concept, while in some ways the most straightforward definition, might, in some cases, require an exchange rate that would involve a large devaluation from the pre-CBA level.

In most modern CBAs, the authorities are likely to see a need for excess coverage, which would imply a somewhat more depreciated rate from the one calculated according to the above criteria. As will be discussed in the later part of this paper, excess coverage could provide some room for future open market operations or a safety margin for banking sector support.[8] In deciding on the issue, the authorities should review whether there are factors in the economy that could lead to the need for significant central bank intervention.

If such factors are present, the approximate magnitude of such intervention, and a safety margin, should be calculated in order to estimate the necessary amount of excess cover, and the level of the exchange rate set roughly to achieve such cover. Finally, taking account of the large psychological component attached to the level of the peg, the authorities should aim to arrive at a "round number" of domestic currency to peg currency – for example, 50 or 100 units of domestic currency for one unit of the peg currency.

III. LEGAL ISSUES

One critical characteristic of a CBA is that the fixed exchange rate is established in law. This means that it will take time to establish the CBA,[9] and will involve bringing parliamentarians – and thus probably the media and the public – into the process. The authorities therefore have to make efforts to explain the purposes of a CBA and to establish a consensus for its introduction.

The authorities will need to identify a team of lawyers to undertake the necessary drafting of the CBA law. The composition of this team will vary from country to country, depending in part upon where the specialized legal skills can best be found. Because of the technical nature of the work, it is likely that the central bank lawyers will play a key role. Lawyers from the Ministry of Justice are also likely to be involved, and they will need to liaise closely with the government and the parliamentary legal experts.

At a minimum, the law needs to specify the fixed exchange rate and that the foreign exchange reserves of the country will be sufficient to cover the domestic liabilities. It will be necessary for the law to define both the reserves and the domestic liabilities that will cover them. Some countries also specify some of the additional constraints on the operation of the CBA in the law, including a prohibition on central bank lending to government, and restrictions on central bank monetary operations. In the final decision on the legal limitations, the authorities should be fully aware of the nature of the trade-off: the more that these additional elements are specified in the law, the more transparent become the operations of the CBA and hence, in some cases, its credibility. On the other hand, excessive legal prescription reduces the ability of the authorities to manage the CBA flexibly, and this may in some circumstances reduce confidence in the sustainability of the arrangement and hence adversely affect its credibility.

There would seem little reason to specify explicitly conditions under which the exchange rate peg can be changed. A CBA is intended to create a fixed arrangement for the foreseeable future; if one specifies an "exit mechanism" at the outset, this may indicate that the authorities are not fully committed to maintaining the arrangement, and may thus undermine credibility in the arrangement.[10] Indeed, the authorities might go in the other direction and tie their hands even more firmly, in the extreme for instance by establishing the CBA law as part of the constitution, or devising some other mechanism that would require a parliamentary super-majority to reverse, to maximize public confidence that the arrangement will be maintained.

In some cases the passage of a CBA law can be taken as an opportunity to review other aspects of the central bank law, for instance to improve the governance of the central bank or to give it greater autonomy. This may help establish the credibility of the CBA at the outset, especially if the CBA is being established as a reaction to past failings of the central bank. On the other hand, broadening the scope of the CBA law may delay the process of establishing the CBA, and may make the possibility of maintaining consensus more difficult.

IV. ORGANIZATION OF A CBA

The primary objective of a CBA is to maintain the foreign exchange cover of the designated domestic liabilities, and to demonstrate frequently that it is doing so. The balance sheet of the central bank – ideally as confirmed by an external audit – must therefore be re-specified so that assets and liabilities of the "currency board" can be separately identified.[11] The authorities have the choice to leave the "currency board" as merely an accounting element within the central bank (such as, for instance, in Argentina); of identifying these assets and liabilities in a separate department within the central bank (such as in Estonia and Bulgaria); or indeed taking the currency board functions out of the central bank into a separate institution. There seem to be advantages in the second of these routes: it maintains the synergies arising from the various central bank functions being conducted within a single institution; and yet it makes clearly visible the functions related to the currency board operations.

If the authorities follow this second route, there needs to be a clear separation of the accounts of the two parts of the central bank, the so-called Issue Department and the Banking Department. The Issue Department would represent the "currency board proper", its main tasks consisting of the management of the country's reserves and issuing domestic currency. The Banking Department would have as its assets the reserves that are in excess of those needed for the full currency board coverage provided by the Issue Department and others as permitted under the CBA law, including possibly domestic paper that can be used for OMOs. Staff should be allocated between the two departments, with service departments – such as administrative and accounting – covering both areas.

The authorities need to decide to what extent the non-core functions of the central bank should be retained within the same institution. Among these, the most important are probably the banking supervision and the fiscal agency functions. Again, the main argument for retention is the synergy of skills and back-room resources; the argument for separation is the need to improve transparency and avoid conflict of interest. One solution is to retain the functions within the central bank, but to establish clear "fire walls" in staffing and accounting between these functions and the core functions of the central bank.[12]

V. BANKING SECTOR REHABILITATION AND SUPERVISION

Reviewing the state of the banking sector, undertaking any necessary rehabilitation measures and strengthening banking supervision have to be crucial ingredients of the move to a CBA. A CBA differs from a standard central bank in that it is generally far more restricted in the extent to which it can provide "lender-of-last resort" support to domestic banks. In fact, the CBA will not have any possibility to lend to banks unless it has accumulated excess coverage, ie a higher level of reserves in the peg currency than that required to cover the specified domestic monetary liabilities. If such excess coverage exists, the CBA can gain credibility by announcing the possibility of limited support to banks in distress, albeit clearly restricted and within well-defined limits.

Given the limitations on the CBA's support to banks, the credibility of the currency board will be higher if, from the outset, the banking system is seen to be sound, with no perception of any looming systemic problems.[13] In addition, interbank markets take on a crucial role for the functioning of the banking system once the possibility of permanent central bank intervention through standing lending and deposit windows has been eliminated. Such markets are likely to function effectively only if the banking system is sound.

Also, while the impetus for interbank trading has to be market driven, it will be important that an adequate legal and institutional framework is put in place prior to the move to a CBA. Examples of supporting measures include a well-functioning payments system and a securities register that allows the effective pledging, transfer of payments for, and ownership of, securities in the secondary market. The process may also be assisted, at least initially when markets can be expected to be relatively thin, by the treasury issuing securities in a range of maturities that are interesting to both primary and secondary market participants.

For countries that have recently undergone severe banking crises, doubts about the soundness of the banking sector are arguably the most difficult obstacle towards making a CBA credible. The problem can best be addressed by the authorities undertaking a broad-based restructuring prior to the start of the CBA. The supervisory authorities will need to assess each bank in the light of established prudential standards, and in the event of non-compliance should agree with the banks' owners and management a timetable for bringing the bank into compliance. In the event that there is no realistic prospect of bringing a bank into compliance in the near future, the authorities should be prepared to resolve the bank's problem, including perhaps through closure. It could be highly damaging to the credibility of a CBA if a banking crisis were to emerge soon after the CBA began.[14] Also vestiges of past crises should be brought to a close – for instance, if a bank closure process is proceeding slowly through the courts, the authorities should make efforts to have the process resolved expeditiously. The soundness of the reformed system should be confirmed by external audits by international firms, and, possibly, by progress towards privatization and international involvement in the sector.

At the end of the banking sector reform process banking supervision should be – and should be perceived to be – strong. A well-designed policy to deal with any further potential problem banks (including possible closures) needs to be in place. This will require that the supervisory authorities have adopted a full set of appropriate prudential regulations, including on capital adequacy, domestic and foreign currency liquidity, loan loss classification and provisioning open foreign exchange positions, insider and large exposure and maturity mismatch limits. Capital adequacy requirements are likely to need to be substantially above the 8 per cent recommended by the Basle Committee for banks in the G10 countries, probably even beyond the 12 per cent discussed for banks in emerging markets generally, in view of the greater riskiness of banking outside the G10 and the need for greater self-reliance in countries with CBAs. Banks should be required to report their positions on the basis of internationally accepted accounting standards.

Once the CBA is established, it will be essential to maintain high-quality supervision staff, with autonomy to undertake supervision on a professional basis, and to enforce fully all prudential requirements.

VI. PUBLIC SECTOR FINANCING ISSUES

A CBA will have important and far-reaching implications for the government's financial operations. Apart from the macroeconomic constraints that rule out any systematic borrowing from the central bank, the CBA in more practical terms also affects both the management of the government's day-to-day liquidity as well as its longer-term debt management

Concerning day-to-day liquidity management, establishment of a CBA requires changes in the usual "banker-client" relationship between the central bank and the government. In most countries, the central bank holds and manages government deposits and often provides some overdraft provisions. However, movements into and out of government deposits are associated with changes in reserve money, so such practices could lead to complications for monetary management under a CBA. For this reason, some currency boards have gone as far as no longer to allow domestic currency government deposits with the central bank and instead pass this function to the market. Other currency boards, for example Bulgaria, have opted to continue to allow government deposits with the central bank.[15] However, for the latter approach to be sustainable, three conditions need to be fulfilled. First, all government deposits will have to be covered by foreign reserve currency holdings, thus avoiding a situation where deposit withdrawals violate the requirement that reserve money be covered by the appropriate amount of the peg currency at all times. Second, government deposits can no longer carry any overdraft provisions, since such provisions would amount to money creation. Third, interest on such deposits can only be paid if the central bank could finance such payments out of its own foreign exchange interest income.[16]

Many central banks are deeply involved in the markets for government debt, often in operations that include the issuance and marketing of treasury bills, as well as the provision of various debt management services to the government.[17] Under a CBA the role of the central bank in this area is curtailed by the fact that it will no longer be able to acquire government paper for its own portfolio, nor to influence monetary conditions through large scale OMOs or primary auction issues.[18] To avoid any potential conflict between debt management and the operations of the CBA, it may be best for the fiscal authorities to take over both debt management and the organization of the primary treasury auctions. Such a separation, if combined with a move of the government's operations account to a commercial bank, would ensure that treasury bill auctions and repayments do not change the outstanding stock of reserve money and, hence, do not affect the CBA. However, where such a clear separation of tasks causes organizational difficulties – for instance, with the transfer of central bank staff to the treasury – an organizational structure in which the CBA undertakes such activities strictly on a "fee for service" basis for the government can be implemented.[19]

VII. DEBT STOCK ISSUES

In simple form, the identify M0=NFA(CB)+NDA(CB) describes the composition of a country's monetary base, where NFA(CB) stands for the central bank's net foreign assets, and NDA(CB) for the central bank's net domestic assets. Under a CBA, foreign assets of the central bank have to at least cover a defined part of the monetary base. In the narrowest definition of a currency board, where NFA(CB) is to cover M0, therefore, net domestic assets (in the form of outstanding stock of credit to the government and to banks) can no longer be held on the books of the central bank.[20, 21]

A number of countries that have established a CBA have had significant stocks of outstanding government debt held by the central bank. A possible solution to the problem, especially where the currency board consists of a separate Issue and Banking Department, is to book these net domestic assets in the Banking Department. The counterpart entry would be the capital of the central bank. Other solutions, where practical, could include the central bank disposing of excess treasury bill holdings in the market, thereby reducing its outstanding monetary liabilities.

While it appears feasible to resolve the issue of an outstanding stock of government debt at the time of change to a CBA, it is not generally consistent with the provisions of a CBA for new debt to be purchased by the central bank. In countries with an IMF programme, a complication – which has occurred in at least two countries – relates to the use of IMF credit. As IMF credit is generally channelled through the central bank, its use by the government – for example for external debt payment – appears impossible as the central bank cannot on-lend the funds in exchange for new NDA.[22] A solution to this problem has to be found on a case-by-case basis. One solution may be for the government, through sales of its securities in the market, to raise the domestic currency counterpart funds for its external debt payments. Alternatively, there may be a renegotiation of the flow payments on the outstanding debt stock, which, in turn, could allow the government to use some of the funds to purchase the necessary foreign exchange. Finally, as in the case of Bulgaria, the on-lending of Fund credit can explicitly be exempted from the rules regarding Government borrowing from the Central Bank.

VIII. FOREIGN EXCHANGE RESERVES MANAGEMENT ISSUES

Under a CBA, the central bank stands ready to exchange unlimited amounts of domestic liabilities for the designated peg currency; it is legally required to have sufficient coverage of foreign exchange reserves, measured in terms of the designated peg currency to meet the designated domestic liabilities. Clearly, these obligations are most easily met by maintaining the country's foreign exchange reserves in the designated peg currency.[23] Conversely, the CBA will be more difficult to operate, the greater the proportion of the coverage of domestic liabilities that is held in assets that have significant fluctuations against the designated peg currency.

This implies that in many countries the desired composition of reserves under a CBA will differ from that existing at the time when the country decides to adopt a CBA. For instance, a country deciding to peg to a European currency may at the outset have a high share of its reserves in dollars. Even more importantly, it may have significant gold holdings in its reserves. The more that a country is constrained by the full coverage requirement (ie the lower the level of excess foreign reserves over the coverage requirement) the more carefully in this regard its reserves will have to be managed.

Immediately after a decision as to the peg currency is made, the central bank should provide an up-to-date listing of the composition of the reserves, as well as the degree to which the reserves are needed to meet the coverage commitment, and the maturity profile of foreign reserves investments as well as any forthcoming foreign exchange liabilities. The central bank may wish to divide the reserves into those needed to provide cover, and the remaining reserves. For the former, it will be important that the major part (say 80 per cent) be in the designated peg currency by the time of the start of the CBA. Assuming that the initial share is lower than this, the foreign exchange department of the central bank should use every opportunity as an investment matures to convert the asset into the designated peg currency. If necessary, the reserve managers should also undertake market sales of assets not in the designated peg currency. In particular, if the country holds sizeable amounts of gold, it may well be appropriate to sell these before the CBA begins.

Especially if a country intends to peg its currency in a CBA to a currency other than the dollar,[24] it will be useful for the central bank to contact its counterpart in the peg currency country at an early stage, and to keep it fully informed. Generally, one would expect that the economy of a country adopting a CBA will be so much smaller than that of the peg currency that there will be no discernible impact on monetary conditions in the peg currency country, but there may be some concerns in this regard which need to be addressed. More positively, the central bank in the peg currency country may be able to give assistance to the CBA central bank in, for instance, the conversion of the latter country's foreign reserves into its currency, and the investing of assets in that currency.

IX. CASH MANAGEMENT ISSUES

An integral element of the establishment of a CBA is the commitment of the central bank to supply unlimited amounts of the designated peg currency against domestic liabilities. Clearly the credibility of the arrangement would be seriously jeopardized if a shortage of banknotes prevented the authorities from being able to honour this commitment. The size of the initial demand for peg currency banknotes is very hard to determine; quite probably, the larger the (visible) supply, the less the amount that will actually be demanded. Indeed, if the launching of the CBA is successful there may well be rapid remonetization leading to excess supply of peg currency by the public seeking to acquire domestic currency and deposits. In this case securing an adequate supply of domestic currency is also of crucial importance.

Concerning the supply of peg currency, the central bank should contract with the central bank of the designated peg currency, or conceivably an alternative source, for the supply of adequate quantities of banknotes by the time that the CBA begins. It should ensure delivery of the currency, and storage in its vaults. It should also make contingent arrangements for immediate acquisition of additional amounts of currency in the event that this is demanded. On the other hand, it should also arrange for the rapid transmittal of peg currency notes abroad, if indeed there are excess receipts, so that the amounts can be invested as quickly as possible.

X. MODALITIES OF THE EXCHANGE WINDOW

The credibility of a CBA is enhanced if it operates an exchange window at the central bank itself, where the public at large can undertake cash exchanges.[25] The operation of this window requires a decision whether or not there should be a trading spread, ie higher exchange rate for buying foreign exchange than for selling the same amount. The arguments for a small spread are straightforward: if the central bank buys local currency at slightly below the par and sells peg currency at slightly above par, it allows private traders to enter (or remain) in the exchange business, by offering an even narrower spread. In addition, insofar as transactions do come to the central bank, it will be able to cover its operating costs and, possibly, gain some profits from the exchange. The establishment of a narrow trading spread is not unusual; it is consistent with the arrangements pertaining in conventional fixed exchange rate systems.

On the other hand, while most central banks do have a trading spread, such an arrangement may, in the case of a CBA, have some costs in terms of credibility as the market exchange rate for customers will differ from the announced peg rate. While largely a psychological issue, the power of a clearly fixed relationship should not be underestimated, especially in cases where the CBA is intended to end a long period of exchange rate instability. Against the psychological advantage of such a system, its economic costs, especially for the private sector, have to be recognized. If the central bank operates an exchange window where it buys and sells foreign exchange without any spread, it will drive many private exchange participants out of this market segment. Since the central bank will generally have, at most, a few branches, and will be open only during core banking hours, there is still likely to be some role for exchange bureaus, since customers can be expected to pay some spread for the convenience of changing through the bureaus. Indeed, it may well be that the central bank becomes supplier for "wholesale" market transitions, and the exchange bureaus suppliers for retail transactions.

To combine the psychological benefits of a peg directly at the peg rate with the benefits of maintaining a spread, an asymmetric peg might be maintained. For example, if a CBA is to be established at the official rate of 100 units of domestic currency (DC) equalling 1 unit of peg currency (PC), the central bank could sell 1 unit of PC at 100 DC but only pay 98 if it buys PC. While the psychological effect of obtaining exactly the official quantity of the designated peg currency in exchange for a given quantity of domestic currency should help confidence, maintaining a spread for the reverse of the transaction means that private traders still would have a sufficient margin for business.[26]

XI. ADDITIONAL MEASURES FOR CREDIBILITY

Mere establishment of a CBA, and even its establishment in law, will not of itself necessarily generate credibility in the arrangement, especially if it is being established at a time of loss of credibility in the earlier arrangements. Credibility should therefore be buttressed by additional measures first to ensure that the arrangements work smoothly and second that they are transparent.

As regards the first, this is achieved by careful attention to the logistics of operating the CBA, as discussed above, for instance through having sufficient volumes of cash on hand at all times. As regards transparency, this can be greatly assisted by a requirement for frequent publication of the accounts of the relevant parts of the central bank; for instance the Bulgarian National Bank has to publish the accounts of its Issue Department on a weekly basis. It can be assisted also by enhancing the independence of the central bank, so that the public has assurances that the operation of the CBA will not be subverted by political forces. Measures to increase central bank independence may therefore well be part of the legal preparations for establishing a CBA, as discussed in section III above.

XII. TIMING AND ANNOUNCEMENT OF THE EXCHANGE RATE LEVEL AND MANAGING THE FOREIGN EXCHANGE MARKET IN THE TRANSITION TO THE CBA

Once the decision to opt for a CBA has been taken, issues of timing and transition will come to the forefront. Regarding timing, the desired macroeconomic benefits of the new system are likely to call for early action. Nevertheless, realism should guide any timetable. Estimates for a feasible time frame should, in particular, take into account the minimum period necessary to change the central bank law and other administrative regulations that have to be in place. Once a schedule has been set out, the announcement of the time frame should be considered binding, given that any delays will cause uncertainty, speculation against the currency, and undermine confidence in the arrangement.

The announcement of the level of the peg will be a second key issue, and one that is likely to generate a great deal of public interest. The public is likely to form a view on the rate that is to be chosen, and the exchange rate – if it is floating at that point, and if the move to a CBA is credible – is likely to move toward this level.

If the public considers that the authorities are seeking a depreciated rate – to allow for additional excess coverage or gains in competitiveness – there is likely to be depreciation toward this level. As such speculation in the run-up to a CBA could be destabilizing and lead to self-fulfilling prophecies, the authorities may opt to announce the exchange rate at an early date.[27] Such an announcement would place constraints on the management of the rate during the period until the CBA was established, but markets would assist in this process by moving the rate toward the announced rate as long as the establishment of the CBA and level of the peg were credible. Hence, an advance announcement should set a rate that could be maintained with a reasonable degree of certainty; a devaluation prior to the introduction of the CBA, while still feasible, might have significant costs in terms of credibility.

XIII. CAPITAL FLOWS AND ARTICLE VIII

A CBA can only work if a sufficient degree of integration in the international economy is assured. Current account convertibility is a necessary ingredient in the international adjustment process, but ideally – for fast interest rate equalization – a country should have full, or at least a high degree of, capital mobility.

Most countries, including some CBA countries, do maintain some forms of capital controls which impede the operation of the well-known interest equalization mechanism.[28] In these cases, if free payments for imports of goods and services are permitted (in more IMF related technical terms, the country accept the obligations of Article VIII, Sections 2, 3 and 4 of the Fund's Articles of Agreement) the adjustment process following a monetary disequilibrium works through a chain of effects involving trade volumes leading to balance of payments surpluses and deficits, which will eventually restore monetary equilibrium, albeit within a time frame dictated by the slower speed of trade flows.

Given that a CBA is usually introduced, among other reasons, to allow countries to benefit from the lower interest rates of the peg country, it obviously works better if the level of capital controls is reasonably low, ie capital is allowed to move relatively unrestricted into and out of the country. In such cases, the initially higher interest rates in a currency board country will rapidly attract foreign (portfolio) investors and deter domestic investors, during the remonetization process, from taking their funds abroad. The increase in available funds, in turn, will put downward pressures on interest rates, thus dampening the net capital inflows.

XIV. TECHNICAL ASSISTANCE

This paper has argued that a wide variety of issues need to be addressed before a country can safely establish a CBA. This is somewhat ironic, since one of the purposes of a CBA may be to create a simple monetary structure that can be operated without requiring great sophistication from the central bank. However, even if the operation of a CBA is relatively simple, it is clear that the authorities may first have to clear up the legacy of monetary, fiscal and financial failings of the past, and this may be rather complicated.

Some central banks may have adequate in-house expertise to address the various identified issues on their own; Argentina is a clear recent example. Also countries starting from a *tabula rasa* should be able to establish a CBA with fewer difficulties.[29] However, the usual preparations for establishing a CBA should not be underestimated, and many countries considering adopting such arrangements may well need to look for outside help to ensure that these preparations are completed properly.[30] Areas in which assistance may be needed include: legal issues, including drafting of the necessary legal texts; banking supervision, including advice on appropriate prudential standards and on monitoring and enforcing compliance with these standards; accounting, including improving the transparency of central bank accounts, and – where relevant – separating the accounts of the Issue Department from the Banking Department; and market management, including the adaptation of the fiscal agency function to the new environment. Such assistance may come from the IMF, but could also be arranged through the World Bank, the regional development banks, or through bilateral assistance. A comprehensive programme of technical assistance, usually involving several sources of support, should generally be an integral part of preparing for the adoption of a CBA.

XV. CONCLUSIONS

Notwithstanding the fact that currency boards are considered simple monetary arrangements, their introduction requires preparatory work on a number of legal and institutional issues. Unless these preparations are made in time and a coherent system is put in place, the credibility of the CBA itself – and with it the entire range of economic benefits desired from the adoption of the arrangement – will be at stake.

Countries that have decided to move to a CBA are therefore well-advised to plan and prepare carefully for its introduction. Given the wide range of issues and institutions involved, this can best be achieved if a committee of all the concerned institutions – including the central bank, Ministry of Finance, and Ministry of Justice – is formed early in the process. Focusing on the various issues discussed in this paper, the committee should develop a task list along with a detailed (possibly even day-by-day) plan towards the fulfilment of these requirements by the target date for the introduction of the CBA. To ensure, and signal, commitment of all parties involved the committee should be chaired by a high level official, in many cases most appropriately the central bank Governor or the Minister of Finance. Given institutional differences across countries, there is not likely to be a single blueprint of an adjustment plan. However all countries planning to introduce a CBA should review the need for preparations in all the various areas outlined in this paper.

References

Baliño, J.T. Tomás and Enoch C. (1997) *Currency Board Arrangements: Issues and Experiences*, IMF Occasional Paper No. 151 (Washington: International Monetary Fund).

Bennett, Adam (1993) "The Operation of the Estonian Currency Board," *Staff Papers*, Washington: International Monetary Fund, Vol. 40, No. 2 (June).

Bennett, Adam (1994) "Currency Boards: Issues and Experiences," *IMF Paper on Policy Assessment* 94/18 (Washington: International Monetary Fund).

Camard, Wayne (1996) "Discretion with Rules? Lessons from the Currency Board Arrangement in Lithuania," *IMF Paper on Policy Analysis and Assessment* 96/1 (Washington: International Monetary Fund).

Williamson, John (1995) "What Role for Currency Boards? Policy Analyses in International Economics" No. 40, Institute for International Economics (September).

Zarazaga, Carlos E. (1995) "Argentina, Mexico, and Currency Boards: Another Case of Rules versus Discretion," Federal Reserve Bank of Dallas, *Economic Review*, Fourth Quarter.

Notes

1. We would like to thank Hugh Bredenkamp, Warren Coats, Alfredo Cuevas, Daniel Dueñas, Vicente Galbis, Daniel Hardy, Alain Ize, Bernard Laurens, George A. Mackenzie, Anne McGuirk, Hassanali Mehran, Elizabeth Milne, Lorenzo Perez, Arne Petersen, Dawn E. Rehm, Christopher Ryan, Veerathai Sanitprabhob, and Vishwapati Trivedi for helpful comments. All errors and omissions remain the responsibility of the authors.
2. See, for instance, Bennett (1994), Williamson (1995) and Baliño and Enoch (1997). The last paper also contains a comprehensive set of references to the currency board literature.
3. In theory a country might wish to peg to a currency basket, such as the SDR. Such an approach, however, would undermine the simplicity and public comprehensibility of the CBA, and might make certain aspects of the operation of the CBA – for example reserve management – more difficult.
4. Some currency boards – mostly for historical reasons – have pegged to currencies of neighbouring countries; eg Brunei is pegged to the Singapore dollar. Most modern currency boards however are pegged to one of the large international reserve currencies.
5. For instance, a country in Central or Eastern Europe with aspirations to integrate into the European Union might expect increasing trade with its European partners over time.
6. We discuss here only the technical issues of choosing the exchange rate. Macroeconomic issues, such as those deriving from the competitiveness of the country, may of course well be critical, but are outside the remit of this paper. While generally macroeconomic and technical factors will both have to be taken into account, in an extreme case – for instance where a country has emerged from hyper-inflation and where its domestic markets are relatively flexible – the authorities may set the exchange rate solely on the basis of the factors discussed here, and then set macroeconomic policy so as to validate that rate.
7. On the issue of the appropriate definition of reserves, see also section VII.
8. Again, there is a trade-off. If the degree of excess cover is insufficient, this may lead to questions as to the robustness of the CBA in the face of likely strains. On the other hand, if coverage is excessive, this may be perceived as permitting the authorities to operate without the necessary degree of discipline.
9. However, the authorities might announce that they are operating as a quasi-CBA during the period until the legal requirements have been put in place.
10. A CBA that specifies an exit strategy would in fact be close to a fixed exchange rate regime; it would be unlikely to benefit from the additional credibility accorded to a policy that eliminates policy discretion in the entire foreseeable future.
11. It will be important that the central bank embark on the process of establishing the balance sheet of the currency board early in the process. Given differences in country's previous central bank functions it is not possible to develop a generic balance sheet; instead the balance sheet will have to reflect a number of case-by-case decisions described elsewhere in this paper.
12. In the final decision on the assignment of auxiliary tasks, the authorities will also have to be mindful about the operating costs of the currency board. Given that the abolition of domestic credit greatly reduces the CBA's income potential, care needs to be taken not to assign it more tasks than can be financed from its income flow.
13. Credibility will also benefit if banks have pre-agreed access to foreign credit lines, as is the case in Argentina (Zarazaga, 1995). It is likely though that, in the case of smaller and less internationally integrated countries, and especially at the outset of a CBA, such arrangements would be expensive and difficult to negotiate.

14. This is particularly the case if the origins of the banking crisis are seen to derive from before the time when the CBA was established. On the other side, if a crisis emerges due to exogenous factors after the establishment of the CBA, and if the CBA is able to handle it successfully, as was the case in Argentina when the "tequila effect" led to withdrawals of 18 per cent of total deposits in 1995, this could even serve to increase the credibility of the CBA.

15. The decision in Bulgaria was mainly motivated by the inability of the commercial banking sector to take over and manage the entire government deposit base in the short run.

16. In practice these interest receipts are usually needed largely to cover administrative expenditures of the CBA, and the decline in seigniorage associated with the lower level of inflation might well put pressure on the central bank's profitability. In such cases, it would be advisable for the CBA to be cautious in setting the rate of interest it pays on government accounts.

17. These services can include organizing auctions, announcing auction results, maintaining the securities register and acting as depository for securities or other collateral.

18. In case of excess coverage, there is room for limited OMOs on the basis of treasury bills. These have been an important feature, in particular, of the operation of the Argentine CBA. Theoretically the CBA could conduct unlimited OMOs based on, ie central bank bills, since this would involve the exchange of one form of its own liability (currency) for another (central bank bill). In practice this would be limited by the amount of interest the CBA is able to offer on such instruments.

19. For example, in Bulgaria, a Fiscal Services Department (FSD) was created within the BNB to take advantage of staff resources as well as existing computer hardware and software. Auction volumes, however, are decided by the Ministry of Finance.

20. As discussed above, in most cases there is some excess coverage. Some countries, most notably Argentina, have also achieved greater coverage by using a relatively broad definition of international reserves. In Argentina, for example, long-term lending by the World Bank would increase coverage. Furthermore, one-third of coverage can be provided by US dollar denominated Argentine Government bonds.

21. Some central banks do hold part or all of a country's long-term external debt on their books. While the definition of net international reserves in this case should probably exclude these liabilities, a CBA might book these liabilities in the banking department, offset by a matching claim on the government. A more transparent solution would be to transfer these claims back to the government.

22. Even in cases where the central bank is not a country's fiscal agent, the central bank is the depository, ie the institution into which the money is being paid.

23. An exception to this rule should apply in cases where the banking system holds a significant share of foreign currency deposits in non-peg currencies. In this case it would be appropriate for the CBA to match these liabilities with an equivalent amount of non-peg currencies in its reserves.

24. For instance, Bosnia-Herzegovina, Bulgaria and Estonia have pegged to the Deutsche mark, and Brunei has pegged to the Singapore dollar.

25. Banks generally would deal with the CBA by exchanging free reserves on their accounts against foreign exchange.

26. An asymmetric spread has been introduced in Bulgaria, where the central bank sells 1 Deutsche mark, for leva 1000, but buys 1 Deutsche mark for leva 995.

27. The central bank could also initially announce a band that would have to be narrowed progressively as the date of the CBA approaches.

28. In these countries interest rates will differ from these in the peg country not only by the country risk premium but also by a wedge accounted for by the capital controls.

29. However, in such cases the level of in-house technical skills may be commensurately low.

30. See Bennett (1993) for details of establishing the CBA in Estonia.

CHAPTER 10

The introduction of the euro

What are the prospects for the greatest monetary experiment in history?

- Introduction
- The benefits and costs of monetary union
- What can we learn from the history of monetary unions?
- What could destroy the greatest monetary experiment in history?
- What is the scorecard on the euro?

INTRODUCTION

On 1 January 1999, the exchange rates of 11 members of the European Union were locked to each other at irrevocably fixed rates. This was a major step towards the establishment of both European Monetary Union (EMU) and of a European Central Bank (ECB). By mid 2002, the 11 domestic currencies will be replaced by one single currency, the euro. It will be circulating in an economic region probably larger than that of any other currency area. 1 January 1999 marked an important transition not only in the history of Europe but also in the history of the global monetary system. The reasoning behind this decision and the attendant risks are the subject of this chapter.

There is a large literature on the benefits and costs of the formation of a monetary union. It is impossible to survey this literature in one chapter. What we intend to do here is to provide the flavour of these benefits and costs, and to survey some of the lessons to be learned from the history of monetary unions. The creation of EMU and the ECB has triggered a discussion of the future of EMU. Many observers have pointed to a number of shortcomings, "flaws" or "faultlines" in the construction and workings of EMU.

These include:

- the absence of a central lender of last resort function for EMU
- the lack of a central authority supervising the financial systems of EMU
- weak democratic control (accountability) of the ECB
- unclear and inconsistent policy directives for the ECB
- the absence of central co-ordination of fiscal policies within EMU (this fact combined with unduly strict criteria for domestic debt and deficits, as set out in the Maastricht rules and the Stability Pact, mean that should the system be faced with asymmetric shocks major problems could occur)
- Euroland is not an "optimal" currency area.

We return to these issues towards the end of this chapter.

THE BENEFITS AND COSTS OF MONETARY UNION

Obstfeld and Rogoff[1] list the four main benefits and four main costs to a pair of currencies from having a common currency. These are listed below.

Benefits of a common currency

1. Reduced transaction costs from currency conversion.
2. Reduced accounting costs and greater predictability of relative prices for firms doing business in both countries.
3. Insulation from monetary disturbances and speculative bubbles that might otherwise lead to temporary unnecessary fluctuations in real exchange rates.
4. Less political pressure for trade protection because of sharp shifts in real exchange rates.

Costs of a common currency

1. Individual regions in a currency union forgo the ability to use monetary policy to respond to region-specific macroeconomic disturbances.
2. Regions in a currency union give up the option to use inflation to reduce the real burden of public debt.
3. Political and strategic problems arise in determining how member countries split seigniorage revenues.
4. Avoiding speculative attacks in the transition from individual currencies to a common currency can be a major problem.

McCallum[2] adds a fifth benefit to the four listed, as follows: the existence of a common currency tends to bring a greater degree of integration to financial and non-financial markets in the two countries.

Insulation from monetary disturbances refers to the benefits gained by eliminating both competitive devaluations and speculative attacks.

Preventing competitive devaluations

Between World Wars I and II, European countries engaged in what are known as competitive devaluations: one country would devalue its currency to boost its export sector, and its trading partners would retaliate by devaluing their currencies at the same time. Reducing the value of currency is inflationary, so competitive devaluations caused an inflationary spiral during that period.

As trade between European countries has increased, the costs to one's trading partners from using a competitive devaluation have increased, but so have the potential gains to any one country. However, the effect on competitive devaluation's on the world's economic welfare is clearly negative, and it can be disastrous if retaliation leads to a devaluation spiral. A single currency eliminates the threat of this type of competition.

Preventing speculative attacks

Although a government can try to thwart speculators by raising interest rates and thereby the return to holding money-market instruments denominated in that currency, there is a downside to doing so. Higher interest rates mean that the business firms face higher borrowing costs, so they will do less borrowing and investing in new plant and equipment, which, in turn, will lead to slower economic growth.

The European exchange rate crisis of 1992 illustrates the effect of speculative attacks on the economy. Europe at that time had been in a deep recession for two full years; the average European unemployment rate was approximately 10 per cent. Short-term political pressures in the countries most badly hit by the recession was a good reason for a low interest rate policy in order to stimulate investment and bring about recovery. But such a policy would be inconsistent with maintaining stable exchange rates unless the policy were pursued across all of Europe. If only one country were to lower its interest rates, financial capital would move out of that country to the ones that still had high rates, given the degree of capital mobility in Europe. This movement of capital would put pressure on exchange rates.

In September 1992 speculators began to borrow British pounds, French francs, and Italian lira and to convert the proceeds into Deutsche marks because they expected the price of pounds, francs and lira to fall after the Governments abandoned their commitment to keep interest rates as high as necessary to maintain a stable exchange rate. As more and more speculators sold these currencies, their value in terms of Deutsche marks continued to fall. In an attempt to attract buyers to their currencies, the British, French and Italian Governments offered very high rates of return on short-term instruments denominated in their home currencies. A side effect of this policy was a deepened recession in those countries, which made adherence to fixed exchange rates increasingly unpopular. That unpopularity, in turn, increased speculation that the policy of fixed exchange rates would not be sustainable. Of the three, only France was able successfully to ward off the speculative attack. Both Britain and Italy abandoned their fixed exchange rates as a result of the speculative pressures.

Since much of the speculative activity within Europe has occurred when speculators have bet that one European currency, would be devalued relative to another, moving to a single currency, it is argued, would eliminate such activity. And again, it is argued, since investors will not have to be compensated for uncertainty about exchange rates, interest rates will fall, thereby stimulating investment and growth within the EMU.

Costs of a single currency

The benefits of switching to a single currency do not come without costs. Probably the biggest cost is that each country cedes its right to set monetary policy to respond to domestic economic problems. In addition, exchange rates between countries can no longer adjust in response to regional problems.

The costs of a single currency and the fault lines which the introduction of the euro involves are discussed in greater detail below.

WHAT CAN WE LEARN FROM THE HISTORY OF MONETARY UNIONS?

> Losing one percentage point of competitiveness a year, if it goes on in time for a number of years, would become a condemnation for Italy and it would be difficult for us to stay in the single currency.

This is a quotation taken from a speech given by Romano Prodi, president-designate of the European Commission, speaking about Italy's ability to remain within the unified currency regime in June 1999. The quotation highlights that the creation of the euro could just as easily be followed by the replacement of the euro!

As discussed earlier, this monetary experiment is not without risks. The decision to introduce the euro contains within it the seeds of a troubled later life. This section describes these seeds, individually manageable, but which maturing together could herald a financial market breakdown the extent of which the world has never seen. Remember that, under the 1992 Maastricht Treaty, monetary union was intended to be an irreversible and irrevocable process and that no mechanism exists in the Treaty to allow a participating Member State to withdraw. Faultlines range from problems associated with the lack of political union within the EU to the ultimate empirical and intellectual discrediting of the whole idea in turn leading to a mutual agreement to dissolve the system. First, it is useful to ask if there are any lessons from history regarding the success or otherwise of monetary unions?

What can we learn from the history of monetary unions?

In the past, many monetary unions have come and gone. Are there any lessons that we can draw from history? The problem with drawing lessons is that EMU is, as Bordo and Jonung comment, "unique in the history of monetary unions".[3] In their work they did not find any clear and unambiguous historical precedence to EMU, a situation where a group of monetary and politically independent countries surrendered their national currencies to form a common monetary union based on a new unit of account under the leadership of a common monetary authority while still retaining political independence. Monetary unification has historically followed political unification – not the other way around.

Table 10.1 lists some of the monetary unions which existed in the 19th century. Bordo and Jonung show that the monetary unification of the US was not finalized until long after its political unification. The US did not establish a central bank with lender of last resort facilities until long after monetary unification. Similarly the formation of the Italian and German monetary unions took place after political unification. The Latin Monetary Union and the Scandinavian Monetary Union broke up under the strain of World War I.

Table 10.1 ● The creation of monetary unions in the 19th century

Monetary area	Time of creation
National monetary unions:	
US	1789–92
Italy	1861
Germany	1875
Multinational monetary unions:	
The Latin monetary union	1865
The Scandinavian monetary union	1873–75

Source: Bordo & Jonung[4]

In analyzing past monetary unions, Bordo and Jonung distinguish between national monetary unions and multinational monetary unions.

● *National monetary unions* are those where political and monetary go hand in hand – the borders of the nation-state are the borders of the monetary area (eg the US).

● *Multinational monetary union* is an international monetary co-operation between a number of independent countries based on permanently fixed exchange rates between their currencies.

Turning to the 20th century monetary unions, Bordo and Jonung stress that the common cause of the break up of monetary unions is found in the political process, not because of monetary or economic forces. See Table 10.2.

The typical collapse has followed two paths. The first path is accompanied by fiscal and monetary turmoil and high inflation in some or all of the new monetary areas. This was the cause of the dissolution of three European empires in the 20th century, Austria-Hungary, Russia and the Soviet Union, as well as the dissolution of Yugoslavia. The second path is a more peaceful and orderly one. The dissolution of the monetary union of Czechoslovakia was an orderly affair, not accompanied by huge fiscal deficits and high inflation.

Table 10.2 ● The dissolution of some monetary unions in the 20th century

Monetary Union	Time of dissolution	Causes of dissolution
National monetary unions		
Austria	1919–27	Defeat at war, creation of several new nation states.
Russia	1918–20	Creation of several new nation states.
Soviet Union	1992–4	Political unrest, creation of several new nation states.
Yugoslavia	1991–4	Political unrest, civil war, rise of new states.
Czechoslovakia	1993	Political divergences, rise of new nation states.

Source: Bordo & Jonung[5]

Bordo and Junong conclude that the break-up of monetary unions and their transformation into new smaller monetary areas has been caused by political forces, most of the causes being due to war with outside enemies or to civil war. When far-reaching political events cause the break-up of existing nation states, monetary separation and divorce follows as a corollary in almost all the cases they studied. We return to these ideas below.

Survival depends on political union

Monetary unions of large sovereign nations which do not have political union eventually fail, sometimes after a long time. For a detailed description of the evolution of monetary unions, see Perlman.[6]

Monetary unions can be divided into four categories as shown in Box 1.

The first category is where political union has ensured the monetary union's success. Many examples fit this category. A recent example is German unification. Longer lasting is last century's Italian monetary union, which followed political unification in 1861. The example many have suggested EMU may try and emulate is the US Federal Reserve, established in 1913 as a decentralized system. The setting of twin policy mandates for the Federal Open Market Committee, as well as accountability to Congress, have ensured a credible yet flexible monetary policy. This has been supported by flexibility in the labour market and in fiscal policy, helping to create the conditions for employment growth that Europe has, so far, been unable to match.

Second, monetary unions of small countries can survive without political union, provided there has been economic convergence. The best example of this was the 1944 Belgian–Luxembourg Economic Union which resulted in a *de facto* monetary union. In actual practice, Belgian money circulates in Luxembourg, but Luxembourg money does not circulate in Belgium. A joint agency manages exchange regulations, but the Belgians were effectively free as to their monetary policy. Luxembourg has had to adjust its monetary policy to Belgium. The monetary union succeeded only because there was a dominant country which could prevent the other country from pursuing a monetary policy which would be incompatible with its own.

The third category is where the survival of the monetary union is dependent on the political system. Once the political system binding it together collapses the monetary union fails. One example is the recent collapse of the Soviet system, another is the failure of the 19th century German monetary union. This was one of three monetary unions which co-existed across Europe a century ago, the other two without political union.

There is a common perception that political union preceded German monetary union in the 19th century. Yet, many elements of monetary union were in place following the creation of the Zollverein in 1834, which removed all internal tariffs and created a single market prior to German political union in 1871. Then followed the formation of the Reichsbank in 1871 and the introduction of the mark in 1876. The collapse came at the end of World War I.

The fourth category is a temporary monetary union that survives for a long time without political union but eventually collapses. The Latin and Scandinavian monetary unions in the 19th century are examples.

The Latin monetary union was formed in 1865 between France and the closely linked economies of Belgium, Italy and Switzerland. Greece joined in 1868. It was a bimetallic union, initially based on silver and then on gold. The precious metal standard, common in old unions, reflected a commitment to fiscal conservatism and small balanced budgets. The union ran alongside Germany's monetary union until World War I.

BOX

1

- **Still surviving but with political union**

British monetary union between England and Scotland	From 1707
Italian monetary union	From 1861
US Federal Reserve System	From 1913
German unification	From 1990

- **Still surviving without political union**

Belgium-Luxembourg union	From 1948
West African CFA franc zone	From 1948

- **Failed once political system collapsed**

German monetary union	1851–WW1
The Soviet system	1917–1993

- **Temporary monetary unions**

Latin monetary union	1865–WW1
Scandinavian currency union	1873–1920

Denmark and Sweden almost joined the Latin monetary union but did not, because of the Franco-Prussian War. Instead, they formed the Scandinavian currency union, which Norway joined in 1875. This was the most stable of all the unions benefiting from economic and political stability and common policy objectives. The suspension of the gold standard at the outbreak of World War I led to volatility in real exchange rates and provided the trigger for the gradual collapse of the Union in 1920.

The lesson is that monetary unions of politically independent, large sovereign nations can fail, particularly when there is an external shock, causing the economic environment to change. It is easier for unions to survive when the economic cycle is favourable. The long time period during which both the Latin and Scandinavian unions survived demonstrates the importance to withhold judgment on the success of a union, until its performance can be judged in an economic downswing or when there is a deflationary shock.

For a monetary union to succeed over a long period, it is necessary for simultaneous political union. The reasoning for this needs to be explained. As Congdon[7] has shown, the explanation is to be sought in the need for someone to be accountable for inflation. When there is one government, one central bank and one money, it is obvious where the responsibility for inflation lies. In the final analysis, it rests with the government of the country concerned.

By contrast, consider the situation under European monetary union where there are several governments and a system of separate national central banks that are subordinate to a Frankfurt-based European Central Bank. Who is to blame for inflation? Is it any one government? Is it all of the governments taken together? Or is it only the European Central Bank's fault?

The single currency project creates the so-called "free-rider" problems, where governments and nations can act irresponsibly and put the blame elsewhere. One free-rider problem is that the larger the budget deficit that any one government runs, the higher the proportion of Europe's resources that this nation can capture for the benefit of its own citizens without paying for them by taxation. But the larger the budget deficits are, the higher the risk of inflation. The Maastricht Treaty has tried to anticipate this danger by spelling out limits on budget deficits and the size of public debt, but governments can, and will, cheat.

In fact, in the run-up to the agreement on membership of the single currency area, virtually all European governments tampered with the definitions of public spending and deficits in order to comply, at least nominally, with their treaty obligations. If they had not fudged the numbers, only one – tiny Luxembourg – would have been eligible.

The second free-rider problem is more complex. Every government has an incentive to borrow at short maturities, where interest costs are traditionally lower. But the likelihood of bank financing of budget deficits, and so of higher money-supply growth increases the more the public debt is short-dated. In the post-war period the German Government has deliberately avoided issuing short-dated paper, because of the lessons learned during its appalling experiences of hyperinflation twice in the 20th century.

But with European monetary union, every government will try to borrow at short maturities and from the banking system. There is nothing in the Maastricht Treaty to prevent them doing so. If governments do borrow at the short end from the banking system, money supply growth and inflation will accelerate.

The conflicts could be resolved if the European Central Bank were fully accountable to a single parliament and if there were one government which had to take the exclusive blame for inflation.

As the passage of events unfolds, Congdon suggests, it will become clear that without political union, the single currency project will collapse.

WHAT COULD DESTROY THE GREATEST MONETARY EXPERIMENT IN HISTORY?

Euroland is not an optimal currency area

Economists have long debated the conditions required if an area is to enjoy the advantages of a single currency without suffering unacceptable costs as a result of the loss of monetary autonomy for each constituent country within the area. It is generally agreed that the necessary conditions for an optimal currency zone go well beyond the narrow shopping-list of convergence criteria included in the Maastricht Treaty. The Treaty focuses principally on the one-time convergence of key variables and not on the sustainability of that convergence into the future. Economies that have converged can, of course, diverge once more, and it is for this reason that many economists insist on the importance, in a prospective single currency area, of removing the structural causes of such sustained divergence in future, and on the need to put in place the non-monetary adjustment mechanisms required to resolve such divergences when they do occur. It is argued that, before it can be appropriate for an area to have one exchange-rate and a single monetary policy, the area should have well-developed alternative means, discussed below, of internal adjustment to enable it to cope either with asymmetric shocks or with any particular region becoming uncompetitive.

The internal adjustment mechanisms usually deemed necessary for a successful currency area, known as an optimal currency area, were set out in a famous paper by Mundell in 1961.[8] They can be put under the following headings:

● capital mobility and diversified asset holdings by residents

● fiscal flexibility within regions or transfers between them

● labour mobility and/or wage flexibility.

The US possesses all three of the broad categories of internal adjustment mechanism required of an optimal currency area. So, for example, if a situation is imagined in which Texas is suffering a negative shock as a result of a sharp drop in the oil price while at the same time California and other states are booming, a number of different mechanisms would cushion the negative impact of the asymmetric shock on the citizens of Texas and make it likely that the divergence of the Texan economy from that of other US states would be limited in extent and duration. The mechanism for this adjustment would take place via three systems of adjustment.

1. Many Texan residents own both directly and indirectly (through pension funds) very significant assets (especially municipal bonds and equities) in other states. This diversification of their asset holdings ensures that the savings and accumulated wealth of Texans are not entirely or even largely geared to the local economy. As a result Texans could offset, to some extent at least, any shortfall in their income resulting from an asymmetric shock by drawing on their diversified asset base.

2. Given the strong US tradition of labour mobility, many Texans would, if necessary, be willing to move to other states in search of a job. Furthermore, in a liberalized labour market, those who are not mobile would usually be willing to accept cuts in nominal wages to protect their jobs. Once wages have dropped, Texas might start to attract more capital investment.

3. The third important adjustment mechanism would be the US federal tax system which serves to redistribute income and thus to soften and spread the negative impact of any asymmetric shocks.

As a result of the efficient operation of these three adjustment mechanisms it is relatively unlikely that an asymmetric shock caused say by a sharp drop in the price of oil would lead Texans to complain that the US dollar and the monetary policy of the Federal Reserve were responsible for their woes, or even that they were an impediment to their recovery.

It is quickly apparent that the position in the EU after monetary union is significantly different. Most residents of the EU countries participating in EMU do not have significant equity assets outside their own economy. Labour mobility across borders is much less pronounced in Europe than it is across state boundaries in the US, not least because of greater language barriers. In the US, 17 per cent of the labour force relocate each year, 25 per cent of which move as far as to another state. In the EU, only 2 per cent of the population even live outside their country of birth. At the same time, labour rigidities, in particular the high cost in many European countries of making people redundant, tend to mean that the pressure for nominal wages to decline during recessions is lower than in the US, making it less easy for Continental European companies to cope with asymmetric shocks and making them less keen to take on labour even when a recovery starts.

On the fiscal side, the contrast is even starker. Whereas the US federal tax system provides a substantial degree of insurance against the negative income effects of asymmetric shocks, the EU has no equivalent system of federal fiscal transfers. The EU budget at $100 billion, 1.2 per cent of GDP is tiny by comparison with that of the US federal government. Recent estimates indicate that 1997 total spending in the US reached 22 per cent of GDP. (See Dwyer and Hafer for a discussion of recent trends in US fiscal policy.[9]) In addition, EU spending is used to subsidize agriculture, finance infrastructure projects and help very poor regions on a long-term basis, rather than being used as a method of stabilizing swings in income resulting from asymmetric shocks.

Individual EU countries could, of course, use their own national budgets as a means of delivering short-term stabilization against demand shocks, but the scope for doing this is severely limited by the Stability and Growth Pact, (described in Box 3 on page 236). This agreement provides for a system of fines for any breach of a 3 per cent ceiling on budget deficits, with automatic exemption only granted in the case of natural disaster or a severe recession involving a decline in GDP of more than 2 per cent over a year. The pact is intended to enforce collective restraint on the fiscal front and to prevent a few countries from free riding on the fiscal prudence of others and imposing monetary externalities on their neighbours by running excessive deficits.

Credibility of the European Central Bank

With effect from 1 January 1999 the European System of Central Banks (ESCB) sets interest rates for the whole euro area. The ESCB is made up of the European Central Bank (ECB) and national central banks in the EMU area. The main aim is to maintain price stability. The proceedings of the meetings of the Governing Council are confidential and there is invariably concern that this lack of transparency will make monetary policy changes more disruptive than need be. This confidentiality comes on top of that already covering European Council meetings. Legislation in secret appears to be inbuilt into EU institutions.

The ECB is not allowed to take instructions from community institutions or bodies, any government or from any other body. This was formally established in the Maastricht Treaty. See Box 2. Its accountability to the European Parliament is limited. The members of the Executive Board are on eight-year non-renewable contracts while the national central bank governors come from independent central banks and are on minimum five-year contracts.

BOX

2

The Maastricht Treaty (1992)

"Neither the ECB nor a central bank shall seek or take instruction from community institutions, bodies or from any government of a Member State."

"The Community institutions and bodies and the governments of the Member States undertake not to seek to influence the members of the decision-making bodies of the ECB or of the national central banks."

The rationale for an independent central bank has always been that it will be less subject to short-term political pressures to try to expand output and employment (say before an election) and will be more committed to maintaining a low inflation rate. Because the public will recognize that an independent central bank is less subject to political pressures, it is argued, announcements made by the central bank should be more credible. Considerable evidence has been marshalled to support the idea that independent central banks are more credible. The most well-known study is by Alesina and Summers.[10] Their study, for the period 1955–88, showed that countries with relatively independent central banks, such as Germany, Switzerland and the US, clearly have lower long run inflation rates than countries without independent central banks, such as the UK, New Zealand, Italy and Spain. They also showed that countries with independent central banks do not have higher long run rates of unemployment. Their evidence supports the idea that increased central bank independence raises credibility and thus lowers the unemployment cost of keeping inflation low.

This mixture of the theory and the evidence has been very influential in the design and operational role of the ECB. However, recent work by Posen[11] and Forder[12] have challenged what had become the academic consensus on central bank independence. They draw attention to two problems. First, that the supposed correlation between central bank independence and low inflation is questionable. Second, even if the correlation turns out to be correct the theory about credibility, they argue, cannot be the reason why.

With regard to the facts, Forder has drawn attention to defects in the litera-ture on the correlation between central bank independence and low inflation. He shows that the definition of independence fluctuates from paper to paper, generally in ways that bolsters the supposed correlation, and when he reworks the data, the correlation disappears altogether.

What then of the underlying rationale? Forder claims that the orthodox story which says that (a) independence increases credibility and (b) credibility reduces the cost of getting inflation down is wrong. To begin with, independence does not seem to increase credibility. If it did, you would expect to see greater rigidity in the setting of nominal wages – reflecting the fact that the banks promise to keep inflation low had been believed. According to research by Posen using data from 17 OECD countries from 1950–89 you do not find this. Moreover, turning from (a) by itself to (a) and (b) taken together, independence not merely fails to reduce the cost of disinflation, it actually seems to increase it. On average, getting inflation down takes as long as and calls for a bigger "sacrifice" of output and jobs in countries with relatively independent central banks.

Apart from the issue concerning the desirability of central bank independence, other problems with the ECB exist. Under EMU, with 11 Member States (Germany, France, Italy, Spain, Austria, Belgium, Finland, Ireland, Luxembourg, Netherlands and Portugal) the Governing Council consists of 17 members. Decision making with such a large committee is difficult, given that committees often try and reach compromise solutions on difficult issues even when decisions are based on a simple majority. Given the potential difficulty in arriving at consensus solutions, there could be considerable inertia in agreeing policy changes. The risk is, therefore, that the ECB Governing Council will tend to be "behind the curve", keeping policy too tight for too long and too loose for too long.

Most countries are relying on the ECB to inherit the credibility of the Bundesbank. But Germany has only one vote on the ECB executive and even less influence on the ECB governing council. Council members are expected to put the interests of the collective economy above that of their own country, but they will hardly ignore what is best for their homeland. Hence, it is argued, there will be a dilution of the strict doctrine of monetary stability. Even if there isn't, it may prove impossible for the ECB to cap the fiscal and public-borrowing discipline of 11 sovereign governments.

A related concern is what prudential functions, if any, the ESCB and within it the ECB and national central banks should perform. The normal prudential functions of a central bank revolve around its "lender of last resort facility" designed to stabilize the banking system should the failure of one bank raise the fear of systemic risk bringing down the whole banking system.

The Maastricht Treaty states that "the ESCB will contribute to the smooth conduct of policies pursued by the competent authorities relating to the prudential supervision of credit institutions and the stability of the financial system". The treaty enables the ECB "to offer advice to and be consulted by the Council, the Commission, and the competent authorities of the Member States on (all relevant legislation)". The ECB can, however, only go beyond a consultative role, to assume a prudential function of its own, after the lengthy procedure outlined in the Treaty, whereby "the Council may, acting unanimously on a proposal from the Commission and after consulting the ECB and after receiving the assent of the European Parliament, confer upon the ECB specific tasks concerning policies relating to the prudential supervision of credit institutions". The absence of clear prudential functions must raise questions over the stability of the banking and financial system under EMU. This is of particular concern given the existence of asset price bubbles in some of the peripheral countries in the early years of EMU as interest rates fell to unprecedently low levels.

Speculative currency attacks: legacy risk exposure

Now that the euro has come into existence the financial markets are faced with a new risk, one of which they have no prior experience and for which the ramifications are enormous. This risk, known as legacy risk exposure, is the possibility and consequent implications of the withdrawal of a Member State from the fixed euro parity. This is quite different from the withdrawal of a Member State from the European Monetary System where individual currencies still existed, albeit nominally pegged to each other.

Individual members of EMU are democracies. Voting into power a party which proposes to lead that country out of EMU may be extraordinarily reckless and dangerous but there is no doubt that, while member countries remain independent democracies, it could happen.

One line of reasoning, for this, of which there could be many others, starts with an examination of unemployment within Europe, at the beginning of year 2000. France has 12.5 per cent unemployment, Spain has 20.8 per cent and Germany has 11.8 per cent. Suppose that by March 2002 France's unemployment rate has risen to over 17 per cent – concentrated particularly among the young and unskilled. This is despite relatively benign economic conditions such as low inflation, low euro interest rates, and exchange rate stability against neighbouring countries. Employers, finding capital cheap and labour expensive substitute one for the other.

The National Front, always an embarrassment through its large natural constituency, let us assume, makes unemployment the keystone of its policy. Its strategy let us say is to leave EMU, reintroduce and devalue the New Franc, which will replace the euro, by at least 20 per cent, impose capital and exchange controls, impose additional tax burdens on non-French companies and individuals in France, and use tax revenues in extensive unemployment reduction schemes.

Assume the National Front is not elected to an absolute majority in the French Parliament. However, no alternative party can survive in government without its support. The National Front imposes EMU exit as a condition of participation in government, and the alternative party accepts.

The withdrawal of a Member State would not, as shown by Record[13] be like an ERM break-up because of two critical differences – banking sector balance sheets and notes and coins. These are not the esoteric points that they may at first seem. Banks operating in EMU countries are required by EU law to treat all euros as the same, and no exchange rate risk is allowed to be admitted between any two euro-denominated balance sheet items.

Banks cannot in any case sensibly determine the domicile of many of their assets and liabilities, so this is practical advice. Say a bank lends money to a pan-European multinational in euros. Where is the debt? Assume a bank takes euro deposits from a US multinational with worldwide interests across its European branches. Where is the deposit? The implication of this is that one country's exit would severely damage, and possibly destroy, the balance sheets of all Europe's major banks. How would this happen?

To appreciate the implications of a potential EMU break up let us assume that the balance sheet of a hypothetical French multinational bank, ParisLyonnais, prior to EMU exit can be represented by Table 10.3. The balance sheet, in this example, reflects a healthy bank.

Table 10.3 ● ParisLyonnais balance sheet prior to EMU exit

Balance sheet denominated in euros

Assets	Loans and advances to customers	60	
	Debt securities	20	
	Loans and advances to banks	15	
	Cash at Central Bank	1	
	Other (property, equities)	4	100
Liabilities	Customer accounts	75	
	Deposits from banks	11	
	Debt securities in issue	5	
	Subordinated liabilities	2	93
Shareholders funds			7

Imagine, say, the looming prospects of France's exit from EMU. As the National Front gain poll support, the financial markets will start worrying. Companies, investors, banks and individuals will all begin to take action to protect what they see as a certainty that, if France exits, a new devalued franc will be introduced. They examine all their euro assets, and judge whether they will remain as euros or get redenominated into New Francs. They will conclude that having deposits (bank liabilities) redenominated in devalued New Francs is unacceptable while having loans (bank assets) redenominated in devalued New Francs is very acceptable.

Most likely, they will judge that having French-issued euro assets relating to bank deposits on French soil is a bad idea. Euro deposits are then withdrawn from France and redeposited in London, Frankfurt or New York, with non-French banks. French corporate and Government Bonds are sold off and replaced with German-issued (or UK, Dutch, etc) bonds. This begins to drive the price of French Bonds down, pushing up market "French" interest rates, and pushing down "German" rates. Bond yields already differ in Euroland largely because of different political risks. But now they start to reflect currency risk, as they did prior to the arrival of the euro. Interest rates in Euroland are now providing information to the markets that the system is under strain.

Inside France, there will be a mix of euro-denominated assets and liabilities, some of which are definitely "French" (French government bonds held by French residents in France), some of which are borderline (multinational euro corporate debt held by French banks), and some are almost certainly non-French (notes and coins – which are a liability of the ECB and which are bearer instruments and so do not have a domicile). The interest rate differential will apply to those instruments deemed most "French", therefore most liable for redenomination.

But there are almost certainly categories of securities whose risk of redenomination can be reduced or eliminated by being moved – either physically or by a change of owner's domicile. This will create a plethora of arbitrage opportunities with bizarre effects. French residents will take all their money out of bank and savings accounts, and put them into euro accounts abroad, possibly in non-French nominee names. They will hoard large quantities of euro notes for their everyday use – much more secure than French bank accounts. They will borrow as much as they can in France, and re-deposit the money offshore. The classic hedging technique of having liabilities denominated in weak currencies and assets denominated in strong currencies will be universally applied.

There will be a credit explosion in the EMU banking sector as French residents and non-residents alike round trip German assets and French liabilities. As the trade turns into a run, and then into a frenzied panic, it will become clear that the banking system will collapse (ie French banks will run out of liquidity) unless action is taken immediately. That action must be an immediate EMU exit – nothing else will halt the flows. It is assumed that, at this point, France exits the euro.

To see the implications of this and to make the arithmetic simple let us assume in Euroland that half of all the balance sheet items of ParisLyonnais are held at branches outside France or by non-French residents. The point about foreign jurisdictions is to ask what happens to the value of ParisLyonnais's assets and liabilities either owed to or from these non-French residents. ParisLyonnais will be forced by the French Government to re-denominate all its assets and liabilities into "New francs". After all, what would be the point of exit otherwise.

Assume a New Franc 20 per cent devaluation from the official conversion rate. ParisLyonnais customers with borrowings in foreign jurisdictions will not complain if they suddenly owe 20 per cent less expressed in euros because their debt has been redenominated. In fact they will demand it. They will argue that they cannot legally be discriminated against purely because of their residence. So in Table 10.4 the assets fall to 80 even though only 50 per cent are owed either outside France or to non-French borrowers. But every individual and bank in a foreign jurisdiction will rightly complain if their euro-denominated asset, deposited with ParisLyonnais is unilaterally redenominated, and consequently worth 20 per cent less. The effect of the devaluation would be to lower the liabilities of ParisLyonnais to 83.7. (I suggest readers should do the arithmetic here if they want to best understand the logic.) It must be said that other European governments will oppose this too, as they will fear that contagion and systemic risk will ensue.

The next morning it will be seen that at the discount that the New Franc is trading at, the assets of ParisLyonnais and other French banks are now worth less than their now non-matching liabilities. See Table 10.4.

Table 10.4 ● ParisLyonnais balance sheet after EMU exit

Denominated in euros (20 per cent devaluation)

Assets	Loans and advances to customers	48	
	Debt securities	16	
	Loans and advances to banks	12	
	Cash at Central Bank	0.8	
	Other (property, equities)	3.2	80
Liabilities	Customer accounts	67.5	
	Deposits from banks	9.9	
	Debt securities in issue	4.5	
	Subordinated liabilities	1.8	83.7
Shareholders funds			(3.7)

With liabilities greater than its assets, the entire French banking sector is insolvent unless redenomination can apply to foreign jurisdictions. In other words, if the banking sectors liabilities can also be reduced by the full 20 per cent. The ECB and the BIS tell France that if redenomination applies to non-French jurisdictions, it will trigger a worldwide banking collapse. The French Government does not agree that it should pick up the full cost of banking sector rescue, and refuses to act as lender of last resort to its own banks. They promptly default, triggering a worldwide banking crisis of previously unseen proportions.

Mass unemployment and Europe-wide recession

Economists consider widespread unemployment and recession to be the most plausible threat to EMU. Certainly lack of synchronicity between the various countries' economic cycles has lead to severe economic and political strain in the first year. The principle that "one interest rate size fits all" is unlikely to be the optimal monetary policy if unemployment in Germany is larger than the total population of Ireland, for example.

Asymmetric shocks to one or more country

The whole future of the euro could be threatened if individual governments pursued expansionary fiscal policies. In an endeavour to prevent this, member governments signed the Stability and Growth Pact in June 1996 at the Amsterdam summit. The Stability and Growth Pact is summarized in Box 3.

This allows a country faced with an annual fall of 2 per cent or more in GDP (less under special circumstance accepted by the EU council of finance ministers) to ease up on the Maastricht criteria and spend itself out of recession. A big enough deflationary shock, however, could put a country beyond the pale, or make it politically impossible to continue membership of EMU.

BOX

3   Stability and Growth Pact

The Stability and Growth Pact seeks to enforce fiscal discipline in EMU by strengthening and clarifying the excessive deficit procedure of the Maastricht Treaty and by building in sanctions to penalize countries found to have excessive deficits. Generally a budget deficit in excess of 3 per cent will lead to sanctions. A budget deficit in excess of 3 per cent of GDP will be only considered exceptional and temporary if it results from an unusual event outside the control of the Member State in question or from a severe economic downturn, provided also that the unusual event or severe downturn have passed, or that EU Commission projections for the following year show the deficit falling back to 3 per cent or less.

A decline in GDP of 2 per cent in the year in question would, as a rule, be regarded as a severe downturn. Countries have agreed not to claim exceptional circumstances for annual output declines of less than 0.75 per cent. However, the Stability and Growth Pact has opened a window of discretion for output declines between 0.75 per cent and 2 per cent. Inside this range, two additional criteria are mentioned explicitly: the "abruptness of the downturn" and the "cumulated output loss relative to past trends". The sanctions would compromise a fixed element equal to 0.2 per cent of GDP plus a variable element equal to the difference between the deficit ratio and the 3 per cent reference value with a ceiling value of 0.5 per cent of GDP. To begin with, the sanctions would take the form of a non-interest rate deposit. The deposit would be returned if the excessive deficit was corrected within two years, otherwise it would become a fine.

Expulsion of a delinquent country

The EU is somewhat reluctant to envisage potential expulsions, except to refuse to deny the possibility. There is no proposal under the Growth and Stability Pact to expel a delinquent country. But fines levied from bad countries and given to the good are like stealing from the poor and giving to the rich. A delinquent country seeing a large percentage of its GDP (0.2 per cent plus a tenth of its deficit excess) going to countries that meet the criteria such as the Netherlands and Luxembourg is unlikely to tolerate this for long. It will "dig in its heels". It will dare the powers in Frankfurt and Brussels to do something. Either they will relent and bail the country out, which is forbidden under the Treaty, or the naughty country will be expelled.

Voluntary exit by a country

A country anticipating being expelled from EMU will make up its mind to leave anyway. Or, despite meeting the Maastricht criteria, it will decide it is unsuited to EMU, or that EMU is a mistake, and leave.

Mutual agreement to dissolve EMU

This would occur if EMU is proved to have been empirically and intellectually to the satisfaction of whatever French and German Government is in power, that EMU was an experiment which failed, and which brought more misery than it did prosperity.

WHAT IS THE SCORECARD ON THE EURO?

A sudden exit from EMU, or even the real fear of it, could unleash chaos on the financial markets. The faultlines discussed earlier – either on their own or in combination – could well result in the monetary experiment falling apart. It is however, unlikely to occur overnight. It is only when those faultlines become the common currency of politicians facing an angry electorate that the real possibility of a mutual agreement to dissolve EMU would become a harsh reality.

References

1. Obstfeld, M. and Rogoff, K. (1996) *Foundations of International Macroeconomics.* Cambridge, MA: MIT Press, pp. 632–4.
2. McCallum, B. J., (1999) *Theoretical Issues Pertaining to Monetary Union.* Paper given at City University Business School Conference on Monetary Unions, May.
3. Bordo, M.D. and Jonung, L. (1999) *What Does the History of Monetary Unions Tell*

Us? Paper given at City University Business School Conference on Monetary Unions, May.

4. Ibid.

5. Ibid.

6. Perlman, M. (1991) *In Search of Monetary Unions*. London School of Economics Financial Markets Group. Special Paper. No. 39, October.

7. Congdon, T.C. (1998) "Could EMU be Europe's 'Maoist Leap Forward'?" in Temperton, P. (ed.) *The euro*. John Wiley & Sons.

8. Mundell, R.A. (1961) "The Theory of Optimum Currency Areas", *American Economic Review*, September.

9. Dwyer, P. and Hafer, R.W. (1998) "The Federal Governments Budget Surplus: Cause for Celebration?" Federal Reserve Bank of Atlanta, *Economic Review*, Third Quarter.

10. Alesina, A. and Summers, L. (1993) "Central Bank Independence and Macroeconomic Performance", *Journal of Money, Credit and Banking*, May.

11. Posen, A. (1996) "Central bank independence and disinflationary credibility: a missing link?" *Oxford Economic Papers*, July.

12. Forder, J. (1998) "The case for an independent central bank: a reassessment of evidence and sources", *European Journal of Political Economy*, Vol. 14.

13. Record, N. (1998) "The Consequences of EMU's Failure", *Off the Record*, Issue 12, 1st Quarter.

CHAPTER 11

How does the introduction of the euro affect the quotation and interpretation of spot and forward exchange rates?

INTRODUCTION

Prior to the arrival of the euro, on 1 January 1999, euro currencies existed for the major European currencies plus the US dollar. Euro currencies were sometimes viewed as another kind of money, although in reality they are simply domestic currencies of one country on deposit in another country. Their value is identical to that of the same currency "at home", and in practice they should simply be seen as interest rate markets. A euro dollar is a US dollar-denominated, interest-bearing deposit in a bank outside the US, normally in London. The bank may be a foreign bank, the overseas branch of a US bank, or a special "offshore" entity called an International Banking Facility (IBF). Following the arrival of the euro, the concept of euro currencies, in the context of a foreign exchange dealing room is no longer used. A euro dollar now means a eurodollar futures contract, although it can still be used as a generic term for US dollars deposited outside the US. A similar situation exists for the other former euro currencies discussed below.

Since the arrival of the euro the former Euro-DM, Euro-BF/Lux Franc, Euro-Franc, Euro-Punt, Euro-Guilder, Euro-Escudo, Euro-Peseta, Euro-Schilling, Euro-FinMark and Euro-Lira have all been replaced by the "euro". The rates at which the conversions to the euro took place are illustrated in Appendix 11.1 and Table 11.18. This chapter illustrates how exchange rates are now quoted, and how the conventions have been altered for both spot and forward rate quotations, given the arrival of the euro.

But first of all let us be clear about some market terminology. A spot exchange rate is a contract simultaneously to buy one currency and sell a second currency. Settlement or value date (the passing of cash) is typically two business days later.

A forward exchange contract is an agreement (between a customer and a bank, or between banks) to buy or sell a currency in the future at a price and date that is agreed upon now. The difference between the present price, the spot rate, and the forward price is a direct reflection of the difference between deposit interest rates of the two currencies for the same period of time, as implied by their relative futures markets. Futures markets drive interest differentials and the extent to which these, in turn, influence forward rates is illustrated in Appendix 11.2 and was discussed in greater detail in Chapter 8.

Since 1 January 1999, the euro has been the base currency in all wholesale spot quotations despite some pre-launch questions over quoting conventions.

The author would like to acknowledge the assistance in writing this chapter provided by Gavin Wells, Foreign Exchange Dealer and Vice President, Citibank, London.

This involved changing former practices for the dollar. Rates are now quoted on a "certain for uncertain" basis (e.g. € 1 = $1.1724; € 1= ¥141.29; € 1 = £0.70582). So this convertion results in the quotations being € 1 = X units of currency Y. Quotation of legacy currencies has now ceased in the interbank market and for large corporate customers.

The "uncertain for certain" basis was not found to be acceptable, eg $1 = € 0.65, despite being the former practice, and was thought likely to create unnecessary confusion for market participants. However, many dealers still feel uncomfortable quoting the more valuable unit as a fraction of the less valuable one, arguing that it feels more comfortable the other way around. Despite this, the convention of quoting the more valuable unit as a fraction of the less valuable unit has now become the market standard, although this has been the standard for the Australian dollar and the New Zealand dollar for a long time.

EXCHANGE RATE QUOTATIONS: A PRIMER[1]

In every exchange rate quotation there are two currencies. The currency being priced is known as the commodity currency. The exchange rate is quoted such that a fixed number of units (usually one) of the commodity currency is expressed in terms of a variable number of units of the other currency. The other currency is known as the terms currency. The commodity currency is sometimes referred to as the base currency. These terms are used interchangeably in a foreign exchange dealing room.

For example, in the exchange rate quotation £1=US$1.5500, the commodity being priced is the pound sterling. One pound is expressed as 1.5500 units of dollars. The unit of account is the dollar. The pound is the commodity currency; the dollar is the terms currency.

In the exchange rate quotation € 1=US$1.04, the euro is the commodity currency and the dollar is the terms currency. The euro is priced in US dollar terms. There is no convention that dictates which currency should be the commodity currency, although in practice the base currency is normally the US dollar.

When the pound sterling was the principal world currency, it was customary for the Commonwealth currency to be quoted as the commodity currency. With the rise to prominence of the US economy, most exchange rates are now quoted with the US dollar as the commodity currency, although this may well change should more countries adopt the euro. The old convention still applies however for several of the former Commonwealth currencies. See Table 11.1.

Table 11.1 ● Exchange rate quotations for Commonwealth currencies

Commodity currency		Terms currency
£1	=	US$1.5500
A$1	=	US$0.7420
NZ$1	=	US$0.6375
US$1	=	€ 0.9660
US$1	=	HK$7.8020

Exchange rate quotations for other currencies

Commodity currency		Terms currency
€ 1	=	US$1.0400
€ 1	=	£0.645
US$1	=	¥120.00
US$1	=	S$1.4370
US$1	=	BHT 25.25

Price and volume quotations

If an exchange rate is expressed such that the foreign currency is the commodity currency and the local currency is the terms currency, this is described as a price quotation. In a price quotation, the foreign currency is priced in terms of the local currency. See Table 11.2.

Table 11.2 ● Price quotations

	Commodity currency		Terms currency
In Germany	€ 1	=	US$1.0400
In Japan	US$1	=	¥120.00
In UK	€ 1	=	£0.625
In US	A$1	=	US$0.6700

If an exchange rate is expressed such that the foreign currency is the terms currency and the local currency is the commodity currency, this is described as a volume quotation. Under the volume quotation system, the local currency is priced in terms of the foreign currency. See Table 11.3.

Table 11.3 ● Volume quotations

	Commodity currency		Terms currency
In US	€ 1	=	US$1.0400
In US	US$1	=	CHF 1.51
In UK	£1	=	€ 1.56
In New Zealand	NZ$1	=	US$0.5600

SPOT EXCHANGE RATE QUOTATION CONVENTIONS FOR THE EURO

A spot deal is a binding agreement between party A and party B to deliver to each other agreed amounts of two currencies, normally two working days later. A deal made on Friday 1 August must be settled on Tuesday 5 August. The difference between a spot and forward deal is illustrated in Table 11.4.

Table 11.4 ● Spot and forward markets

Agreement on Price: Day 0

Settlement or delivery date (days forward)	Contract
0	Cash; value same day
1	"Tom next" or Tomorrow next
2	Spot rate
More than 2	Forward rate

Note: Canadian dollar Spot deals are settled one business day later.

Assume the spot rates for the rate of the euro against the US dollar, generally quoted as EUR/USD, were 1.1000–1.1010, then on the Bid side the price maker buys 1 euro and sells US$1.1000 and on the Offer side the price maker sells 1 euro and buys US$1.1010. See Table 11.5.

Table 11.5 ● Spot rate euro/US dollar (EUR/USD)

Bid	Offer
$1.1000..$1.1010	
Bank (price maker)	Bank (price maker)
Buys	*Sells*
€ 1	€ 1
Sells	*Buys*
$1.1000	$1.1010

Turning now to the pound sterling, assume the spot rate for the euro against the pound sterling, generally quoted as EUR/GBP, was 0.6790–0.6800. This means that on the Bid side the price maker buys 1 euro and sells £0.679 and on the Offer side the price maker sells 1 euro and buys £0.680. See Table 11.6.

Table 11.6 ● Spot rate euro/sterling (EUR/GBP)

Bid	Offer
£0.6790	£0.6800
Bank (price maker)	Bank (Price maker)
Buys	Sells
€ 1	€ 1
Sells	Buys
£0.6790	£0.6800

The market is sometimes asked to quote the rates as GBP/EUR, in which case the rate is € 1.4715–1.4725 and the convention in Table 11.6 is reversed. See Table 11.7.

Table 11.7 ● Spot rate sterling/euro (GBP/EUR)

Bid	Offer
€ 1.4715	€ 1.4725
Bank (price maker)	Bank (price maker)
Buys	Sells
1 pound sterling	1 pound sterling
Sells	Buys
€ 1.4715	€ 1.4725

DAY COUNT COMPLICATIONS

It is necessary to introduce at this stage what are known as "day count conventions". On Tuesday 5 October 1999, the spot date for the Japanese yen is 7 October. The one-year forward rate would be 7 October 2000, which is 366 days. However, 7 and 8 October 2000 in Japan are a weekend and 9 October 2000 is a holiday in the US, and 10 October 2000 is a holiday in Japan. Thus the value date of the one-year Yen forward will be 11 October – making this a 370-day year. The traditional 365-day year has to be adjusted for these holidays and weekends.

Even more odd is the effect of what is confusingly referred to as "End End" in the dealing room. When the spot date is the last working day of a month, the maturity date of all tenors (1m, 2m, 3m etc) will also be the last date of their respective month. See Table 11.8.

Table 11.8 ● The effect of End End

On	Normal 24 May 1999	Days	End End 27 October 1999	Days
Spot	26 May	2	29 Oct	2
1m	28 June	33	30 Nov	32
2m	26 July	61	31 Dec	63
3m	26 Aug	92	31 Jan	94
4m	27 Sept	124	29 Feb	123
5m	26 Oct	153	31 March	154
6m	26 Nov	184	28 April	182
7m	29 Dec	217	31 May	215
8m	26 Jan	245	30 June	245
9m	28 Feb	278	31 July	276
10m	27 March	306	31 Aug	307
11m	26 April	336	29 Sept	336
12m	26 May	366	31 Dec	368

FORWARD EXCHANGE RATE QUOTATION CONVENTIONS FOR THE EURO

The forward markets are markets for borrowing one currency and lending another currency. The forward outright market is the market whereby exchange rates for transactions taking place in the future can be fixed today. This market enables companies/investors facing exchange rate uncertainty in the future to lock in the rates today, thereby eliminating the risk that currency volatility can damage their profit margins or investment returns. The rationale for the existence of the forward market is illustrated in Appendix 11.2 and was discussed in detail in Chapter 8.

Before discussing how forward rates are quoted, it is first essential to explain what swap points are, more commonly referred to as "forward points", or simply "points". A "point" is the last digit of a quotation and convention dictates the number of decimal points in each quotation. Quotations of the euro are made to four decimal places. Hence a point is equal to 0.0001 of the currency. See Figure 11.1. Should the quotation involve a fifth decimal place this is known as a pip, although the two terms are often used interchangeably.

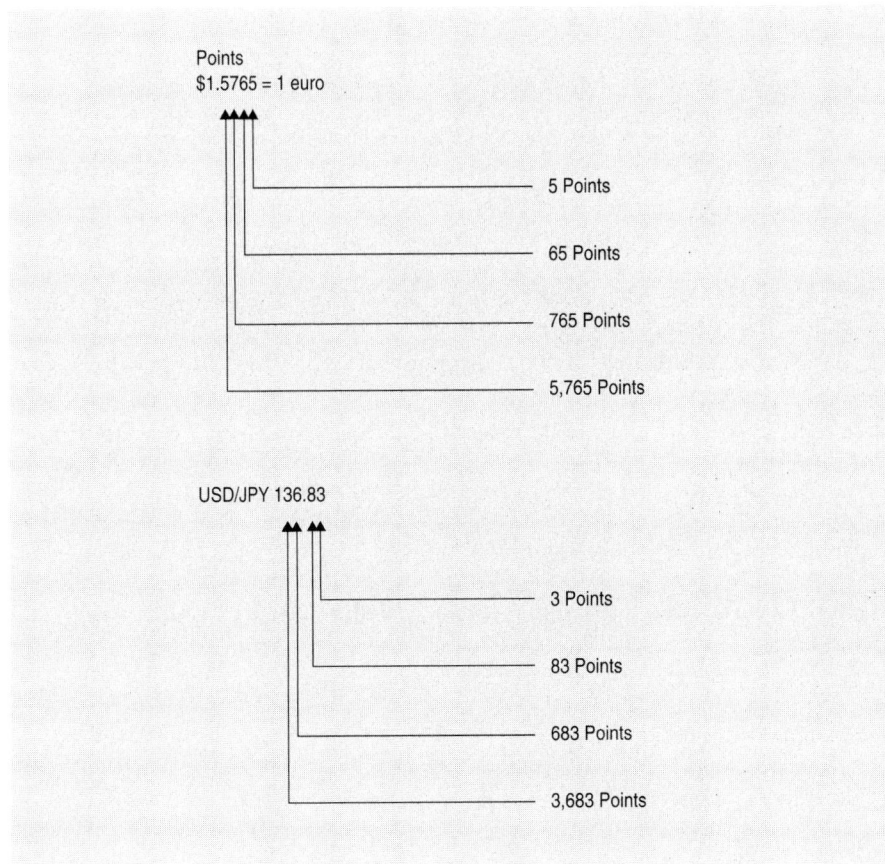

Fig 11.1 ● What are swap points?

The difference between the spot rate and the forward rate is known as the forward margin. If the forward margin is positive (points) the commodity currency is said to be at a forward premium, ie the forward price is higher than the spot price. If the forward margin (points) is negative, the commodity currency is said to be at a forward discount. The exact principle is illustrated in Table 11.9.

A currency with high interest rates trades at a forward discount against one with a lower interest rate, and vice versa. If this was not the case speculators would constantly borrow and deposit in the higher interest rate markets and enter into a forward foreign exchange contract to cover the repayment of the loan. Efficiently priced markets ensure that arbitrageurs cannot print money.

Table 11.9 ● How do we know whether to add or subtract swap "points"?

Base/Commodity currency	Term currency	Forward points	Swap points
High	Low	Discount	Subtract
Low	High	Premium	Add

Table 11.10 sets out the swap formula that foreign exchange dealers use to calculate forward exchange rates.

As discussed in Appendix 11.2, swap points and forward outright rates are derived from interest rate differentials. Assume that one-year euro rates are 3 per cent and one-year US Eurodollar rates are 5.25 per cent. Using the swap formula from Table 11.10 and applying it in Table 11.11, with a spot rate of $1.1000, the swap points for EUR/USD of 243.5 are derived. (We take the mid point rate of 243.5 and then create a 2 point spread, giving 242.5–244.5.)

Table 11.10 ● The swap formula for commodity/terms currency forward rate calculations

$$\text{Spot} \times \left[\frac{1 + \left(L_T \times \dfrac{d}{b_T} \right)}{1 + \left(L_c \times \dfrac{d}{b_c} \right)} - 1 \right] = \text{Forward points}$$

Where L_T = interest rate of terms currency
L_c = interest rate of commodity currency
d = no. of days in forward tenor
b_T = day basis of terms currency
b_c = day basis of commodity currency

where all currencies apart from GBP, GRD are 360 days
GBP, GRD are 365 days

Table 11.11 ● How to calculate the euro/dollar forward rate (EUR/USD) (swap points added)

$$1.1000^* \left[\frac{1 + \left(0.0525 \times \dfrac{365}{360} \right)}{1 + \left(0.03 \times \dfrac{365}{360} \right)} - 1 \right] = 243.5$$

And so with a spot rate of $1.1000-1.1010 these are then added to the spot rate giving forward outright rates of $1.12425–1.12545. See Table 11.12.

Table 11.12 ● Forward rate euro/dollar (EUR/USD)

One-year	euro rate is 3%
One-year	Dollar rate is 5.25%
	Forward points are at a premium

Spot rate	$1.1000...............	$1.1010
Forward points	242.5	244.5
Forward rate	$1.12425...............	$1.12545
	Bank	Bank
	Buys	*Sells*
	€1	€1
	Sells	*Buys*
	$1,124,25.............	$1,125,45

Having illustrated the case whereby the EUR/USD forward points are at a premium, let us assume that the situation is reversed. Assume now that one-year US eurodollar rates are at 3 per cent and one-year euro rates are at 5.25 per cent. Using the same formula as in Table 11.10, we derive the following swap points:

Case A If EUR/USD is the quotation

$$1.1000 \times \left[\frac{1 + \left(0.03 \times \frac{365}{360}\right)}{1 + \left(0.0525 \times \frac{365}{360}\right)} - 1 \right] = -238.25$$

Case B If USD/EUR is the quotation

$$0.909 \times \left[\frac{1 + \left(0.0525 \times \frac{365}{360}\right)}{1 + \left(0.03 \times \frac{365}{360}\right)} - 1 \right] = -201.25$$

Creating a two-point spread and ensuring that the bid rate is lower than the offer rate gives us forward outright rates of \$1.076075–1.077275, in Case A. See Table 11.13. Case B gives us the forward outright rates of € 0.929025–0.930225.

Table 11.13 ● Forward rate euro/dollar

Case A (EUR/USD)		or	Case B (USD/EUR)	
\$1.1000	−\$1.1010		€ 0.9090	€ 0.9100
−239.25	−237.25		200.25	202.25
\$1.076075	\$1.077275		€ 0.929025	€ 0.930225

Swap points for forward sterling against the euro (EUR/GBP) are calculated in a similar way to the dollar with the exception that sterling calculations use a 365-day year convention, while the US dollar uses a 360-day year convention. Table 11.14 illustrates that this gives us swap points of (129.25) and again creating a two-point spread gives us one-year forward outright rates of £0.692825–0.694025. See Table 11.15.

Table 11.14 ● How to calculate euro/sterling forward rates (EUR/GBP)

If 1-year EUR rates are 3%, 1-year GBP rates at 5% and EUR/GBP spot is 0.6800, using the formula in Table 11.10 we get:

$$0.6800 \times \left[\frac{1 + \left(0.05 \times \frac{365}{365}\right)}{1 + \left(0.03 \times \frac{365}{360}\right)} \right] = \text{Forward points} = 129.25$$

Table 11.15 ● Forward rate euro/sterling (EUR/GBP)

One-year
Euro rate is 3%
Sterling rate is 5.25%
Euro at a premium

Spot rate	£0.6800	.£0.6810
Forward points	128.25	130.25
Forward rate	£0.692825	£0.694025
	Bank	Bank
	Buys	*Sells*
	€ 1	€ 1
	Sells	*Buys*
	£0.692,825	£0.694,025

If we are seeking sterling/euro forward rates (GBP/EUR) we use the formula in Table 11.10. Sterling is now the base currency. So we then insert the rates into the formula in Table 11.10. See Table 11.16.

Table 11.16 ● **Swap points for sterling/euro (GBP/EUR)**

$$1.4705 \times \left[\frac{1 + \left(0.03 \times \frac{365}{360}\right)}{1 + \left(0.05 \times \frac{365}{365}\right)} - 1 \right] = -274.25$$

In this case we subtract the swap points giving forward outright sterling/euro (GBP/EUR) rates of € 1.442975–1.444175. See Table 11.17.

Table 11.17 ● **Forward rates for sterling/euro (GBP/EUR)**

Spot rate	€ 1.4705	–	€ 1.4715
Forward points	–275.25		–273.25
Forward rate	€ 1.442975		€ 1.444175
	Bank		Bank
	Buys		*Sells*
	1 pound		1 pound
	Sells		*Buys*
	€ 1,442,975		€ 1,444,175

In conclusion, the introduction of the new currency, the euro, means that foreign exchange calculations involving hedging, arbitrage, and overseas foreign investment decisions must now take note of the fact that foreign exchange rate quotations are now quoted in a way not previously observed for the major currency transactions. The euro has usurped the dollar as the commodity currency.

Reference

1. These principles are discussed in more detail in Anthony, S. (1997) *Foreign Exchange in Practice*, LBC Information Services.

Euroland exchange rates disappear. The era of the "euro" has arrived

On 1 January 1999, the euro was born after EU finance ministers set the irrevocable conversion rates between the euro and the "in" currencies for the 11 nations in EMU. From midnight on 31 December 1998, one euro was worth:

1.95583	Deutsche marks
6.55957	French francs
1936.27	Italian lire
166.386	Spanish pesetas
2.20371	Dutch guilders
40.3399	Belgian francs
13.7603	Austrian schillings
200.482	Portuguese escudos
5.94573	Finnish markkas
0.787564	Irish pounds
40.3399	Luxembourg francs

During the 1999–2002 transition period, notes and coins will continue to circulate in legacy currencies. However, with the introduction of the euro, each legacy currency legally became a denomination of the euro rather than a currency in its own right. Where funds are held in a legacy currency, the bilateral conversion rates are also fixed (as declared in the 1998 May summit).

Table 11.18 ● Euro conversion rates

	100 BFr/LFr	100 French franc	100 D-Mark	1 Irish £	100 Guilder	100 Escudo	100 Peseta	100 Schilling	100 Markka	100 Lira
Belgium/Luxembourg		614.977	2062.55	51.2210	1830.55	20.1214	24.2447	293.162	678.468	20.8338
France	16.2608		335.386	8.32893	297.661	3.27189	3.94237	47.6704	110.324	3.38773
Germany	4.84837	29.8164		2.48338	88.7517	0.975559	1.17547	14.2136	32.8947	1.0101
Ireland	1.95232	12.0063	40.2676		35.7382	0.3923834	0.473335	5.72347	13.2459	0.406743
Netherlands	5.46285	33.5953	112.674	2.79812		1.099220	1.32445	16.0150	37.0637	1.13812
Portugal	469.984	3056.34	10250.5	254.56	9097.53		120.492	1456.97	3371.88	103.541
Spain	412.462	2536.54	8507.22	211.267	7550.3	82.9929		1209.18	2798.42	85.9313
Austria	34.1108	209.774	703.552	17.4719	624.415	6.86357	8.27006		231.431	7.10657
Finland	14.7391	90.6420	304.001	7.54951	269.806	2.96571	3.57345	43.2094		3.07071
Italy	4799.90	29518.3	99000.2	2458.56	87864.4	965.805	1163.72	14071.5	32565.8	

Where do forward exchange rates come from?

Forward exchange points are the interest rate differential of two currencies expressed as a percentage of the exchange rate. The futures markets determines where these interest rate differentials come from. A swap is an agreement to buy a currency now (spot) and at the same time sell it back at a later date (forward), or conversely, to sell a currency now (spot) and agree to repurchase it forward.

Swaps may be arranged between a customer and a bank, or between a bank and another bank, but in all cases the rates are based on the interbank market, as explained below. Consider the following.

> High Interest Bank has US $1,000,000 which could earn 5% pa for 360 days in the interbank market. Low Interest Bank has 4,000.000 euros which could earn 4% pa for 360 days in the interbank market. Assume the present price for dollars (spot rate) is € 4.000 per US dollar, in order to make the arithmetic easier.

Low Interest Bank wants dollars during the above period and agrees with High Interest Bank to swap its euros for dollars for 360 days. (Some countries use a 365-day year but in this appendix we will use the simpler and more usual 360 days.) If High Interest Bank were to convert dollars to euros and euros back to dollars at the same price one year from now, it would be sacrificing the use of a 5% pa currency for the use of a 4% pa currency without any compensation for the opportunity loss of 1% pa. Compensation therefore comes through the difference between the spot rate, point (a) on Figure 11.2 and point (b) the forward rate. One per cent of € 4.000 is 0.400 or 4 centimes. This is equal to the extra amount of interest earned per dollar by Low Interest Bank with its newly acquired dollars. On day 360, High Interest Bank deducts 4 centimes, ie 4.0000 minus 0.400 = <u>3.9600</u> (theforward rate) when it repays euros to Low Interest Bank. Four centimes by itself may sound minimal, but to put it in perspective this difference on $1,000,000 would amount to € 40,000 ($10,000). In other words, Low Interest Bank would exchange € 4,000,000 for $1,000,000 today but in 360 days it would only receive € 3,960,000 to offset the extra € 40,000 (equivalent) earned on the dollars it temporarily acquired. Due to the difference between the spot and forward rates, Low Interest Bank still earns a net 4% pa and High Interest Bank earns a net 5% pa as they would have with their original currencies had they not swapped them.

If the agreement had covered six months instead of one year, the extra amount of interest earned by Low Interest Bank would have been one half of 4 centimes per dollar deposited, ie two centimes (€ 20,000 [$5,000]), point (c) on Figure 11.2, so the forward rate would be 4.000 minus 0.0200 = <u>3.9800</u>. A ten-day forward rate between two currencies with a 1% pa interest difference (5% pa − 4% pa) would be a 3.9989, point (d) on Figure 11.2, practically the same as 4.0000. Putting it the other way around, for every day Low

Interest Bank holds dollars, it earns an extra 0.011 centimes (ie 4 centimes/360) per day deposited or € 110 per day on $1,000,000. As shown by the diagonal line of the diagram, for each additional 0.011 centime earned per day, the discount increases by the same amount, ultimately reaching 4 centimes for a 360-day period. The basic formula for determination of the forward rate is shown below:

$$\frac{\text{Difference between spot and forward rates}}{\text{Spot rate}} \times \frac{360}{\text{days}} \times 100 = 1\% \text{ pa}$$

$$\frac{0.0200}{4.0000} \times \frac{360}{180} \times 100 = 1\% \text{ pa}$$

In practice, the relationship is not linear. The precise relationship depends on the shape of the yield curve.

It is helpful to remember that a company converting forward, from a low interest currency (4% pa) to a high interest currency (5% pa) benefits from an exchange saving compared to today's price (spot rate). The reverse is true when converting from a high interest currency (5% pa) to a low interest currency (4% pa).

In conclusion, it is the difference between euro-deposit rates that determines the forward discount or premium, ie 1% difference between 4% and 5%. The wider the euro-deposit interest rates differential, the larger the forward discounts and premiums. Similarly, the narrower the euro-differentials, the smaller the forward discounts and premiums.

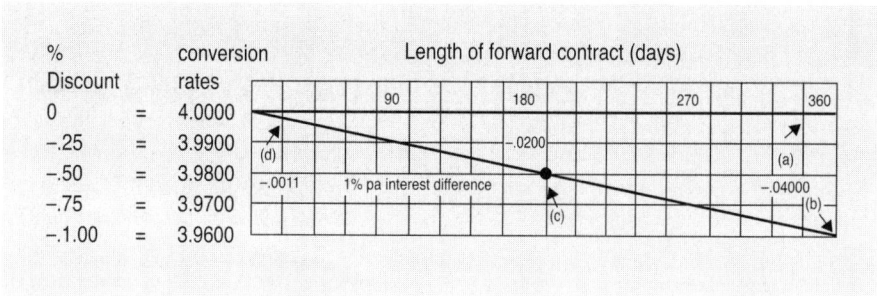

% Discount		conversion rates
0	=	4.0000
−.25	=	3.9900
−.50	=	3.9800
−.75	=	3.9700
−.1.00	=	3.9600

Fig 11.2 ●

CHAPTER 12

What is the impact of the introduction of the euro on the money markets?

From LIBOR to EURO-LIBOR, EURIBOR, EONIA and EURONIA

INTRODUCTION

The introduction of the new currency, the euro, on 1 January 1999 and the subsequent abolition of 11 currencies of the European Union meant that a parallel change in the money markets was also necessary. A glance at the money rates section of Table 12.1 indicates that a new world of money markets and subsequent terminology has been introduced. This chapter describes these changes which have, in turn, generated a whole new set of money market acronyms.

Table 12.1 ● Domestic money rates

	Over night	One month	Three months	Six months	One year	Lomb. inter.	Dis. rate	Repo rate
Euro-zone	$4\frac{1}{16}$	$4\frac{3}{32}$	$4\frac{1}{16}$	$4\frac{5}{8}$	$4\frac{15}{16}$	–	–	3.75
Switzerland	$1\frac{15}{16}$	$2\frac{3}{4}$	$3\frac{3}{32}$	$3\frac{3}{16}$	$3\frac{27}{32}$	–	0.50	–
US	$6\frac{11}{16}$	$6\frac{19}{32}$	$6\frac{25}{32}$	$7\frac{1}{16}$	$7\frac{1}{2}$	–	6.00	–
Japan	$\frac{3}{32}$	$\frac{1}{16}$	$\frac{1}{16}$	$\frac{1}{8}$	$\frac{7}{32}$	–	0.50	–
■ $ LIBOR BBA fixing*								
Interbank fixing	–	$6\frac{19}{32}$	$6\frac{13}{16}$	$7\frac{1}{16}$	$7\frac{1}{2}$	–	–	–
US Dollar CDs	–	6.46	6.69	6.96	7.35	–	–	–
Euro Linked Ds	–	$4\frac{3}{16}$	$4\frac{3}{8}$	$4\frac{5}{8}$	$4\frac{7}{8}$	–	–	–
SDR Linked Ds	–	$3\frac{3}{8}$	$3\frac{17}{32}$	$3\frac{11}{16}$	$4\frac{1}{32}$	–	–	–
BBA EURO LIBOR	–	$4\frac{1}{4}$	$4\frac{15}{32}$	$4\frac{21}{32}$	$4\frac{31}{32}$	–	–	–
EURO EURIBOR	–	4.266	4.476	4.655	4.986	–	–	–
EONIA	4.02	–	–	–	–	–	–	–
EURONIA	4.0218	–	–	–	–	–	–	–

*London interbank fixing rate (LIBOR) is the BBA London rate fixed at 11am (London time).
Mid rates are shown for the domestic Money Rates, US$ CDs, Euro & SDR Linked Deposits (Ds).

Source: Financial Times, 18 May 2000

With the advent of the euro, the former Eurocurrencies quoted in London, namely Euro-French Franc, Euro-Deutsche mark, Euro-Lira, Euro-Guilder, Euro-Peseta, Euro-Punt, Euro-Escudo, Euro-Fin Mark, Euro-Belgian Franc have now disappeared and new money market benchmark rates have been created. See Table 12.1. These currencies remain quoted, but their significance is now different.

The various authorities that publish the new money market reference rates make a distinction between the "in" euro-zone and "out" euro-zone currencies and these are summarized in Table 12.2.

Table 12.2 ● Which zones use which rates?

In euro-zone	Out euro-zone
EURIBOR	BBA LIBOR
	BBA EURO-LIBOR
EONIA	EURONIA

But first of all it is important to be clear about what a money market is, taking the example of the London Money Markets, and seeing as to where they fit into the global financial marketplace.

WHAT IS THE MONEY MARKET?

The money market is a wholesale market for low risk, highly liquid, short-term IOUs. It is important to define these terms.

The money market is "wholesale" in that it is dominated by financial intermediaries handling large cash flows. There is limited participation by retail investors.

The market trades instruments that are low risk. The traditional role of the money market lies in intermediating the monetary surpluses and deficits, of the financial community. It is vital that credit risks in the money market should be minimized by limiting access to high-quality counterparties. Credit quality is assured by a mix of:

● limiting participation in the money market to names perceived as creditworthy: large areas of the money market continue to rely on this so-called name recognition

● internal credit analysis

● credit rating by specialist agencies: this has become the norm

● security through some form of credit enhancement:
  – collateralization;
  – guarantees.

Collateralization is rare in the money market compared with the capital market. It is usually limited to some deposits (such as UK call money) and to sale-and-repurchase agreements, a major source of short-term funds. Guarantees are found in the form of acceptances of commercial bills.

The money market is also a liquid market. The need for liquidity reflects the traditional role of the money market in intermediating working balances. The role of working balances as a buffer to absorb the impact of the unexpected (and therefore unpredictable) on the cashflow of an institution makes it crucial that any such funds lent in the money market are liquid, meaning that such lending can be liquidated quickly and without significant capital loss.

Money market instruments are naturally liquid by virtue of being short term and homogenous. The shorter the period of investment, the more likely it is that funds will be or will become available when needed.

In order to provide additional liquidity to money market lenders, while ensuring adequate tenors for borrowers, most money market instruments are negotiable or transferable – meaning that title to instruments can be sold by lenders to other parties, without specific permission from borrowers – thereby providing assurance that funds can be retrieved before the maturities of the instruments. The new holders of the transferred instruments can do the same, creating a secondary market.

All money market instruments, except deposits and sale-and-repurchase agreements, are negotiable. In practice, many negotiable money market instruments (particularly commercial paper) are retained until maturity by their original investors and are rarely traded in secondary markets. In other words, liquidity is provided by the short-term tenor of the instruments.

The short-term horizon of the money market is conventionally set at 12 months. Beyond 12 months the money market merges in with the capital market. Several money market instruments are limited by law or other regulations to tenors of 12 months and less.

The short-term nature of the money market reflects its traditional function in matching the supply of and demand for cash balances, employing temporary surpluses and funding temporary deficits in cashflow.

The overlap between the UK money and capital markets has been increasing. The money market has increasingly been used for capital funding and investment. Short-term borrowing and lending is renewed or rolled over for longer-term periods, thereby combining capital market tenors with money market pricing. In the 1970s, such borrowing and lending mainly took the form of syndicated loans. In the 1980s, loans were securitized into floating-rate notes. In the 1990s, euronotes and medium-term notes – short-term securities issued through medium-term programmes – have further blurred the distinction between money and capital markets.

The size of the transaction is important in a short-term market. Borrowing and lending for short periods is only economic for large amounts.

Because money markets are wholesale, most money market securities are usually exempted from the registration requirements which are imposed on domestic and foreign issues of capital market securities in order to protect retail investors. This makes them quicker and cheaper to issue, and is one of the reasons behind its growth.

There are a number of other points to note about the money market.

- the money market lacks a single physical location or centralized communication network. Rather, it is an over-the-counter (OTC) market, with participants very widely dispersed and connected by telecommunication networks.

- instruments in the money market are quoted in terms of yield rather than price. This is in contrast to the capital market and reflects:
  - the need to quote in comparable terms to deposits
  - the limited secondary market in some money market instruments, which means that the principal form of return is the interest or discount paid at maturity rather than the differences between buying and selling prices, which would be important in trading.

The short-term tenor of most money market instruments means that there is usually only a single payment of principal and return back to investors and this is made at maturity. On longer-term (capital market) instruments, on the other hand, investors usually receive returns in a series of interim payments before maturity. These interim payments reduce the duration of the credit risk to which investors are exposed. Such serial returns take the form of interest. For short-term (money market) instruments, on which there is only one payment of return to investors, there are alternatives to interest as a means of paying returns. Traditional negotiable money market instruments use the simpler mechanism of paying returns in the form of a discount between the purchase price and the face value of the instruments. A discounted investment is issued to investors at a price below face value, but is repaid by issuers at face value: investors realize their return at maturity as a capital gain, on the difference between the issue price and face value. Traditional negotiable instruments, bills and commercial paper tend to be discounted.

The only negotiable money market instrument which is normally interest bearing is the non-traditional certificate of deposit (although eurocommercial paper is sometimes issued in interest-bearing form). Non-negotiable money market instruments, such as deposits and sale-and-repurchase agreements are interest bearing. The only pure discounted instrument found in the capital market is the zero-coupon bond.

Given the short tenors of money market instruments and the role of some money market instruments as close substitutes for cash, it is impracticable and undesirable to register ownership with the issuer. Negotiable money market instruments are therefore issued as bearer securities, more usually, or as global notes held within a clearing system, eg commercial paper in the Central Money-markets Office (CMO).

London Interbank Offered Rate (LIBOR)

Prior to the introduction of the euro, the key money market rate of interest was the London Interbank Offered Rate, more normally referred to using its acronym of LIBOR. LIBOR remains the key money market rate for the Australian Dollar (AUD), the Canadian Dollar (CAD), the Swiss Franc (CHF), the British Pound (GBP), the US Dollar (USD) and the Japanese Yen (JPY). LIBOR is the rate of interest charged for Euro currency transactions in London. Euro currencies, discussed in Chapter 1 are currencies traded outside their home currency, so Eurodollars would be dollars traded outside the US.

What does the term "euro" really mean?

The term "euro" simply means that the subject currency is being traded or used outside the country which issues that currency.

Example 1: If you deposit US dollars in a British bank, you now hold a "Euro-dollar deposit".

Example 2: If a Japanese firm issues (sells) a bond in London which is denominated in Japanese yen, it is a "Euro-yen bond".

Does the term apply just to the currencies of Europe?

The markets or currencies are not necessarily European. The term is used for any currency outside of its home market anywhere in the world.

The significance of euro-currency markets

1. Governments normally accept no responsibility for other country's currencies.
2. No responsibility normally means no regulations. This means no deposit insurance, no reserve requirements and no restrictions on capital flows in and out of the country.
3. No regulations or restrictions mean the capital is "pure", or the rates are the most representative of world market forces.

There are important differences between interest rates for dollars quoted in London and those quoted in the US.

The fact that US-based banks have to place reserve requirements with the Federal Reserve and have other banking restrictions placed on them means that their cost of funds is higher than for the same transactions undertaken elsewhere. As there are no restrictions in dollars (or other euro currencies) traded in London, there are two important effects.

1. Lenders provide loans to borrowers at lower rates than in domestic markets.
2. Depositors earn higher rates than in domestic markets.

The effect of this is that the spread between domestic rates and rates in London for US dollars is wider, as can be seen in Figure 12.1.

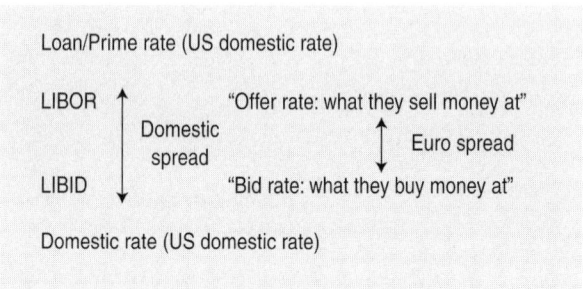

Figure 12.1 ● US dollar deposits and loans in London

It must be stressed that following the introduction of the euro that market practice, at least inside a foreign exchange dealing room, has moved away from using the term "euro-currency". A eurodollar now refers to a Eurodollar futures contract. Similarly with the other euro currencies. We now turn to these new money market acronyms.

LIBOR BBA London Interbank fixing

The British Bankers' Association (BBA) LIBOR is the primary benchmark used by banks, securities houses and investors to fix the cost of borrowing in the money, derivatives and capital markets around the world.

BBA LIBOR is the BBA fixing of the London Inter-Bank Offered Rate. For each currency, rates are fixed daily for maturities of one week and from one month to 12 months inclusive. A panel of Contributor Banks, selected by the BBA on the basis of market activity and perceived market reputation, is surveyed for their views of the market rate. An individual BBA LIBOR Contributor Panel Bank contributes the rate at which it could borrow funds, were it to do so by asking for and then accepting inter-bank offers in reasonable market size just prior to 11am. All Contributor Panel Bank inputs are published on-screen to ensure transparency.

BBA LIBOR fixing evolved in the early 1980s with the growth of syndicated lending and early developments in the derivatives markets. Since then the fixings have assumed an increasing importance with well over 20 per cent of all international bank lending and more than 30 per cent of all foreign exchange transactions taking place in London.

BBA LIBOR is now used to calculate the interest rates applying to a wide range of contracts including OTC instruments such as swaps, loan agreements, Floating Rate Notes (FRNs), Forward Rate Agreements (FRAs) and Exchange Traded Short-Term Interest Rate contracts traded on LIFFE, Eurex, CME and the DTB, among others.

BBA LIBOR has traditionally been fixed for the following currencies:

Pound Sterling (GBP)
United States Dollar (USD)
Japanese Yen (JPY)
Swiss Franc (CHF)
Canadian Dollar (CAD)
Australian Dollar (AUD)
Deutsche mark (DEM)
French Franc (FRF)
Netherlands Guilder (NLG)
Italian Lira (ITL)
Portuguese Escudo (PTE)
Spanish Peseta (ESP)

All currencies are fixed on a spot basis on each London business day, apart from sterling, which is fixed for same day value. During the euro transition period, 1999 to 2002, the BBA continues to publish LIBOR fixings in the national currency rates which already have BBA LIBOR benchmarks. The rates for national currency units are identical to those for euro units from 1 January 1999. There are not separate panels for rates in the former national currencies which have now become the euro.

LIBOR is provided as a free service to the market by the BBA. There is no comprehensive list of all its users or uses, but it is generally acknowledged as an international benchmark. BBA LIBOR is published simultaneously on more than 300,000 screens throughout the world, being distributed by, among others, the following major information vendors:

ADP	Datastream	Reuters
Bloomberg	Nomura Research	S & P Comstock
Bridge Telerate	Quick	

Bridge Telerate manages the fixing process on behalf of the BBA, collecting data from Contributor Panel Banks, applying quality control tests to it and calculating the Fixing, releasing it just before noon, London time.

Note that in Table 12.3, former euro-currency rates have been replaced in the *Financial Times* by international money rates.

Table 12.3 ● International money rates

	Short term	7 days notice	One month	Three months	Six months	One year
Euro	3 29/32 – 3 13/16	4 1/16 – 3 31/32	4 5/32 – 4 3/16	4 15/32 – 4 3/8	4 21/32 – 4 5/8	5 1/16 – 4 15/16
Danish Krone	4 3/16 – 4	4 7/32 – 4 1/16	4 7/16 – 4 3/16	4 3/4 – 4 21/32	5 5/16 – 5 3/16	5 19/32 – 5 1/2
Sterling	5 3/4 – 5 5/8	5 3/4 – 5 5/8	6 1/32 – 5 29/32	6 3/16 – 6 3/32	6 3/8 – 6 1/4	6 23/32 – 6 5/8
Swiss Franc	2 – 1 1/2	2 3/16 – 2 1/16	2 11/16 – 2 5/8	3 1/16 – 3	3 13/16 – 3 3/8	3 13/16 – 3 21/32
Canadian Dollar	5 13/16 – 5 11/16	5 13/16 – 5 11/16	5 27/32 – 5 23/32	5 31/32 – 5 7/8	6 3/16 – 6 3/32	6 1/2 – 6 3/8
US Dollar	6 19/32 – 6 15/32	6 25/32 – 6 21/32	6 19/32 – 6 17/32	6 13/16 – 6 3/4	7 3/32 – 7 1/2	7 17/32 – 7 13/32
Japanese Yen	1/8 – 1/32	1/8 – 1/32	3/32 –	1/8 – 1/32	5/32 – 3/32	9/32 – 5/32
Asian $Sing	3/4 – 1/2	3 3/8 – 3 1/8	3 3/8 – 3 1/8	3 3/8 – 3 1/8	3 7/16 – 3 3/16	3 19/32 – 3 3/8

Short term rates are call for the US Dollar and Yen, others: two days' notice.

Source: Financial Times, 18 May 2000

ERM Euro-rates for the EU members who either did not qualify under the Maastricht convergence criteria, Greece, or who did not choose to join, Denmark, are published. Greece and Denmark are participants in ERM II, as discussed further in Chapter 4. In addition the rates for the non-ERM member, sterling, continues to be quoted. See Table 12.4.

Table 12.4 ● ERM Euro-rates

	Euro cen. rates	Rates against Euro €	Change on day	% +/– from cen. rate	% spread v weakest	Div. ind.
Greece	340.75	336.70	+0.1	−1.19	1.19	8
Denmark	7.46038	7.4592	+0.0004	−0.02	0.00	0
NON ERM MEMBERS						
UK	0.653644	0.60390	+0.0052	−7.61	8.22	–

Euro central rates set by the European Central Bank. Sterling central rate set by the European Commission. Percentage changes are for Euro; a positive change denotes a weak currency. Divergence shows the ratio between two spreads: the percentage difference between the actual market and Euro central rates for a currency, and the maximum permitted percentage deviation of the currency's market rate from its Euro central rate.

Source: Financial Times, 18 May 2000

BBA EURO-LIBOR

BBA EURO-LIBOR, sometimes referred to as Euro BBA LIBOR, is a measure of the cost of euro funds based on the offer rates quoted by 16 of the most active banks in the London market. So despite the fact that sterling is not one of the in-zone currencies, and consequently is not part of the euro zone, rates on euro money markets are determined, for the purpose of this benchmark, in London.

When the euro was introduced the BBA ceased fixing LIBOR for the ECU and replaced it immediately with a fixing rate for the euro.

The 16 banks that comprise the EURO BBA LIBOR panel are:

ABN Amro	Chase Manhattan	Midland	RBC
Bank of America	Citibank	JP Morgan	SocGen
Bank of Tokyo-Mitsubishi	CSFB	Lloyds	UBS
Barclays	Deutsche	Nat West	Westdeutsche

The banks were chosen on the basis of their London based activity in the "in-zone" currency interbank deposit and loan market as well as the short dated (up to one year) foreign exchange swap market. (A short dated foreign exchange swap is analogous to an interbank placement or deposit.)

Table 12.5 illustrates the currencies for which BBA EURO-LIBOR is quoted.

Table 12.5 ● BBA LIBOR for European currencies

From 1 January 1999			
EUR		Act/360	Spot
DEM	**EUR**	Act/360	Spot
FRF	**EUR**	Act/360	Spot
NLG	**EUR**	Act/360	Spot
ITL	**EUR**	Act/360	Spot
PTE	**EUR**	Act/360	Spot
ESP	**EUR**	Act/360	Spot
GBP		Act/365	Same Day

EURO INTERBANK OFFERED RATE (EURIBOR)

The European Monetary Institute, the forerunner of the European Central Bank indicated, prior to the introduction of the euro, that it was unhappy that the money market reference rate for the euro should be set outside the euro area, viz. in London, and they wanted to see a reference rate based on the rates in the euro area.

A new benchmark was sponsored by the European Banking Federation, in collaboration with the ACI, the Financial Markets Association. This benchmark is EURIBOR, referred to in the *Financial Times* as EURO EURIBOR. EURIBOR is the rate at which euro interbank term deposits within the euro zone are offered by one prime bank to another prime bank. The rates for EURIBOR are fixed by a panel of 57 banks: 47 selected by national banking associations to represent the euro markets in the participating Member States and 10 international or 'pre-in' banks active in the euro market with an office in the euro area.

Most euro in-zone countries have now announced that they are replacing their domestic benchmark rates with EURIBOR for both new and existing contracts. This is illustrated in Table 12.6.

Table 12.6 ● Announced changes in price sources for first wave currencies

Currency	Rate	EMU successor rate	Change
Austrian Schilling	ATS VIBOR	ATS VIBOR	None
Belgian Franc	BEF BIBOR	EURIBOR	Yes
German	DEM FIBOR	EURIBOR	Yes
Deutsche mark	DEM LIBOR	Euro LIBOR	Yes
Dutch Guilder	NLG AIBOR	EURIBOR	Yes
	NLG LIBOR	Euro LIBOR	Yes
Finnish Marka	FIM HELIBOR	FIM HELIBOR	None
ECU	XEU PIBOR	EURIBOR	Yes
	XEU LIBOR	Euro LIBOR	Yes
French Franc	FRF PIBOR	EURIBOR	Yes
	FRF LIBOR	Euro LIBOR	Yes
Irish Punt	IEP DIPOR	EURIBOR	Yes
Italian Lira	ITL RIBOR	EURIBOR	Yes
	ITL LIBOR	Euro LIBOR	Yes
Portuguese Escudo	PTE LISBOR	EURIBOR	Yes
	PTE LIBOR	Euro LIBOR	Yes
Spanish Peseta	ESP MIBOR	ESP MIBOR	Yes
	ESP LIBOR	Euro LIBOR	None

Source: Bank of England

EURIBOR creates a new term structure of interest rates replacing PIBOR, FIBOR, MIBOR, etc.

EURIBOR tends to be fixed at 10am GMT, 11am Frankfurt time, earlier than LIBOR, and is quoted on an actual/360-day basis, displayed to three decimal places.

WHAT IS THE DIFFERENCE BETWEEN BBA EURO-LIBOR AND EURIBOR?

A comparison of BBA EURO-LIBOR with EURIBOR is not straightforward because of the differing sizes of the Panels. On average BBA EURO- LIBOR Panel banks have twice as much capital and double the asset base of the average EURIBOR bank, as measured in the July 1998 *The Banker* survey of the top 1,000 banks. Eleven of the BBA EURO-LIBOR banks are in the top 20 world banks compared with only 8 of the EURIBOR banks. Furthermore, 9 of the BBA EURO-LIBOR banks are in the May 1998 *Euromoney* foreign exchange poll's top 10 indicating that the BBA EURO-LIBOR Panel banks are among the most active in the world in the wholesale interbank market.

The averaging method of BBA EURO-LIBOR (wherein the top and bottom quartiles are discarded and the middle 50 per cent averaged to produce the LIBOR fixing) is similar to EURIBOR's although only the top and bottom 15 per cent are rejected in the FBE/ACI process. This differential topping and tailing results in there being a greater ratio of smaller banks to larger banks in EURIBOR. This could lead to the conclusion that the average credit quality of the EURIBOR banks will be somewhat lower than that of the BBA EURO-LIBOR Panel.

Differential credit quality would be one factor influencing any disparity between the EURIBOR fixing and the BBA EURO-LIBOR fixing. Another one would be the impact of reserve requirements on mainland European interest rates. The European Central Bank is using minimum reserves to manage money market rates and these are being remunerated on the basis of its repo rate.

The evidence so far indicates that the two reference rates largely move together. This is despite the markets former expectations that EURIBOR would fix above BBA EURO-LIBOR and that banks consequently would prefer to index loans to EURIBOR and that corporate borrowers would insist on lending rates fixed to BBA EURO-LIBOR.

EONIA: EURO OVERNIGHT INDEX AVERAGE

There has also been a need for a new overnight reference rate to replace the ones formerly designated prior to the introduction of the euro. EONIA is the overnight rate computed as a weighted average of all overnight unsecured lending transactions in the interbank market initiated within the euro area by the contributing panel banks.

EONIA is calculated by the European Central Bank (ECB). The panel of reporting banks is the same as for EURIBOR, so that the most active banks located in the euro area are represented on the panel and the geographical diversity of banks in the panel is maintained.

So EONIA is the effective in-zone overnight rate in the euro. This is basically a market rate as it is based on the unsecured lending transactions of the euro banks.

EURONIA: EURO OVERNIGHT INDEX AVERAGE

EURONIA is the average interest rate, weighted by volume, of all unsecured overnight euro deposit trades arranged by eight money brokers in London. In this case it is the London equivalent, or euro out-zone equivalent, of EONIA.

EURONIA is the weighted average overnight deposit rate for each business day. Each rate in the average is weighted by the principal amount of deposits which were taken on that day. The average is calculated to four decimal places.

EURONIA effectively benchmarks the cost of funds in the overnight euro market in London. It was introduced by the Wholesale Markets Brokers' Association and is endorsed by the British Bankers' Association.

The spread between EONIA and EURONIA has, since the inception of the scheme, been very small, typically less than one basis point, with occasional volatility around the end of reserve maintenance periods.

CHAPTER 13

Can currency collapses be predicted?

- The rules of the game
- Can currency crashes be predicted?

Economies that had been hailed as paragons of sound macroeconomic management, largely based in Asia, recently suddenly found themselves with large-scale currency devaluations, a collapse of both asset prices and of economic activity. The 1994 currency collapse in Mexico was also just as surprising to observers. This chapter examines the extent to which currency collapses can be predicted.

THE RULES OF THE GAME

It is relatively easy to point the finger at the causes of a currency collapse after the event. What is more useful is some sort of model which correctly predicted a currency collapse and which subsequently took place, before the event. To qualify for this more useful role it is necessary to set out, at the outset, precisely what exactly any such form of analysis, or model, must and must not be able to do. Chang and Velasco[1] set out the criteria below.

Rule 1: *It must not rely on government misbehaviour to generate the crisis*

A striking fact of recent crises is that government budgets were either in balance or showed surpluses. This has been stressed by Velasco[2] for the case of Chile, by Sachs, Tornell and Velasco[3] for Mexico and by Radelet and Sachs[4] for Asia. This means that so called "first generation" models of currency crises, pioneered by Krugman,[5] which rely on large money-financed fiscal deficits to generate reserve erosion and an eventual currency crash, are not well suited to explain these recent crashes.

Rule 2: *It must be general enough to accommodate a wide variety of macroeconomic circumstances*

As Frankel and Rose[6] and Sachs, Tornell and Velasco[7] have shown, there is no unique pattern of behaviour for basic macroeconomic variables in the build-up to a crisis. Sometimes the current account is in deficit, but not always. The same is true for private consumption and investment. In the Frankel and Rose study of macroeconomic behaviour over a large set of currency crises, there is often a contraction in output the year of the crisis but, as the authors themselves point out, causality could run in either direction. This suggests that so-called "second generation" models, pioneered by Obstfeld,[8] in which the government devalues in reaction to mounting unemployment and/or a growing external imbalance, are not particularly useful either.

Rule 3: It must be specific enough to explain why in some of these macroeconomic scenarios a crisis occurs, and in some it does not

First, the model must answer the question of why there is a crisis now and not before. Take the case of the current account, whose behaviour is often blamed for currency crashes. East Asian countries often had large current account deficits in the 1980s and early 1990s, but the crash did not happen until late 1997/early 1998. Why? Second, it must also answer the question of why it happened where it did and not elsewhere. In 1996 Malaysia, Korea, the Philippines and Thailand had large current account deficits (above 4 per cent of GDP), but so also did Brazil, Chile, Colombia and Peru. Yet the crisis happened in Asia and not in South America.

Rule 4: It must account for the high observed correlation between exchange rate collapses and banking crises

In the Southern Cone of the Americas in the early 1980s, Scandinavia in the early 1990s, Mexico in 1995 and Asia in late 1997 and early 1998, currency collapses and a financial system collapse occurred simultaneously. Casual observation suggests that the price of assets (real estate, the stock market) tend to rise before a crash occurs. Formal econometric work, such as that reported by Kaminsky and Reinhart,[9] confirms that financial variables, unlike real ones, do seem to be reasonably good predictors of crises. Sachs, Tornell and Velasco, for instance, found that the previous speed of bank credit growth helped explain which countries were affected by the Tequila effect, that is the effect on other South American currencies of the 1994 Mexico peso devaluation.

Rule 5: It must replicate the puzzling fact that the punishment is much larger than the crime

The real consequences of these crises are large. Chile's GDP contracted by 14 per cent in 1982 and Mexico's by almost 7 per cent in 1995. The economies of once fast-growing Korea, Indonesia and Thailand shrunk in 1998 and 1999. Yet we saw above that not in all cases were the underlying macro fundamentals weak –

and certainly not so weak as to justify the depressions observed in Chile and Mexico. A necessary correction in the current account of, say, three percentage points of GDP naturally requires a contraction in aggregate demand, which in turn may be associated with higher interest rates and dampened activity.

Is there a model that satisfies these rules?

Chang and Velasco have produced just such a model for emerging economies. Their story places international liquidity, which may result in outright collapse of the financial system, at the centre of the problem. Illiquidity – defined as a situation in which the financial system's potential short-term obligations exceed the liquidation value of its assets – may emerge naturally as a response to some features of the environment. However, it may also make this system vulnerable to costly bank runs.

The Chang and Velasco model places emphasis on six factors which must be closely monitored when predicting currency crises:

- capital flows from abroad
- financial liberalization
- the financial system
- rise in land and real estate prices
- government deposit guarantees and investment subsidies
- attempts to stabilize the banks and maintain a stable exchange rate.

Capital flows from abroad

Capital flows from abroad, caused by an opening of the capital account and/or an increase in the country's access to international credit, can magnify the illiquidity problem. In particular, the vulnerability of domestic banks can be sharply increased when these foreign loans are of short maturity. A creditors' panic, that is, a creditors' refusal to roll over the short-term loans, may render a self-fulfilling bank run possible.

Financial liberalization

The illiquidity problem may also be aggravated by a round of financial liberalization, which accentuates the maturity mismatch between assets and liabilities that is typical of commercial banks. In particular, Chang and Velasco show how two kinds of financial liberalization, lowering of reserve requirements and increasing competition in the banking sector, can increase banks' vulnerability to runs.

The financial system

The financial system may greatly magnify the effects of small changes in exogenous circumstances (ie terms of trade, competitiveness, world interest rates). Small shocks may result in financial distress, implying costly asset liquidation, an unnecessarily large credit crunch, and large drops in asset prices and economic activity.

Rise in land and real estate prices

Prices of assets that are in inelastic supply (such as land and real estate) will typically rise as financial flows from abroad are intermediated by the financial system, and then crash in the event of a bank collapse. But the initial increase is not, in and of itself, evidence of an "asset bubble". Similarly, the crash need not be an indication that prices are returning to their "fundamental level". In their model Chang and Velasco stress that the meaning of "fundamental" is conditional on the absence or occurrence of a bank collapse. If a financial run occurs and asset prices crash the resulting price drop is unnecessary, since it results from inefficient asset liquidation. A higher price (and associated higher welfare) would have prevailed if the run had not taken place.

Government deposit guarantees and investment subsidies

The main danger of unsound policies of the kind described by Krugman[10] and allegedly pursued in East Asia (government deposit guarantees and investment subsidies, leading to overinvestment and overborrowing) is that they can increase the fragility of banks. If banks collapse as a result, the associated costs far outweigh the conventional efficiency losses caused by such policies.

Attempts to stabilize the banks and maintain a stable exchange rate

An exchange rate peg may collapse because, if and when a bank crisis comes, both stabilizing the banks and keeping the exchange rate peg become mutually incompatible objectives. A Central Bank may attempt to fight a bank crisis by keeping interest rates from rising (which would further wreck the banks) or by providing lender-of-last-resort funds. But then agents will use the additional domestic currency to buy reserves, eventually forcing the abandonment of the fixed exchange rate. It is in this sense that one observes "twin crises": a financial crisis and a balance of payments crisis.

While potentially illiquid banks exist in emerging and mature economies alike, Chang and Velasco believe that their story is most relevant for emerging markets, because of two reasons. First, banks play a much larger role in emerging than in mature economies. This observation justifies a focus on banks to the detriment of other credit mechanisms such as debt or equity markets. Second, focusing on illiquidity is natural for emerging markets because their access to world capital markets is more limited. If fractional reserve banks in mature economies face a liquidity problem (as opposed to a solvency one) they are likely to get emergency funds from the world capital markets. This seldom occurs in emerging economies. A private bank in Bangkok or Mexico City will receive many international loan offers when things go well, and none when it is being run on by depositors. The combination of fractional reserve (and hence potentially illiquid) banks and external credit ceilings is potentially devastating. It is this combination which is the focus of their model.

CAN CURRENCY CRASHES BE PREDICTED?

Accurate forecasting of currency crises remains elusive. However, recent empirical and theoretical work has identified warning indicators that at least improve our understanding of the likelihood that currency crises can, in some sense, be foreseen. So, applying the rules set out by Chang and Velasco, what are the factors that will improve the ability to foresee future currency crises and what are the strengths and weaknesses of such an approach?

What is a currency crisis?

The first problem in identifying leading indicators of currency crises is one of defining exactly what a currency crisis is. Defining currency crises as instances when a "large" currency depreciation takes place excludes situations where a currency was under substantial pressure but the authorities managed a successful defence by, among other measures, raising interest rates and/or intervening in the foreign exchange market. As a result, most researchers define currency crises by using indices that weight changes in the exchange rate, foreign exchange reserves and (if available) short-term interest rates. The construction of these indices as well as the thresholds used for identifying crises differ across researchers. Even this definition may not completely capture crisis situations because in several instances, the authorities have responded to exchange market pressures by introducing capital controls.

Leading indicators of currency crises

Research on currency crises is taking place at both the theoretical and empirical level. Any theoretical methodology must be tested empirically. Two types of empirical methodologies have been used in the search for leading indicators of currency crises: the signals approach and the probit approach.

The "signals" approach to predicting currency crises

Many researchers have identified leading indicators by comparing the behaviour of a variable prior to crises with its behaviour in tranquil periods. A variable is a useful leading indicator if it displays anomalous behaviour prior to crises while not providing false signals of an impending crisis in normal or tranquil times. What is construed as anomalous behaviour for a particular variable is defined by choosing a selection rule that achieves a balance between decreasing the probability of not predicting crises and decreasing the probability of giving false signals of stress. The advantage of such "univariate" event analyses is that they are easy to implement and do not impose much a priori structure on the data. However, when multiple indicators are available one has to address the question of combining them for predicting the possibility of a crisis. In this section we draw on the work of Kaminsky, Lizondo and Reinhart.[11]

The "signals" approach to forecasting currency crises essentially involves monitoring the evolution of a number of economic indicators that tend to systematically behave differently prior to a crisis. Every time that an indicator exceeds a certain threshold value, this is interpreted as a warning "signal" that a currency crisis may take place within the following 24 months. The threshold values are calculated so as to strike a balance between the risk of having many false signals (if a signal is issued at the slightest possibility of a crisis) and the risk of missing many crises (if the signal is issued only when the evidence is overwhelming).

The framework for classifying signals is illustrated in Figure 13.1.

Figure 13.1 ● Framework for classifying signals

	Within 12 months, currency turbulence	
State of the signalling variable	...occurs	...does not occur
Warning signal is issued	A	B
No warning signal is issued	C	D

Source: Deutsche Bundesbank, August 1999

The signals are correct if:

● the crisis indicator exceeds a given threshold value and currency turbulence ensues within the predefined run-up period (here: 12 months) (A)
● the crisis indicator remains below the threshold value and no currency turbulence ensues within the run-up period (D).

The signal is false if:

● the threshold value is exceeded yet currency turbulence does not occur (B)
● the threshold value is not exceeded although currency turbulence occurred (C).

This can be used as a basis for calculating a measure of the goodness-of-fit of the results known as the "adjusted noise-to-signal" ratio. This ratio, Q, is the quotient of:

● the number of false warning signals divided by the number of observations in tranquil periods (B/(B+D))
● and the number of correct warning signals divided by the number of observations in the run-up period (A/(A+C)):

$$Q = \frac{(B/(B+D))}{(A/(A+C))}$$

This quotient has the following features:

● in the case of a purely random process, it is expected to be 1
● it approaches 0 the more correct warning signals are sent prior to currency turbulence or the fewer false signals are sent during period of tranquillity.

The matrix can be made operational using Figure 13.2.

In this matrix, A is the number of months in which the indicator issued a good signal, B is the number of months in which the indicator issued a bad signal or "noise", C is the number of months in which the indicator failed to issue a signal (which would have been a good signal), and D is the number of months in which the indicator refrained from issuing a signal (which would have been a bad signal).

The effectiveness of the signals approach can be examined at the level of individual indicators (the extent to which a given indicator is useful in anticipating crises) and at the level of a set of indicators (the extent to which a given group of indicators taken together is useful in anticipating crises).

A perfect indicator would only produce observations that belong to the northwest (A) and southeast cells of this matrix (D).

	Crisis (within 24 months)	No crisis (within 24 months)
Signal was issued	A = Signal	B = Noise
No signal was issued	C = Noise	D = Signal

Signal indicates a good leading indicator
Noise indicates a poor leading indicator

Fig 13.2 ● **Distinguishing between "noise" and "signals"**

The system would issue a signal in every month that is to be followed by a crisis (within the next 24 months), so that $A>0$ and $C=0$, and it would refrain from issuing a signal in every month that is not to be followed by a crisis (within the next 24 months), so that $B=0$ and $D>0$. Of course, in practice, none of the indicators fit the profile of a perfect indicator. However, the matrix above provides a useful reference to assess how close or how far each indicator is from that profile.

Information on the performance of individual indicators is presented in Table 13.1. For each indicator, the first column shows the number of crises for which data on the indicator are available. The number of crises range from 33 to 72, with an average of 61 crises per indicator.

The second column of Table 13.1 shows the percentage of crises correctly called, defined as the number of crises for which the indicator issued at least one signal in the previous 24 months (expressed as a percentage of the total number of crises for which date on the indicator are available). Virtually every indicator called correctly at least half of the crises in their respective samples. On average, the various indicators correctly called 70 per cent of the crises.

The third column shows an alternative measure of the tendency of individual indicators to issue good signals. It shows the number of good signals issued by the indicator, expressed as a percentage of the number of months in which good signals could have been issued $A/(A+C)$, in terms of the matrix in Figures 13.1 and 13.2. While obtaining 100 per cent in the *second* column of Table 13.1 would require that *at least one signal* be issued within the 24 months prior to each crisis, a 100 per cent in the *third* column would require that a signal be issued *every month* during the 24 months prior to each crisis.

In terms of the results in the third column, the real exchange rate is the indicator that issued the highest percentage of possible good signals (25 per cent), while imports issued the lowest percentage of possible good signals (9 per cent).

The fourth column measures the performance of individual indicators regarding sending bad signals. It shows the number of bad signals issued by the

Table 13.1 ● "Signals" approach performance of indicators

	Number of crises for which there are data (1)	Percentage of crises called (2)	Good signals as percentage of possible good signals[a] (3)	Bad signals as percentage of possible bad signals[b] (4)	Noise/signal (adjusted)[c] (5)	P(Crisis/Signal) (6)	P(Crisis/Signal) – P(Crisis) (7)
In terms of the matrix in Figures 13.1 and 13.2			A/(A+C)	B/(B+D)	[B/(B+D)]/ [A/(A+C)]	A/(A+B)	
Real exchange rate	72	57	25	5	0.19	67	39
Exports	72	85	17	7	0.42	49	20
Stock prices	53	64	17	8	0.47	49	18
M2/international reserves	70	80	21	10	0.48	46	17
Output	57	77	16	8	0.52	49	16
"Excess" M1 balances	66	61	16	8	0.52	43	15
International reserves	72	75	22	12	0.55	41	13
M2 multiplier	70	73	20	12	0.61	40	11
Domestic credit/GDP	62	56	14	9	0.62	39	11
Real interest rate	44	89	15	11	0.77	36	6
Terms of trade	58	79	19	15	0.77	36	6
Real interest differential	42	86	11	11	0.99	29	0
Imports	71	54	9	11	1.16	26	–3
Bank deposits	69	49	16	19	1.20	25	–4
Lending rate/deposit rate	33	67	13	22	1.69	18	–9

[a] the higher the percentage the better is the indicator
[b] the lower the percentage the better is the indicator
[c] the lower the number the better is the indicator

Source: Kaminsky, Lizondo and Reinhart[12]

indicator, expressed as a percentage of number of months in which bad signals could have been issued B/(B+D) in terms of the above matrix in Figures 13.1 and 13.2. Other things being equal, the lower the number in this column the better is the indicator. The real exchange rate, once again, shows the best performance (issuing only 5 per cent of possible bad signals), while the ratio of lending to deposit interest rate shows the poorest performance (issuing 22 per cent of possible bad signals).

The information about the indicators' ability to issue good signals and to avoid bad signals can be combined into a measure of the "noisiness" of the indicators. The fifth column shows the "adjusted" noise-to-signal ratio, discussed earlier. This ratio is obtained by dividing false signals measured as a proportion of months in which false signals could have been issued, by good signals measured as a proportion of months in which good signals could have been issued. This is the Q ratio, ([B/(B+D)]/[A/(A+C)] in terms of the matrix in Figures 13.1 and 13.2. Other things being constant, the lower the number in this column the better is the indicator.

The various indicators differ significantly with respect to their adjusted noise-to-signal, or Q, ratios. While this ratio is only 0.19 for the real exchange rate, it is 1.69 for the ratio of lending to deposit interest rates. The adjusted noise-to-signal ratio can be used as a criterion for deciding which indicators to drop from the list of possible indicators. A signalling device that issues signals at random times (and thus has no intrinsic predictive power) would have (with a sufficiently large sample) an adjusted noise-to-signal ratio equal to unity. Therefore, those indicators with an adjusted noise-to-signal ratio *equal to or higher than unity* introduce excessive noise, and thus are not helpful in predicting crises. Thus, on the basis of the results presented in Table 13.1, there are four indicators that should be removed from the list of those to be used within the signals approach. These indicators are: the ratio of lending interest rates to deposit interest rates, bank deposits, imports, and the real interest rate differential.

The previous discussion ranked the indicators according to their ability to predict crises while producing few false alarms. However, such criteria are silent as to the lead times of the signal. More importantly for predicting currency crises one must distinguish between an indicator that sends signals well before the crisis occurs and one that signals only when the crisis is imminent. In focusing on the 24 months window prior to the onset of the crisis, the criteria for ranking the indicators presented in Table 13.1 does not distinguish between a signal given 12 months prior to the crisis and one given one month prior to the crisis.

To examine this issue, it is necessary to tabulate for each of the indicators considered the average number of months in advance of the crisis, known as the lead-time, when the first signal occurs. This, of course, does not preclude the fact that the indicator may continue to give signals through the entire period immediately preceding the crisis. The results are shown in Table 13.2. The most striking observation about these results is that, on average, all the indicators send the first signal anywhere between a year and one and a half years before the crisis erupts, with the real exchange rate offering the longest lead-time. Hence on this basis all the indicators considered are leading rather than coincident, which is consistent with the spirit of an "early warning system".

Table 13.2 ● Average lead-time before a currency crisis takes place

Indicator	Number of months in advance of the crisis when first signal occurs
Real exchange rate	17
Real interest rate	17
Imports	16
M2 multiplier	16
Output	16
Bank deposits	15
"Excess" M1 balances	15
Exports	15
Terms of trade	15
International reserves	15
Stock prices	14
Real interest differential	14
M2/international reserves	13
Lending rate/deposit rate	13
Domestic credit/GDP	12

Source: Kaminsky, Lizondo and Reinhart[13]

The main conclusion that follows from the signals approach is that it can be useful as the basis for an early warning system of currency crisis. Within this approach a number of indicators have been shown to be helpful in anticipating currency crises.

The indicators that have proven to be particularly useful in anticipating currency crises include the behaviour of international reserves, the real exchange rate, domestic credit, credit to the public sector, and domestic inflation. Other indicators that have found support include the trade balance, export performance, money growth, real GDP growth and the fiscal deficit.

The probit approach to predicting currency crises

A second approach to predicting currency crashes has been to directly estimate the probability of a currency crisis (using limited-dependent variable models) and to identify the variables that statistically aid in predicting crises. See Frankel and Rose.[14] This technique, known as a probit model, estimates the probability of devaluation. It has the advantage that it summarizes the information about the likelihood of a crisis in one useful number, the probability of devaluation. It has the added advantage that it considers all the variables simultaneously, and it disregards those variables that do not contribute information that is independent from that provided by other variables already included in the analysis.

This methodology, however, also has some important limitations. First, the methodology does not provide a system for ranking the indicators according to their ability to accurately predict crises and avoid false signals, since a variable either enters the regression significantly or it does not. While measures of statistical significance can help pinpoint which are the more reliable indicators, they provide no information on whether the relative strength of that indicator lies in accurately calling a high proportion of crises at the expense of sending numerous false alarms, or instead missing a large share of crises but seldom sending false alarms.

Second, this method does not provide a transparent reading of where and how widespread the macroeconomic problems are. Within this approach, it is difficult to judge which of the variables is "out-of-line", making it less-than-ideally suited for the purpose of predicting which variables should be closely monitored.

The results of an IMF study[15] applying the probit model are illustrated in Table 13.3.

The study found that only a handful of variables may be considered to consistently provide information about vulnerability to a currency crisis – in the sense that it correctly signalled crises a significant number of times and did not sound frequent false alarms, and also provided signals early enough for countermeasures to be taken. These variables were the real exchange rate, credit growth, and the M2-to-reserves ratio. Together they can provide some useful information about the risks of a possible crisis. Specifically, if these variables have been consistently above their average levels during normal times, then a country would seem potentially vulnerable to a crisis in the event of, say, a rise in world interest rates or some other disturbance that adversely affects investor confidence.

The overvaluation of the real exchange rate was one of the earliest and most persistent signals of vulnerability. As early as 13 months before a crisis, real appreciation of the domestic currency relative to its previous two-year average tended to signal a currency crisis. Other variables that displayed these properties were the M2-to-reserves ratio and the growth of domestic credit. Stock price declines significantly signalled currency crises only for industrial countries. Low domestic real interest rates, reflecting easy monetary conditions, also were a useful indicator variable. Terms of trade deteriorations at around eight months prior to the crisis provided a strong signal for the emerging market countries.

Table 13.3 ● Significance of early warning indicators of vulnerability to currency crises

Indicator	Country group	Months prior to crisis		
		13	8	3
Real exchange rate appreciation	Industrial country	●	●	●
	Emerging market	●	●	●
Domestic credit expansion	Industrial country		●	●
	Emerging market		●	●
M2-to-reserves ratio	Industrial country	●	●	●
	Emerging market	●	●	●
Stock price decline	Industrial country	●	●	●
	Emerging market			
Low domestic real interest rates	Industrial country	●	●	
	Emerging market			
Terms of trade deterioration	Industrial country			
	Emerging market		●	
World real interest rate increase	Industrial country			●
	Emerging market			●

Table 13.3 shows the results of a series of *probit regressions* of the binary crisis indicator on the previous 6-month lagged average of each variable at 3, 8 and 13 months before the crisis date. Each regression included a dummy for the industrial countries and an interaction term of the dummy with the variable. A variable was deemed to be a significant indicator at the indicated lag if the appropriate estimated coefficients were significant at least at the 10 per cent level. A bullet denotes that the variable is significant at the indicated lag. The regressions were based on monthly dates from January 1975 to November 1997 for a sample of 50 countries, which included 20 industrial countries.

Source: IMF (1998)[16]

References

1. Chang, R. and Velasco, A. (1998) *Financial Crises in Emerging Markets: A Canonical Model*. Federal Reserve Bank of Atlanta. Working Paper 98-10. July.

2. Velasco, A. (1987) "Financial and Balance of Payments Crises," *Journal of Development Economics* 27, 263–83.

3. Sachs, J., Tornell, A, and Velasco, A. (1996a) "The Collapse of the Mexican Peso: What Have We Learned?" *Economic Policy* 22, 13–56.

4. Radelet, S., and Sachs, J. (1998) "The Onset of the Asian Financial Crisis", mimeo Harvard Institute for International Development, March.

5. Krugman, P. (1979) "A Model of Balance of Payments Crises," *Journal of Money, Credit and Banking*, 311–25.

6. Frankel, J. and Rose, A.K. (1996) "Currency Crashes in Emerging Markets: An Empirical Treatment," *Journal of International Economics 41*, pp. 351–68.

7. Sachs, J., Tornell, A, and Velasco, A. (1996b) "Financial Crises in Emerging Markets: The Lessons from 1995," *Brookings Papers on Economic Activity,* No. 1, 147–98.

8. Obstfeld, M. (1994) "The Logic of Currency Crises," *Cahiers Economiques et Monétaires* No. 34.

9. Kaminsky, G. and Reinhart, C. (1996) "The Twin Crises: The Causes of Banking and Balance of Payments Problems," International Finance Discussion Paper No. 544, Board of Governors of the Federal Reserve System, March.

10. Krugman, P. (1998) "What Happened in Asia?", mimeo, MIT.

11. Kaminsky, G., Lizondo, S. and Reinhart, C.M. (1997) "Leading Indicators of Currency Crises", IMF Working Paper.

12. Ibid.

13. Ibid.

14. Frankel, J. and Rose, A.K. (1996) "Currency Crashes in Emerging Markets: An Empirical Treatment," *Journal of International Economics 41*, pp. 351–68.

15. IMF (1998) *Financial Crises: Characteristics and Indicators of Vulnerability.*

16. Ibid.

TRAINING IN FINANCIAL MARKETS

Brian Kettell, author of *What Drives Currency Markets*, runs training courses on financial markets for banks, financial institutions, investment banks and for institutional and retail investors.

The courses are taught in-house and can be modified according to the needs of the client. Courses currently being taught range from graduate trainee programmes to courses on specific instruments and markets.

Among the courses offered are:

- graduate training programme for newcomers to financial markets
- financial markets for dealers/fund managers/investors
- US economic indicators – which ones should you watch?
- foreign exchange market fundamentals for dealers/fund managers/investors
- portfolio management and investment analysis: the basics
- Fed-watching for dealers/fund managers/investors
- economics of financial markets – what lies behind all this volatility?
- finance for non-financial managers
- statistics and mathematics for financial markets: what you really need to know.

For further information on in-house training, please contact:
Brian Kettell
Managing Director
9A South End Road
Hampstead
London NW3 2PT
United Kingdom
Telephone 020 7435 4487
Fax 020 7431 8410
E-mail: brian@bkettell.com
Web site: www.bkettell.com

INDEX